Entrepreneurial Innovation for Securing Long-Term Growth in a Short-Term Economy

Jorge Gamez-Gutierrez
Universidad de la Costa, Colombia

Jose Manuel Saiz-Alvarez
Universidad Católica de Santiago de Guayaquil, Ecuador & Universidad Autónoma de Manizales, Colombia & CEIEF-Universidad de Santiago de Chile, Chile

A volume in the Advances in Business Strategy and Competitive Advantage (ABSCA) Book Series

IGI Global
PUBLISHER of TIMELY KNOWLEDGE

Published in the United States of America by
IGI Global
Business Science Reference (an imprint of IGI Global)
701 E. Chocolate Avenue
Hershey PA, USA 17033
Tel: 717-533-8845
Fax: 717-533-8661
E-mail: cust@igi-global.com
Web site: http://www.igi-global.com

Library of Congress Cataloging-in-Publication Data

Names: Gámez Gutiérrez, Jorge Alberto, editor. | Sáiz Álvarez, José Manuel, editor.
Title: Entrepreneurial innovation for securing long-term growth in a short-term economy / Jorge Gamez-Gutierrez and Jose Manuel Saiz-Alvarez, editors.
Description: Hershey : Business Science Reference, 2020. | Includes bibliographical references and index. | Summary: "This book is a collection of research on the methods and applications of corporate decision making on the overall success of a company in the long term"-- Provided by publisher.
Identifiers: LCCN 2019055627 (print) | LCCN 2019055628 (ebook) | ISBN 9781799835684 (hardcover) | ISBN 9781799835691 (paperback) | ISBN 9781799835707 (ebook)
Subjects: LCSH: Decision making. | Business planning. | Success in business.
Classification: LCC HD30.23 .E538 2020 (print) | LCC HD30.23 (ebook) | DDC 658.4/063--dc23
LC record available at https://lccn.loc.gov/2019055627
LC ebook record available at https://lccn.loc.gov/2019055628

This book is published in the IGI Global book series Advances in Business Strategy and Competitive Advantage (ABSCA) (ISSN: 2327-3429; eISSN: 2327-3437)

British Cataloguing in Publication Data
A Cataloguing in Publication record for this book is available from the British Library.

All work contributed to this book is new, previously-unpublished material.
The views expressed in this book are those of the authors, but not necessarily of the publisher.

For electronic access to this publication, please contact: eresources@igi-global.com.

Advances in Business Strategy and Competitive Advantage (ABSCA) Book Series

ISSN:2327-3429
EISSN:2327-3437

MISSION

Business entities are constantly seeking new ways through which to gain advantage over their competitors and strengthen their position within the business environment. With competition at an all-time high due to technological advancements allowing for competition on a global scale, firms continue to seek new ways through which to improve and strengthen their business processes, procedures, and profitability.

The **Advances in Business Strategy and Competitive Advantage (ABSCA) Book Series** is a timely series responding to the high demand for state-of-the-art research on how business strategies are created, implemented and re-designed to meet the demands of globalized competitive markets. With a focus on local and global challenges, business opportunities and the needs of society, the **ABSCA** encourages scientific discourse on doing business and managing information technologies for the creation of sustainable competitive advantage.

COVERAGE

- Resource-Based Competition
- Adaptive Enterprise
- Business Models
- Differentiation Strategy
- Innovation Strategy
- Customer-Orientation Strategy
- Joint Ventures
- Economies of Scale
- Value Chain
- Tacit Knowledge

IGI Global is currently accepting manuscripts for publication within this series. To submit a proposal for a volume in this series, please contact our Acquisition Editors at Acquisitions@igi-global.com or visit: http://www.igi-global.com/publish/.

The Advances in Business Strategy and Competitive Advantage (ABSCA) Book Series (ISSN 2327-3429) is published by IGI Global, 701 E. Chocolate Avenue, Hershey, PA 17033-1240, USA, www.igi-global.com. This series is composed of titles available for purchase individually; each title is edited to be contextually exclusive from any other title within the series. For pricing and ordering information please visit http://www.igi-global.com/book-series/advances-business-strategy-competitive-advantage/73672. Postmaster: Send all address changes to above address.

Titles in this Series

For a list of additional titles in this series, please visit: http://www.igi-global.com/book-series/

Revolutionizing Institutional Theory Through Stakeholder Capitalism
Neslihan Aydogan-Duda (UC Berkeley Extension, USA)
Business Science Reference • © 2021 • 300pp • H/C (ISBN: 9781799844921) • US $235.00

Creating Social Value Through Social Entrepreneurship
Mine Afacan Fındıklı (Beykent University, Turkey) and Duygu Acar Erdur (Beykent University, Turkey)
Business Science Reference • © 2021 • 369pp • H/C (ISBN: 9781799847274) • US $195.00

Handbook of Research on International Business and Models for Global Purpose-Driven Companies
Rafael Ignacio Perez-Uribe (EAN University, Colombia) Carlos Largacha-Martinez (Fundación Universitaria del Área Andina, Colombia) and David Ocampo-Guzman (EAN University, Colombia)
Business Science Reference • © 2021 • 589pp • H/C (ISBN: 9781799849094) • US $345.00

Cases on Internationalization Challenges for SMEs
António Carrizo Moreira (University of Aveiro, Portugal)
Business Science Reference • © 2021 • 333pp • H/C (ISBN: 9781799843870) • US $185.00

Impact of Disruptive Technologies on the Sharing Economy
Ford Lumban Gaol (Bina Nusantara University, Jakarta, Indonesia) Natalia Filimonova (Vladimir State University, Russia) and Chandan Acharya (City University of New York, USA)
Business Science Reference • © 2021 • 350pp • H/C (ISBN: 9781799803614) • US $245.00

Innovation Management and Growth in Emerging Economies
Heather C. Webb (Higher Colleges of Technology, Dubai, UAE) Wendy Wu (Edinburgh Napier University, UK) and Hussain Al Numairy (Higher Colleges of Technology, Dubai, UAE)
Business Science Reference • © 2021 • 288pp • H/C (ISBN: 9781799841951) • US $195.00

IGI Global
PUBLISHER of TIMELY KNOWLEDGE

701 East Chocolate Avenue, Hershey, PA 17033, USA
Tel: 717-533-8845 x100 • Fax: 717-533-8661
E-Mail: cust@igi-global.com • www.igi-global.com

Table of Contents

Detailed Table of Contents

concludes that the transition to sustainability is possible if technology is not just regarded as a tool to reduce carbon emissions, but used to materialize the sustainable design philosophy and integrated into the sustainability rebranding process in the whole supply chain from beginning to end.

The fashion industry employs more than 300 million workers in the world with a turnover of more than a trillion dollars, which is equivalent to being the seventh economic power on the planet. The presence of Latin America and the Caribbean in this industry is growing, where Carolina Herrera is of fundamental importance. The objective of this chapter is to analyze the critical success factors of this company to recognize it internationally as an icon-brand and to study the entrepreneurial spirit of the company to be an example for new generations (and even to competitors). A SWOT analysis will be made complemented by a PESTEL analysis to achieve these goals. The chapter ends with conclusions and perspectives after COVID-19.

This chapter presents the fundamental elements related to the success factors of social organizations. The first step was bibliographic research on social entrepreneurship. This research established that social entrepreneurship improves the quality of life of vulnerable communities, which stands out for the social construction of products, services, and processes that allow social inclusion. Social entrepreneurship in Colombian companies has become a topic of analysis; however, it is still a developing area. The second step was to conduct a quantitative and descriptive investigation in the Colombian coffee region, specifically in the departments of Caldas, Risaralda, and Quindío. The sample distribution of the proportions determined the sample. The information was collected from non-profit companies. The results showed that the success factors are to offer quality services, to have committed human talent, and the adequate management of resources that the competitive advantage is the social need they satisfy, and the social benefit is the reduction of poverty.

The violence that hits Colombia for more than 50 years forced many people, families, and communities to leave their original territories and seek refuge in the principal cities, especially in Bogotá, where displaced people from various regions of the country arrived. Victims of this situation, the Wounaan-Nonam community, were relocated in the periphery of Bogotá, under challenging conditions, some without the necessary infrastructure to live with a minimum quality of life standards, and in a completely different context and culture than the one they were used to live. This research seeks to help artisan women for developing production processes around Wérregue products. As a result, this community will improve their productivity, structure their organization, define marketing strategies, and promote their sustainability and growth while protecting and respect their cultural essence and heritage to generate higher and sustainable income for the artisans.

This chapter describes the implementation of the Open Collaborative Innovation Program in Colombia's National Spectrum Agency (from Spanish, ANE). Six universities participated in the program. The model implemented was based on previous models developed by Ramírez-Salazar; Chesbrough; VanGudy; and Davila, Epstein, and Shelton (2008). The objective of the implementation was to propose solutions to reduce the number of complaints related to the illegal use of the spectrum in Colombia. The innovation challenge for universities was to find answers to solve the problem previously mentioned. Three solving teams were formed. Movimiento Espectral was the winning team with its solution called "Clausula de la Cultura." The model was validated by ANE executives who deemed it adequate to conduct external projects that provide solutions to institutional challenges.

Generational analysis and studies are a recent research trend that analyzes social, cultural, political, and economic changes within the framework of the digital revolution. In this work, an approach is made to the generational phenomena in the SMEs. The objective is to identify the correlations between entrepreneurship and management operations from the logic of individual values and the practices of SMEs managers and owners in Bogotá, from the Blackman model, according to their correspondence with the generational classification taking into account your date of birth. The sample is 383 entrepreneurs from Bogotá, and it was found that there are significant differences associated with generations in skills and abilities, risk management, honesty, responsibility, and work in the provision of services and facilities.

Foreword

The current health and economic crisis caused by the coronavirus is leading to structural changes in the world economy. Changes that will be permanent over time and whose social, geopolitical, and economic repercussions will continue for a long time. In this situation of change, the countries with the highest levels of business innovation and entrepreneurship will take the positions of world leadership, which will cause a substantial displacement of human and productive resources towards the countries with the highest technological and economic efficiency on the planet.

In this challenging context, this excellent Book of Research was born. Readers will find in these pages new visions and aspects related to entrepreneurial innovation, based on economic and social concepts linked to solidarity and social entrepreneurship. Also, the authors propose cases and business models to increase efficiency and productivity in the value chain, both SMEs and multinationals. Twenty-three experts, from different countries and institutions, have collaborated to propose models on issues related to entrepreneurial innovation.

In short, this Book of Research entitled *Entrepreneurial Innovation for Securing Long-Term Growth in a Short-Term Economy* provides an understanding of this complex and multi-faceted process linked to entrepreneurial innovation. I hope that its readers will enjoy learning and taking useful ideas from it. Finally, I congratulate both the authors and editors for the excellent work fulfilled.

Jorge Moreno Gómez
Universidad de la Costa, Barranquilla, Colombia

Preface

In times of uncertainty, it seems appropriate that governments, firms, organizations, people, and HEIs (higher education institutions) set their goals and think in the short term only. The pandemic caused by COVID-19 has taught us that the most affected actors are people who fall ill or die, added to the effects on the economy including unemployment, less consumer confidence, weakness in the service and productive sectors, social distancing measures, and uncertainty. As a result, the economic recovery will be long and painful. This pandemic has caused high monetary losses derived from the confinement measures every nation has been forced to put into force, which has caused substantial social and economic costs worldwide.

Entrepreneurial innovation is playing a crucial role in overcoming this double sanitary and economic crisis caused by Covid-19, also known as SARS-CoV-2 or Coronavirus. Due to the Coronavirus pandemic, new social and economic priorities have emerged. Tens of millions of people have dabbled their lives in telework, and children and young people entered distant education. Humanity's priorities focus on addressing the high rates of poverty generated during this pandemic situation while the economy is collapsing, hoping that old employment will, at least partially, will recover. The beginning of the third decade of the 21st century confronts humanity with complex scenarios, in which interest is renewed in the supply economy and in the factors that can contribute to economic growth through entrepreneurial innovation.

Stagnation and unemployment produced worldwide by COVID-19, a process accelerated by globalization expressed in new technologies and large population flows, require recent efforts from entrepreneurs to recover the economy. In this situation, humanity values each contribution, especially the entrepreneurial efforts rooted in innovation and coming from SMEs (small and medium enterprises) and their innovation-related proposals.

This Book shows some issues and cases that seem to be a priority for entrepreneurs. They include the right and smart management of SMEs, the use of technology in firms, and the emerging of new forms of cooperativism and social entrepreneurship, social innovation, and ethical values. As a result, the target audience of this Book are researchers, students, practitioners, and in general, people interested in different aspects related to entrepreneurial innovation as a mechanism for social change and economic growth in a competitive and globalized environment. The economic crises caused by SARS-CoV-2 that affect economies in the short term have the risk of impacting in a long time if there is not a robust public-private collaboration and growing international cooperation. SMEs and multinationals must have a stronger reconsideration, given their potential for job creation, innovative dynamism, and the ability to adapt to changes with the final objective of maintaining social stability and fostering economic growth.

Therefore, society must open space to social entrepreneurs who are leaders of this transformation process through entrepreneurial leadership, with the proposal of appropriate approaches and solutions to improve the lives and socioeconomic circumstances of the less favored. New forms of social innovation are required to set the process of how, where, and why developing entrepreneurial innovation is an asset for achieving their socioeconomic goals, where management approaches based on values must play a crucial role.

ORGANIZATION OF THE BOOK

This book is divided into two sections. The first section (Chapters 1 to 6) deals with entrepreneurial innovation, and the second section (Chapters 7 to 10) is related to some cases of entrepreneurial innovation in Colombia. Both parts comprise theoretical and empirical studies, including experiences and models linked to entrepreneurial innovation in China, Colombia, Ecuador, Mexico, and the USA.

Regarding Section 1, the Chapter 1 entitled "Inventory Control and the Use of Technology in Businesses: A Survey Study of Micro-companies in Mexico" and written by Miguel Ángel Gil Robles (https://orcig.org/0000-0001-7824-6367), and Raúl F. Montalvo Corzo (https://orcid.org/0000-0002-9124-1787) explores the relationship between inventory control and the use of technology. To cope with this goal, A survey was conducted in the city of Guadalajara, Mexico, covering 466 micro-companies. The authors use a logit analysis to calculate the probability for the micro-companies to implement formal inventory controls. The study found that using technology in micro-companies fosters formal inventory control. This chapter contributes to other Management Control studies which claim that technology might promote the use of formal inventory controls. Furthermore, the authors advise practitioners to adopt technology in their business as a way to facilitate the implementation of formal inventory controls.

In this line of discussion, Chapter 2 titled "Monopolistic Business Practices: Opportunities for Entrepreneurs? The Case of the Big Four Accounting Firms," written by Md. Jahidur Rahman (https://orcid.org/0000-0003-4336-1941), and

Rob Kim Marjerison (https://orcid.org/0000-0003-1181-8695), analyzes how monopolistic business practices result is a situation that, while it creates a unique set of challenges, can also be a compelling opportunity for new ventures to enter the market. This chapter aims to explore the market conditions that enable and encourage monopolistic behavior, specifically in the Accounting and Audit services sector. The Big Four auditing firms, as industry leaders, have been identified as creating monopolistic market conditions. The authors use an integrated literature review approach to explore the existing research on the topic. Findings indicate that there are three causes of monopolies in this sector: partner's compensation, revenue-generating purpose, and better auditing service and disclosure advice compared to other companies. The authors include the influence of the increasing prices in the audit industry and fraud. The chapter contributes to the body of knowledge related to an understanding of how monopolies can occur and how new ventures can seek to enter into competition with those firms.

In Chapter 3, called "Chamber of Popular Micro-Businesses, Popular Brands, and Multi-Place Fairs: Entrepreneurial Association in Monte Sinai (Guayaquil, Ecuador)," written by Uriel Hitamar Castillo-Nazareno, Jessica Silvana Matute-Petroche, and María-Teresa Alcívar-Avilés, studies a town named Monte Sinai located in the northwest of the city of Guayaquil, Ecuador. The authors affirm that this urban agglomeration is in the process of being transformed into a satellite city due to entrepreneurial innovation. Despite this fact and the acceleration of startups, extreme poverty has increased from 7.9% to 15% from 2010 to 2020. There are approximately 12,152 businesses in Monte Sinai: cyber shops (spaces for renting Internet services by the hour or fraction thereof), grocery stores, canteens, pharmacies, bazaars, hairdressers, chicken restaurants, and creative entertainment services, among others. This fact implies an economically active population of 34,584 (there are no rigorous statistics on the population), which means the possibility of disposing of a very varied number of retailers. The objective of this chapter is to propose the creation of a Chamber of Popular Entrepreneurs to foster popular brands through the use of Multiplazas Itinerant Fairs of popular micro businesses.

Entrepreneurial innovation is also intense in technology-related issues. Chapter 4, entitled "A Proposal for the Transformation of Fossil Fuel Energy Economies to Hydrogen Economies Through Social Entrepreneurship," and written by Jossie Esteban Garzon Baquero (https://orcid.org/0000-0001-9470-7581), and Daniela Bellon Monsalve (https://orcid.org/0000-0001-8374-108X), studies how to avoid severe sustainability problems caused by fossil fuel energy. The promise of hydrogen fuel has led large nations to invest in transitioning their fossil fuel economies to a hydrogen-based model. This change will result in significant social impacts, leading to the question, "how should it be done?". The authors propose how social entrepreneurship can integrate socioeconomic actors and agents and help them to devise and implement new forms of energy innovation, which will open spaces for new business models. The current study conceptualizes within a present-day context the connotations of the hydrogen economy at an international level, its implications to society, and its synergy with social entrepreneurship to observe how the models used to manage these undertakings play a vital role.

Another industry where entrepreneurial innovation is crucial is the Fashion industry. Related to this fact, Chapter 5, titled "Scope for Sustainability in the Fashion Industry Supply Chain: Technology and its Impact," written by Kiara Carranza Gudiel, Rob Kim Marjerison (https://orcid.org/0000-0003-1181-8695), and Yuxi Zhao, seeks to determine whether entrepreneurial technological innovation can mitigate the intrinsic contradiction between short-term fashion and the long-term fashion industry in the supply chain to achieve environmental, economic, and social sustainability. The current fashion industry is driven by the ephemeral nature of fashion and its associated wastes, which are not very sustainable. Although the literature has demonstrated that operations research can be used to reduce inventory wastes, whether emerging technologies can reformat the whole mode of production in the fashion industry to be more sustainable remains unknown. After having interviewed practitioners specialized in the supply chain, the authors conclude that the transition to sustainability is only possible if the technology reduces carbon emissions to achieve sustainability by redesigning and rebranding the supply chain.

This study is complemented with Chapter 6 entitled "Entrepreneurship in the Fashion Industry: The Case of Carolina Herrera," written by José Manuel Saiz-Alvarez (https://orcid.org/0000-0001-6435-9600) from Universidad Católica de Santiago de Guayaquil, Ecuador, and Universidad Autónoma de Manizales, Colombia. The author affirms that the fashion industry employs more than 300 million workers in the world with a turnover of more than a trillion dollars, which is equivalent to being the seventh economic power on the planet. The presence of Latin America and the Caribbean in this industry is growing, where Carolina Herrera is of fundamental importance. This chapter aims to analyze the critical success factors of this company to recognize it internationally as an icon-brand, and (2) to study the entrepreneurial spirit of the company to be an example for new generations (and even to competitors). A SWOT analysis is made (Strengths, Opportunities, Weaknesses, and Threats) complemented by a PESTEL analysis to achieve these goals. This chapter ends with conclusions and perspectives after COVID-19.

Section 2 of this book relates to some cases of entrepreneurial innovation in Colombia. In this regard, Chapter 7, titled "Social Entrepreneurship: Successful Factors of Organizations Developed by Adults in the Colombian Coffee Region," written by Jairo Alberto Vasquez Bernal (https://orcid.org/0000-0002-8726-8960) presents the fundamental elements related to success factors in social organizations. Social entrepreneurship improves the quality of life of vulnerable communities, which stands out for the social construction of products, services, and processes that allow social inclusion. Social entrepreneurship in Colombian companies has become a topic of analysis; however, it is still a developing area, especially in the Colombian coffee region, specifically in the departments of Caldas, Risaralda, and Quindío. The authors have collected the information from non-profit companies only, and the results show that success factors relate to offering quality services, disposing of human talent, and adequate management of resources. Their competitive advantage is the social need they satisfy, and the main social benefit is the reduction of poverty.

Entrepreneurial innovation is also seen in displaced communities caused by the conflict in Colombia. In Chapter 8, titled "From Displacement to Entrepreneurship: Case of the Wounaan-Nonam Community," written by Javier Andrés Reyes Ardila, Omar Alonso Patiño Castro (https://orcid.org/0000-0002-4897-4897), Catalina Lucía Ruiz Arias (https://orcid.org/0000-0001-9171-9499), and Paula Echeverry Pérez, studies how the violence that hit Colombia for more than 50 years forced many people, families, and communities to leave their territories and seek refuge in the biggest Colombian cities, especially in Bogotá, where displaced people arrived from various regions of the country. Victims of this situation, the Wounaan-Nonam community, was relocated in the periphery of Bogotá, under challenging conditions, without the necessary infrastructure to live with a minimum quality of life, and in a completely different context and culture, they used to live. This chapter seeks to help artisan women for developing production processes around Wérregue products. As a result, this community will improve their productivity, structure their organization, define marketing strategies, and promote their sustainability and growth while protecting and respecting their cultural essence and heritage to generate higher and sustainable income for the artisans.

In Chapter 9, titled "Open Collaborative Innovation at Colombia's National Spectrum Agency," written by María del Pilar Ramírez-Salazar (https://orcid.org/0000-0002-9462-0897), Carlos Salcedo-Pérez (https://orcid.org/0000-0002-4433-5537), and Sara Esperanza Castañeda Valenzuela, describes the implementation of the Open Collaborative Innovation Program in Colombia's National Spectrum Agency (from Spanish, ANE). Six universities participated in the program to propose innovative solutions for reducing the number of complaints related to the illegal use of the spectrum in Colombia. Three solving teams were formed, and the team named "Movimiento Espectral" won the conquest with the entrepreneurial innovation called "Cláusula de la Cultura" (Culture clause). The model was validated by ANE executives who deemed it adequate to conduct external projects that provide solutions to institutional challenges.

Finally, Chapter 10, entitled "Values and Administrative Practices for Generations Associated With Organizational Innovation," written by Gustavo Adolfo Gil Angel (https://orcid.org/0000-0002-6924-9993), Jorge Gámez-Gutiérrez (https://

orcid.org/0000-0002-1550-0804), and Robinson Ernesto Calvo, develops a recent research trend that analyzes social, cultural, political, and economic changes within the framework of the digital revolution. In this work, an approach is made to the generational phenomena in SMEs. The goal of this chapter is to identify the correlations between entrepreneurship and management operations from the logic of individual values and the practices of SMEs managers and owners in Bogota (Colombia) using the Blackman model (2003). The authors used a sample composed of 383 entrepreneurs from Bogota (Colombia). They found that there are significant differences associated with the generation of skills and abilities, risk management, honesty, responsibility, and work in the provision of services and facilities.

To conclude, this Book constitutes an outstanding compilation of studies carried out by 23 research-professors, specialists, and practitioners from 4 nations and two continents in themes related to entrepreneurial innovation. The combination of a multidisciplinary perspective on this topic, and the inclusion of real cases related to this area of knowledge, show new views in this field and contributes to the subject matter. We expected that this Book would be of your interest to find it fruitful, valuable, and applicable to your professional work and personal life.

Jorge Gámez-Gutiérrez
Universidad de la Costa, Colombia

José Manuel Saiz-Alvarez
Universidad Católica de Santiago de Guayaquil, Ecuador & Universidad Autónoma de Manizales, Colombia & CEIEF-Universidad de Santiago de Chile, Chile

Acknowledgment

We thank our families for being always a source of strength during these pandemic times.

We thank the outstanding academic and research work made by the twenty-three authors from four countries and two continents finally selected after a rigorous double-blind review process. We also thank the referees for their invaluable work during this selection process.

We show our gratitude to the Editorial Advisory Board for their stand up for the book.

We truly acknowledge the IGI Global Book Development Team for their understanding during these difficult times.

We appreciate Universidad de la Costa (Colombia), Universidad Católica de Santiago de Guayaquil (Ecuador), and Universidad Autónoma de Manizales (Colombia) for their financial support.

Finally, we express gratitude to Nicolás Gámez Abril and Rubén Mauricio Muñoz Morales for their revision to a previous draft of this book.

Section 1
Entrepreneurial Innovation

Chapter 1
Inventory Control and the Use of Technology in Businesses:
A Survey Study of Micro-Companies in Mexico

Miguel Angel Gil Robles
https://orcid.org/0000-0001-7824-6367
Tecnologico de Monterrey, Mexico

Raul F. Montalvo Corzo
EGADE Business School, Tecnologico de Monterrey, Mexico

ABSTRACT

This research explores the relationship that exists between inventory control and the use of technology. A survey was conducted in the city of Guadalajara, Mexico, covering 466 micro-companies. A logit analysis was used to calculate the probability for the micro-companies to implement formal inventory controls. The study found that using technology in micro-companies fosters formal inventory control. This chapter contributes to other management control studies which claim that technology might foster the use of formal inventory controls. Furthermore, this chapter aims to advise practitioners to adopt technology in their business as a way to facilitate the implementation of formal inventory controls.

DOI: 10.4018/978-1-7998-3568-4.ch001

INTRODUCTION

The relationship between inventory control and the use of technology has been studied in the existing accounting literature (Song and Zipkin, 1993; Tao et al., 2017). The current understanding of technology and inventory control is that an investment in technology would foster inventory control (Hitomi, 2017). In particular, studies found that organizations that adopted technological improvements implemented more formal inventory control tools (Tayal et al., 2016). Nevertheless, scholars argued that implementing novel technology was not the only factor that fostered the implementation of formal inventory control tools. Some studies found that hiring an accountant, paying taxes, combined with incorporating new technologies, allowed organizations to implement more formal tools of inventory control (Hajej et al., 2017; Hamilton, 1997). However, these empirical studies focused on large organizations that already had corporate accounting practices that benefited from the more intensive use of new technology (Li, 2013). Little is known about the effect of incorporating new technologies in micro-economies and its impact on inventory control (Nyathi and Benedict, 2017).

The current literature has ignored the context of micro-companies, where capital is scarce, and the owners usually work in the organization that they own (Kelliher and Reinl, 2009; Lin, 1980). Micro companies are defined as organizations with less than ten employees and with total assets less than 400,000 USD (Jaouen and Lasch, 2017). Such unique characteristics of micro-companies affect how organizations implement their control practices (Jaouen and Lasch, 2017). Additionally, micro-companies tend to centralize control due to its small size. Thus, owners monopolize organizational management, and they perceive that implementing formal control tools is a threat to the legitimacy of their position (Assenova and Sorenson, 2017). Besides, micro-companies owned that are also family businesses have even more pressures to centralize control. The purpose of this paper is to find out whether implementing new technologies in micro-companies fosters the implementation of formal inventory control tools (Ignaciuk, 2013).

Using a scale of formal inventory controls (Daft and Macintosh, 1984), this paper measures the effect of technology on the formality of inventory control in micro-companies. This study examines whether using the internet, a computer, and a mobile phone, increases the probability of implementing formal inventory control tools. The current literature has explored the effect of technology improvements and their impact on inventory control only in large and complex organizations (Van der Laan and Salomon, 1997). This paper focuses on the effects of technology on micro-companies, as it is unknown if the conclusions about large organizations can be generalized into the context of micro-companies (Ojala et al., 2016).

The main contribution of this chapter is to incorporate the use of technology as a factor that fosters formal inventory control in micro-companies. This contribution highlights the importance of implementing technology in a micro company to improve formal inventory control but also recognizes the boundaries of such a conclusion (Want, 2006). Furthermore, the context of this study is important; Mexico, as a developing country, presents fundamental challenges for micro-companies that hinder the implementation of formal control practices (Kakihara, 2010). Thus, the context in which the micro-companies operate is incorporated in this research in the form of control variables.

LITERATURE REVIEW

Micro companies are defined as organizations with no more than ten employees and with an annual income that does not surpass 50,000 USD (Pavon, 2010). Also, micro-companies are generally family firms (Fernandez and Nieto, 2005) and are controlled by an individual or a group of people who own the firm. Furthermore, micro-companies attend a regional market (Nikunen et al., 2017). Micro companies usually only sell to a local market as they are not aiming to achieve geographical expansion. Another vital characteristic of micro-companies is that they usually started business informally without an organizational or managerial structure (Duong, 2013).

Besides the internal characteristic of micro-companies, another essential factor is the context in which they operate. Usually, micro-companies have problems when trying to access capital or, in some cases, they find that it can be expensive (Hamilton, 1997). Furthermore, micro-companies are usually closely controlled and managed by an individual or partners that generally have the same interests (Lin, 1980). Thus, owners of micro-companies do not sense the need to implement formal management control tools in their organizations. However, micro-companies need to have a certain degree of management control to perform their day to day operations. An example of this is the control of the inventory. Without inventory control, even micro companies can fall short in operating efficiently (Collis, 2012).

Inventory control is a relevant issue with micro-companies (O'Dwyer and Ryan, 2010). Managers and owners of micro-companies need to have control of their inventories to complete their operations. Otherwise, firms may lack products available for sale (Llach and Alonso-Almeida, 2015). Thus, the focus of inventory control is to provide relevant data for the operation of the company.

Due to the nature and needs of micro-companies, inventory control generally relies on informal tools (Marginson, 2002). Such informal tools are usually related to visits from the owners or managers to the store, who typically do not document operations related to the inventory (Cravens et al., 2004). Although in some cases, micro-companies operate with such informal control practices, in other cases, managers and owners completely lose track of inventory control, so affecting the performance of the firm (Pant, 2001). At this point, formal inventory controls become relevant, even in small organizations where managers and owners work closely in the day to day operations of the firm. Thus, an important question arises: 'What can foster the implementation of formal control tools in a micro-company?'

The current literature only answers the question in the context of larger organizations. Several studies have concluded that technology fosters the implementation of formal inventory controls in large organizations (Mandal and Gunasekaran, 2002). For example, large manufacturing companies implement more formal control practices after a digital transformation process (Bowersox and Closs, 2005). Moreover, large retailers have more standard forms of inventory control after implementing Enterprise Resource Planning (ERP) in their operations (Hicks and Stecke, 1995). However, it is not clear if technology would foster the implementation of formal inventory control practices.

Regarding the geographical context of this study, the current literature has focused more on the management processes of micro-companies in Guadalajara and Mexico. For instance, Navarrete (2013) analyzed the decision-making process of local micro-companies in Guadalajara. He stated that micro-companies in Guadalajara make decisions through complex and sometimes chaotic processes. His results imply, to some degree, the lack of formal management control in micro-companies. Besides, Camarena (2002), in his study about the footwear industry in Guadalajara, found that micro-companies imitate the institutional rules that other larger firms have. Such results imply that micro-companies might be in pursuit of more formal control tools.

Regarding technology, micro firms have different technologies to that of larger organizations. For instance, larger organizations focus on automatization, while micro-companies tend to use technology to document data and perform core operations (Hicks and Stecke, 1995). Additionally, the type of technologies that larger organizations implement are usually ERPs, while micro-companies implement the use of a computer, a mobile telephone, and the internet (Guang-wen, 2012). Thus, the analysis of the implementation of technology in micro-companies should focus on these specific implementations rather than more complicated investments such as ERPs. The research question of this study is: 'Does the use of technology in business foster the implementation of formal inventory control tools in micro-companies?'

HYPOTHESIS

Due to the characteristics of micro-companies and the type of technologies these firms implement, we test the following hypotheses,

H1 = The use of a computer increases the probability that a micro company will implement formal inventory control practices

H2 = The use of a mobile phone increases the likelihood that a micro company will implement formal inventory control practices

H3 = Internet access increases the probability that a micro company will implement formal inventory control practices

METHOD

The authors surveyed the second semester of 2017 in the city of Guadalajara, Mexico, to collect the data for this study. The survey was of 500 micro-companies that had an inventory. More specifically, the surveyed companies were: grocery stores, clothing retailers, general stores, and pharmacies. To be considered a micro company, it had to have no more than five employees and an income of less than USD 10,000 per month.

The context of Guadalajara, Mexico, is also crucial for this study. Guadalajara has become the third major city in the country in terms of economic activity and population. Besides, must of the companies that have emerged in the region are micro-companies. At the same time, several international large firms have developed factories and offices in the city. This combination of technology and micro-companies becomes exceptionally relevant when answering the research question in this study.

The researchers aimed to survey 500 organizations to have a significant amount of data that would allow for statistical analysis. Besides, the researchers calculated that 500 micro-companies would represent about 10% of the total number of micro-companies in the city center of Guadalajara. Thus, such a number would convey the total population of micro-companies in that specific area of the city.

As part of the survey, the owners or managers of the companies answered a questionnaire. The answers were typed into an Excel spreadsheet, which was later used for the statistical analysis. From a total of 500 surveyed companies, 34 were discarded due to omissions and errors committed by owners or managers while answering the questionnaire.

The independent variable of this study is whether or not the micro company uses formal inventory control tools. To determine if the company used formal inventory control tools, the company had to be able to answer 'yes' to at least 3 of the following questions: (i) Does the company have an inventory form (physical or virtual) with the current quantities?; (ii) Does the company have an established procedure to count and verify the current inventory?; (iii) Does the firm know the price of their goods in the inventory?; (iv) Does the organization know the goods that go to waste in their inventories?; (v) Is there a person in charge of supervising the inventory of the company? It was necessary to have a dummy variable since the research design included a logit analysis that aimed to calculate which variables correlate more with the probability of implementing formal inventory control tools.

Regarding the variables that measure the use of technology in the company, three dummy variables were used. The first variable is whether the company uses the internet; this means that the micro company has internet service in the physical place where the business is conducted. The second variable is whether the micro company has and uses a computer. In the case of this second variable, the computer does not necessarily need to be connected to the internet. The third variable is whether the company uses mobile phones. As with the second variable, having a mobile phone does not mean it needs to be connected to the internet.

Methodologically, it is essential to differentiate whether the company is connected to the internet or if they only own a computer or a mobile phone. Contrary to what happens in developed countries where internet connections are relatively cheap[1], common, and easy to install, in Mexico, the reality is very different. Internet penetration is scarce, and there are certain areas, even in cities, where Internet Service Providers do not have the infrastructure to provide the service. Similarly, mobile phone companies are expensive, and they usually charge for the data used. Thus, consumers tend to minimize their use of the internet on the mobile phone to reduce costs.

Five control variables were used to test if specific characteristics of the companies affected the results of the regression analysis. The control variables were: (i) whether the company hired an accountant; (ii) if the owner of the company received managerial training; (iii) if the company pays its taxes correctly; (iv) the income of the company, and; (v) the number of employees.

STATISTICAL ANALYSIS

The descriptive statistical analysis is shown in this section. Table 1 shows the descriptive statistics of each of the variables.

As mentioned earlier, from 500 surveys that were competed in the data collection period, only 466 could be used in this study. The other 34 surveys were not used due to errors and omissions. From the 466 micro-companies surveyed, only 107 qualified as having formal inventory control tools. The other 359 micro-companies were cataloged as not having formal inventory control tools.

Table 1. Descriptive Statistic

	Inventory	Internet	Computer	Mobile	Accountant	Training	Taxes	Income	Employees
Mean	0.770386	0.772532	0.757511	0.761803	0.465665	0.495708	0.429185	2.412017	1.532189
Median	1	1	1	1	0	0	0	2	2
Maximum	1	1	1	1	1	1	1	5	5
Minimum	0	0	0	0	0	0	0	1	0
Std. Dev.	0.421036	0.419648	0.429049	0.426438	0.499356	0.500519	0.495492	1.111903	1.093497
Skewness	-1.285764	-1.300258	-1.201668	-1.229176	0.137664	0.017168	0.286146	0.330144	0.006655
Kurtosis	2.65319	2.690671	2.444007	2.510874	1.018951	1.000295	1.08188	2.108743	1.913029
Jarque-Bera	130.7332	133.1666	118.1535	121.9899	77.67364	77.66667	77.79684	23.88866	22.94434
Probability	0	0	0	0	0	0	0	0.000006	0.00001
Sum	359	360	353	355	217	231	200	1124	714
Sum Sq. Dev.	82.43133	81.88841	85.59871	84.56009	115.9506	116.4914	114.1631	574.8927	556.0172
Observations	466	466	466	466	466	466	466	466	466

Source: Author

REGRESSION ANALYSIS

The regression analysis used in this study is the logit regression. A logit regression analysis is relevant when the objective of the study is to determine which variables affect the probability of a particular phenomenon to occur. In the case of this study, the aim is to determine if the use of technology affects the likelihood that a company will implement formal inventory control tools. Thus, due to the research question stated earlier, this study uses a logit regression analysis.

The stated equation to complete the logit analysis is shown as follows:

$$\log it\,(inv) = \alpha + \beta_1\,(\text{int}\,ernet) + \beta_2\,(computer) + \beta_3\,(mobile) + \gamma_1\,(controls) + \mu$$

From the previous equation, "inv" represents whether the micro company uses formal inventory control tools. "Internet" is whether the micro company has and uses the internet service. "Computer" is whether the micro company owns a computer. "Mobile" is whether the micro company uses a mobile phone. Finally, "controls" is the vector of control variables that were stated in the previous section.

RESULTS

This section provides the answer to the Research Question stated previously. As mentioned in the method section, this study uses a logit regression to evaluate if certain variables affect the probability of a micro company to implement formal inventory control tools. This section provides the result of such regression analysis and provides an answer to the research question stated previously: Does the use of technology in business foster the implementation of formal inventory control tools for micro-companies?

Descriptive statistics provide a general overview of the relationship between the variables. The following is the correlations table of the variables used in the regression.

As seen in Table 2, the use of the internet, computers, and mobiles are correlated in, between, and also with the implementation of formal inventory controls. The correlations within the other variables are much weaker. The results from the analysis of the table of correlations are not conclusive; therefore, it is necessary to complete the regression analysis of the sample to answer the research question.

Table 2. Correlations Table

	Inventory	Internet	Computer	Mobile	Accountant	Training	Taxes	Income	Employees
Inventory	1	0.8844	0.8340	0.8685	-0.0325	0.0310	-0.2482	-0.0318	0.0371
Internet	0.8844	1	0.7799	0.8743	-0.0374	0.0158	-0.2431	-0.0292	0.0113
Computer	0.8340	0.7799	1	0.7885	-0.0339	0.0002	-0.2175	-0.0606	0.0190
Mobile	0.8685	0.8743	0.7885	1	-0.0435	0.0002	-0.2479	-0.0647	0.0142
Accountant	-0.0325	-0.0374	-0.0339	-0.0435	1	-0.0221	0.0510	-0.0519	0.0060
Training	0.0310	0.0158	0.0002	0.0002	-0.0221	1	0.0074	0.0109	0.0671
Taxes	-0.2482	-0.2431	-0.2175	-0.2479	0.0510	0.0074	1	-0.0484	-0.0494
Income	-0.0318	-0.0292	-0.0606	-0.0647	-0.0519	0.0109	-0.0484	1	0.0934
Employees	0.0371	0.0113	0.0190	0.0142	0.0060	0.0671	-0.0494	0.0934	1

Source: Authors

The logit regression aims to find the variables with higher correlations. By identifying such variables, it is possible to answer the hypotheses established in the previous sections. The following table shows the result of the logit regression.

Table 3. Logit Regression

Variables	Coefficient	Std. Error	z-value
Constant	-5.256799***	1.3291	-3.9552
Internet	3.376611***	0.7375	4.5786
Computer	3.453181***	0.6456	5.3488
Mobile	2.36944**	0.7412	3.1966
Accountant	0.2966	0.6331	0.4685
Training	0.5380	0.6390	0.8418
Taxes	-0.8709	0.6663	-1.3070
Income	0.2212	0.3019	0.7326
Employees	0.4319	0.3129	1.3807
R-square	0.8230	*p > 0.90, **p>0.95, ***p>0.99	
Observations	466		

Source: Author

As Table 3 shows, the three stated hypotheses pass with 99% significance. The three variables have a positive effect on the implementation of formal inventory control tools. The variable with the most impact (higher coefficient) is the use of a computer, followed by the use of the internet in the business and, finally, the use of a mobile phone for business purposes. The results of the regression show that the research question, 'Does the use of technology in business foster the implementation of formal inventory control tools for micro-companies?' can be answered as 'yes.'

An interesting result from the control variables is that the increase in the number of employees is not significant in affecting the probability of adopting formal inventory control tools. A possible explanation for this is that the number of employees varies from 0 to 5, which, in perspective, is a shallow level and doesn't contradict the argument by Davila and Foster (2005) that, in general, the number of employees affects the Control Systems significantly.

DISCUSSION

The use of technology and management control are popular topics in recent literature. However, most of the studies focus on developed countries and on organizations that can be considered as small, medium, or large. Researchers have practically ignored micro-companies. Micro companies are crucial actors in the economies of developing countries, where capital is scarce, and businesses tend to be much smaller compared to those in developed economies. This study aims to understand if the use of technology can foster the implementation of formal inventory tools, specifically in the context of micro-companies in a developing country.

The study found that there is a higher probability of implementing formal inventory control tools in micro-companies when such businesses use the internet, a computer, and a smartphone. The three variables proved to have a 99% significance in the implementation of formal inventory control tools. This study is consistent with the findings of Mandal and Gunasekaran (2012), who already stated that increasing the use of technology in the business might foster formal management control. However, this study adds to the literature by examining the context of micro-companies in a developing country.

The analysis of the results in the regression of the control variables can also provide exciting conclusions. For instance, the number of employees was not significant in influencing the probability of implementing formal inventory control tools. This result contradicts previous studies on organizational control, which argues that increasing the number of employees in the organization leads to more formal management control (Davila & Foster, 2005).

Surprisingly, hiring an accountant and the owners attending training in management techniques were not significant variables either. Such finding is contradictory to other studies that have found a positive relationship between hiring accountants and formal control (Hamilton, 1997). A possible explanation for these results is that those variables may affect the probability of implementing controls when the companies are larger. In this case, the micro size of the companies affected how owners perceive technology and control. It might be interesting to replicate this study with small companies (larger than micro but smaller than medium companies) to verify these conclusions.

CONCLUSION

The theoretical implications of this study are twofold. First, to strengthen the notion that the use of technology in businesses is related to the implementation of more formal management control tools. Second, in the case of micro-companies in Mexico, the use of technology fosters the implementation of such controls. The results of this paper are in line with the findings of Mandal and Gunasekaran (2012), thus expanding the current knowledge of the use of technology and management control.

Moreover, as highlighted earlier in the paper, this research takes into consideration the context of micro-companies in developing countries. This approach contributes to bridging the gap in the existing literature, where most of the researchers focus their studies on more complex organizations and developed countries.

The practical contribution of this research is for practitioners and policymakers to realize the importance of technology in management control. Practitioners should be aware of the management control benefits of implementing technology and how it might facilitate the implementation of formal inventory control tools. Regarding policymakers, it is relevant to notice that if micro-companies adopt technologies, it is more probable that they would implement more formal management control tools. Therefore, it might be a good idea for policymakers in developing economies to fund programs that aim to improve the technology of micro-companies.

This study is aware of its limitations; focusing on a single city in Mexico draws its conclusions from only one local community. However, these concluding remarks can be expanded to other geographical areas with similar socio-economical contexts. As the size of the organizations is the focus of this study, the results do not permit generalizations for more complex organizations. However, larger organizations can adopt some concepts, such as the positive effect of technology on management control.

Further research should aim to replicate this study in a similar context to validate the results. Additionally, an interesting future study could focus on a sample where the government has intervened to improve the use of technology and compare its results. Finally, another interesting future research to compare the effect of technology in management control could also include small organizations.

REFERENCES

Assenova, V. A., & Sorenson, O. (2017). Legitimacy and the benefits of firm formalization. *Organization Science*, *28*(5), 804–818. doi:10.1287/orsc.2017.1146

Bowersox, D. J., Closs, D. J., & Drayer, R. W. (2005). The digital transformation: Technology and beyond. *Supply Chain Management Review*, *9*(1), 22–29.

Camarena, D. E. S. (2002). La intervención institucional en las micro y pequeñas empresas de la industria del calzado de Guadalajara. *México y la Cuenca del Pacífico*, (17), 53–59. doi:10.32870/mycp.v5i17.178

Collis, J. (2012). Determinants of voluntary audit and voluntary full accounts in micro-and non-micro small companies in the UK. *Accounting and Business Research*, *42*(4), 441–468. doi:10.1080/00014788.2012.667969

Cravens, D. W., Lassk, F. G., Low, G. S., Marshall, G. W., & Moncrief, W. C. (2004). Formal and informal management control combinations in sales organizations: The impact on salesperson consequences. *Journal of Business Research*, *57*(3), 241–248. doi:10.1016/S0148-2963(02)00322-3

Davila, A., & Foster, G. (2005). Management accounting systems adoption decisions: Evidence and performance implications from early-stage/startup companies. *The Accounting Review*, *80*(4), 1039–1068. doi:10.2308/accr.2005.80.4.1039

Duong, L. (2013). *Effective Risk Management Strategies for Small-Medium Enterprises and Micro Companies: A case study.* Viope Solutions Ltd.

Fernández, Z., & Nieto, M. J. (2005). Internationalization strategy of small and medium-sized family businesses: Some influential factors. *Family Business Review*, *18*(1), 77–89. doi:10.1111/j.1741-6248.2005.00031.x

Guang-wen, Y. H. F. H. (2012). Can Commercial Micro Credit Companies Benefit Small Customers? *Finance and Trade Research*, (1), 8.

Hajej, Z., Rezg, N., & Gharbi, A. (2017). Ecological optimization for forecasting production and maintenance problem based on carbon tax. *International Journal of Advanced Manufacturing Technology*, *88*(5-8), 1595–1606. doi:10.100700170-016-8877-9

Hamilton, J. T. (1997). Taxes, torts, and the toxics release inventory: Congressional voting on instruments to control pollution. *Economic Inquiry*, *35*(4), 745–762. doi:10.1111/j.1465-7295.1997.tb01961.x

Hitomi, K. (2017). *Manufacturing systems engineering: A unified approach to manufacturing technology, production management and industrial economics.* Routledge. doi:10.1201/9780203748145

Ignaciuk, P. (2013). LQ optimal and robust control of perishable inventory systems with multiple supply options. *IEEE Transactions on Automatic Control*, *58*(8), 2108–2113. doi:10.1109/TAC.2013.2246093

Jaouen, A., & Lasch, F. (2015). A new typology of micro-firm owner-managers. *International Small Business Journal*, *33*(4), 397–421. doi:10.1177/0266242613498789

Kakihara, T. (2010). *The Small and Medium Sized Enterprises (SMEs) in Mexico: the Case of Jalisco State*. Institute for Economic Studies, Seijo University.

Kelliher, F., & Reinl, L. (2009). A resource-based view of micro-firm management practice. *Journal of Small Business and Enterprise Development*, *16*(3), 521–532. doi:10.1108/14626000910977206

Li, S. (2013). Emission permit banking, pollution abatement and production–inventory control of the firm. *International Journal of Production Economics*, *146*(2), 679–685. doi:10.1016/j.ijpe.2013.08.023

Lin, E. (1980). Inventory Control Systems for Small Business. *American Journal of Small Business*, *4*(4), 11–19. doi:10.1177/104225878000400404

Llach, J., & Alonso-Almeida, M. D. M. (2015). Integrating ICTs and Supply Chain Management: The Case of Micro-Sized Firms. *Human Factors and Ergonomics in Manufacturing & Service Industries*, *25*(4), 385–397. doi:10.1002/hfm.20559

Mandal, P., & Gunasekaran, A. (2002). Application of SAP R/3 in on-line inventory control. *International Journal of Production Economics*, *75*(1-2), 47–55. doi:10.1016/S0925-5273(01)00180-3

Marginson, D. E. (2002). Management control systems and their effects on strategy formation at middle-management levels: Evidence from a UK organization. *Strategic Management Journal*, *23*(11), 1019–1031. doi:10.1002mj.271

Navarrete Baez, F. E. (2015). Las prácticas de desarrollo sustentable: Un acercamiento descriptivo a las pequeñas empresas de Guadalajara, México. *Cuadernos Americanos*, *31*(53), 48–58. doi:10.25100/cdea.v31i53.16

Nikunen, T., Saarela, M., Oikarinen, E. L., Muhos, M., & Isohella, L. (2017). Micro-Enterprise's Digital Marketing Tools for Building Customer Relationships. *Management, 12*(2).

Nyathi, M., & Benedict, O. H. (2017). An Analysis of Bookkeeping Practises of Micro-Entrepreneurs in the Retail Clothing Industry in Cape Town, South Africa. *J Entrepren Organiz Manag*, *6*(216), 2.

O'Dwyer, M., & Ryan, E. (2000). Management development issues for owners/managers of micro-enterprises. *Journal of European Industrial Training*, *24*(6), 345–353. doi:10.1108/03090590010373334

Ojala, H., Collis, J., Kinnunen, J., Niemi, L., & Troberg, P. (2016). The demand for voluntary audit in micro-companies: Evidence from Finland. *International Journal of Auditing*, *20*(3), 267–277. doi:10.1111/ijau.12070

Pavón, L. (2010). *Financiamiento a las microempresas y las pymes en México (2000-2009)*. Cepal.

Song, J. S., & Zipkin, P. H. (1996). Inventory control with information about supply conditions. *Management Science*, *42*(10), 1409–1419. doi:10.1287/mnsc.42.10.1409

Tao, F., Fan, T., Lai, K. K., & Li, L. (2017). Impact of RFID technology on inventory control policy. *The Journal of the Operational Research Society*, *68*(2), 207–220. doi:10.105741274-016-0030-5

Tayal, S., Singh, S. R., & Sharma, R. (2016). An integrated production inventory model for perishable products with trade credit period and investment in preservation technology. *International Journal of Mathematics in Operational Research*, *8*(2), 137–163. doi:10.1504/IJMOR.2016.074852

Van der Laan, E., & Salomon, M. (1997). Production planning and inventory control with remanufacturing and disposal. *European Journal of Operational Research*, *102*(2), 264–278. doi:10.1016/S0377-2217(97)00108-2

Want, R. (2006). An introduction to RFID technology. *IEEE Pervasive Computing*, *5*(1), 25–33. doi:10.1109/MPRV.2006.2

KEY TERMS AND DEFINITIONS

Dummy: A type of a dichotomous and quantitative variable that can take on any of two quantitative values.

ERP: Acronym of Enterprise Resource Planning is a type of software used to manage day-to-day business activities.

Inventory Control: Also known as 'Stock Control,' it consists of how firms regulate and maximize the company's warehouse inventory.

Logit: It is a type of regression used for modeling a categorical outcome variable.

Micro-Company: They are the smallest companies in the market whose limits on the number of employees and turnover vary between countries.

Policymaker: A member of a government department who is responsible for making new rules to rule firms and society from the public sector.

Retailer: It is a type of intermediary between the wholesaler and the final consumer.

Technology: The practical application of knowledge to benefit society and firms.

ENDNOTE

1 In Mexico, the monthly average fee of an Internet Service Provider is 5 days work on minimum wages (25 USD).

Chapter 2
Monopolistic Business Practices:
Opportunities for Entrepreneurs? The Case of the Big Four Accounting Firms

Md.Jahidur Rahman
https://orcid.org/0000-0002-0534-0181
Wenzhou-Kean University, China

Rob Kim Marjerison
https://orcid.org/0000-0003-1181-8695
Wenzhou-Kean University, China

ABSTRACT

Monopolistic business practices result is a situation that, while it creates a unique set of challenges, can also be a compelling opportunity for new ventures to enter the market. This chapter aims to explore the market conditions that enable and encourage monopolistic behavior, specifically in the accounting and audit services sector. The big four auditing firms, as industry leaders, have been identified as creating monopolistic market conditions. The integrated literature review approach is used to explore the existing research on the topic. Findings indicate that there are three causes of monopolies in this sector: partner's compensation, revenue-generating purpose, and better auditing service and disclosure advice compared to other companies. The influence of the increasing prices in the audit industry and fraud are included in the work. The chapter contributes to the body of knowledge related to an understanding of how monopolies can occur, and how new ventures can seek to enter into competition with those firms.

DOI: 10.4018/978-1-7998-3568-4.ch002

INTRODUCTION

Monopolistic business practices (MBPs) are not uncommon, especially in the era of globalization and multinational corporations (Bertoletti and Etro, 2017; Fischer and Normann, 2019). MBPs create market conditions that are unique and often difficult for Small and Medium-Sized Businesses (SMEs), and for new ventures, but may result in a business environment where there are unexpected opportunities for entrepreneurial activity (Cheng and Tabuchi, 2019; Elert and Henrekson, 2016; Salop, 1979).

There are many examples of monopolistic market conditions where new ventures have successfully entered the market successfully, often resulting in considerable disruption. An extensive list is outside the scope of this paper, but a few examples can be identified easily. The duopoly for men's shaving products in the US, long dominated by Schick and Gillette was entered by two new ventures in the recent years (Esty and Fisher, 2019; Martins, 2019); *the Dollar Shave Club*, a subscription based online model, and *Harry's* also initially and online offering both succeeded in gaining considerable market share and resulted in the two larger firms lowering their prices considerably (Esty and Fisher, 2019).

The commercial aircraft manufacturing industry for medium and large planes, long dominated by *Airbus* and *Boeing,* Robertson (2018) competing for market share in the rapidly growing Asian market, He et al. (2017) will soon face pressure from the new venture based in Beijing (Cassagnard and Regibeau, 2018; Zhu et al., 2019).

The mobile phone services market in the US, dominated by another duopoly of *ATT Mobility* and *Verizon Wireless* resulted in market conditions where the two were both able to achieve greater value added, and a host of smaller operators were able to successfully enter the market with value and prepaid pricing models (Zhou et al., 2020). This situation also created an opportunity for distant 3rd and 4th place carriers Sprint and T-Mobile to join and enter the market as equals to complete with Verizon and ATT (Curwen and Whalley, 2017; Vorobiyenko et al., 2015). This list could go on extensively, the message is that where monopolistic business practices result in prices for consumers that are beyond the fair market value of the products and services offered, there are opportunities for new ventures to successfully enter the market (Elert and Henrekson, 2016; Parenti et al., 2017).

This paper will explore in detail one such market, the accounting and audit services sector, long dominated by the "quadropoly" of the "Big Four" accounting firms; Deloitte, Ernst and Young, KPMG, and PricewaterhouseCoopers.

In this research, an integrated literature review approach was utilized, and it was determined that there are three main causes of monopolies in the accounting and professional services sector: partner's compensation, revenue-generating purpose and better auditing service and disclosure advice than other smaller accounting firms. These, therefore, are the areas of focus for this paper. A review of various related literature was used to draw conclusions.

This study contributes to the literature in several ways. Most importantly, this study hopes to provide initial evidence on the topic of the reasons for the Big Four's monopolization in the market. Strong evidence is provided to support the monopolistic practices of the big four which results in such huge market share of the auditing market. The paper also contributes to drawing attention to the need for the Big Four to improve internal control processes.

This paper is organized as follows; Section one, the instruction, the situation and overview. In Section 2, some emerging issues pertaining to the auditing profession are discussed and in section 3, the theoretical contribution is discussed. In section 4, The findings and conclusions are presented.

DISCUSSION

What is the Issue and What Contributed to the Formation of This Issue?

The Big Four occupies a large proportion of market and form monopolies. According to Alali's (2017) due to regulatory and economic changes, the Big Four pricing strategies have differed over time. However, for most of the recent decades, Big Four pricing was continuously escalating. Significantly, Big the Four charged premium prices to small companies during Sarbanes–Oxley Act (SOX) period (2002-2003), Auditing Standard 5 (AS5) period and the Great Recession period (Alali et al., 2019). It has been reported that the pricing is related to firm size and transaction cost. Based on the assumption that all audit firms in an industry have the necessary expertise to audit their customers, the relative operational scale of audit companies in an industry should be the most relevant determinant for auditors to change transaction costs in the industry (Chu et al., 2018). In Chu's explanation, the transaction cost (that is, the learning cost of the audit company and the conversion cost of the client) is extraordinary. That is the main reason that why clients tend to keep the same audit firm for many years instead of replacing it every few years (Chu et al., 2018). Under this circumstance, even though the prices of the Big Four are higher than those of the Non-Big Four, the Big Four still account for the majority of the market because of Big Four's fixed customers and high exchange costs. This is an important reason why the Big Four continue to dominate the market and have been able to form a monopoly of sorts.

In addition to its high pricing strategies, the high concentration of suppliers in the national audit market has become the most challenging issue. In most major economies, the audit market for public companies is dominated by the Big Four audit firms (Francis and Michas, 2012). In the European Union, according to the turnover of listed clients, Sigel et al. (2008), the average composite market share of the four major audit firms is about 94%. In terms of statutory auditing of listed companies, the four major auditing firms; Deloitte, Ernst and Young, Price Waterhouse Coopers and KPMG, provide auditing services to more than 60% of listed companies and occupy most of the national auditing market (Heß and Stefani, 2012). As mentioned in the article, due to audit market regulations and supplier concentration around the world, smaller audit service providers face serious market access barriers. It has proven difficult to acquire new auditors of Listed Companies in oligopoly markets. According to Guo et al. (2017) market concentration severely limits auditors' options for firms. In particular, if one of the Big Four firms fails, the lack of options could lead to market disruption.

Apart from the issues discussed above, which are results of the Big Four monopoly, there is another serious issue that is increasingly gaining attention. Due to the Big Four monopoly, there is a concern that if the vitality and competitiveness of the audit market is low, the audit quality may be low (Heß and Stefani, 2012; Mueller et al., 2015; Whittle et al., 2014). As Gao (2017) pointed out, and was reinforced by Bloom (2008) the concentration has adverse effect on the selection, which reduces the chance of Big Four customer changing auditors, especially considering the Sarbanes–Oxley act of 2002 that gives new auditor independence requirements. In turn, fewer options for clients may be perceived as increasing auditor stubbornness and complacency and may result in more lenient and less skeptical audits of clients. As a result, the quality of audits will be adversely affected. On the contrary, there is a phenomenon that smaller firms have a comparative advantage in helping customers conduct mergers and acquisitions.

According to Louis (2005), the performance of buyers audited by non-Big four accounting firms is better than that of firms audited by The Big Four accounting firms. This effect is more evident when these firms are privately held, and auditors are more likely to play an important advisory role. Based on the view that non-Big Four accounting firms have a better understanding of the local market and good customer relationship, Louis (2005) concluded that non-Big Four accounting firms may provide better acquisition suggestions for customers. Although the Big Four may have more expertise in M&A activities, non-Big Four accounting firms may have more experience and the resultant expertise in private holding companies (Louis, 2005). As a result, the Big Four are not necessarily the best at every aspect of the audit and accounting services sector.

One factor worth exploring is partner's compensation and revenue-generating purpose. There is extensive research suggesting that partner's compensation can be one of the reasons why the Big Four has such a huge market share in the auditing market. Researchers have also taken a strong interest in clientele selection of the Big Four for better auditing service and disclosure advice. The Big Four's specialized work in auditing industry and its large market share would lead customers to pay more attention to seeking to engage them as their auditing service provider, which in turn results in exacerbating the issue of a monopoly in the market (Balsam et al., 2003)

The Big Four, are generally organized as partnerships. Instead of the equal sharing across partners, partners' profits are more dependent on their attributes and revenue generating activities on behalf of the firm. Firstly, revenue generation. Due to revenue-generating opportunities, the partners' compensation of Big Four is positively related to the size of their clientele. the number of publicly traded clients, and the number of billable hours that the Client is able to tolerate. This becomes one of the main reasons that the Big Four focus their attention on seeking customers in the auditing area (Knechel et al., 2013).

In the research of Huddart, (2013) six related empirical relationships have been discussed: (1) partner compensation increases with the book value of the assets audited by the partner; (2) partner compensation depends on the number of office auditors and is higher for partners working in the capital cities; (3) for the partners who are experts in auditing a specific industry or auditing listed companies, compensation is higher; (4) the amalgamator compensation is higher when gaining new customers and lower when losing existing customers; (5) for more advanced partners, the salary level for acquiring new customers is higher; (6) Partner compensation is lower when (i) the audit opinion includes continuing operations disclosure and the company is not bankrupt, or (ii) does not include continuing operations disclosure and the company does go bankrupt (Huddart, 2013).

Except segments two and three, all four incentives above lead partners in the Big Four to be more ambitious in the acquisition of new customers and gaining book value of audited assets to increase their own compensation. In the article on 'Empirical Evidence on the Implicit Determinants of Compensation in Big 4 Audit Partnerships', Knetchel et al. (2013), based on a case study in Sweden, the authors found that performance-related incentives can affect the income of a Big Four's Partner significantly by focusing on such activities as attracting new clientele, and, as partners progress in their career, and retaining of old clients, which also influences the market share of the auditing firms. As the mode of partners' compensation, which determines that the benefit partners can earn is determined by their contributions to the firm, actually is reasonable, and hard to change to the equal-sharing method, which as recognized as not suitable for the companies' development and growth (Knechel et al., 2013).

The second reason is that clientele select Big Four for auditing service and disclosure advice.

According to previous research, different type of providers, their specific knowledge and professional skills, and their reputational capital can derive the differences between the possible levels of auditing and sustainability assurance (Balsam et al., 2003) Based on the analysis in this article, the brand name of the audit firms can also be complemented by the degree of industry special expertise (Craswell et al., 1995). And according to Balsam et al. (1995), large auditing firms, such as the Big Four, will be the choices of many customers, because they are regarded as having the most extensive base of specialist knowledge and expertise in assurance services. high standards and good reputations.

The Big Four experienced more repetition in similar settings, gaining and retaining clients in similar market segments, and also due to their large volume of business in auditing industries, which in turn leads these companies to become more trusted and more reliable (Balsam et al., 2003). It is claimed by Craswell et al. (1995) that thc Big Four has experts in auditing some specialty or difficult to audit industry segments that some small audit firms do not have the ability or expertise to deal with including such industries as education, oil, minerals, and emerging technology-based enterprises.

When choosing targeted auditors as part of their overall disclosure strategy, clients require industry professional auditors to provide value-added benefits from an industry-specialized perspective, including potentially lower fees, disclosure recommendations, improved audit quality and as a signaling mechanism to investors, that the client intends to provide better disclosures. Based on the research discussed above, as the audit companies' level of specialization, as measured by the market share of the firms, increases, the companies obtain larger economic scale (Dunn and Mayhew, 2004) As mentioned above, the market share of the auditing industry has already been dominated by the Big Four in most of countries of the world. Also based on previous research, the Big Four's specialized work in the auditing industry and its large market share would lead customers to pay more attention to engaging them as their auditing service provider, which only serves to further perpetuate the issue of monopolistic business practices in the audit and accounting professional services sector.

What Series of Events Have led to Changes in Standards/Laws/Regulations?

Prior to 2018, the Big Four were auditors for 97% companies of the FTSE 350. In the last survey of the Competition Commission in 2012/13, this figure was 95%, which means that the market competition has decreased rather than increased in recent years (Kend et al., 2014).

The continuous and ongoing trend towards more monopolistic market conditions not only results in a decline the market competition but also drives a more severe problem, that of auditing quality and auditing ethics. This has drawn the attention of auditing regulators in many countries, largely as the result of some high-profile cases.

Carillion, a British construction company with a history 200 years of operations, declared bankruptcy in January 2018. Carillion's business scope was very broad, with a revenue of 5.2 billion pounds in 2016 and a market value of nearly 1 billion pounds in July 2017 (Thomas, 2018). Towards the end, Carillion was too risk tolerant, and ambitious, taking on a number of risky and low-margin contracts that ultimately resulted in huge and unmanageable amount of debt. The banks ultimately refused to provide any further financial support to this company, and it was forced into bankruptcy and liquidation. Carillion's bankruptcy liquidation sparked concerns about the work and pensions of the company's 43,000 employees worldwide, as well as the prospects of the company's 450 ongoing project (Wren-Lewis, 2018).

KPMG, one of the Big Four, had been providing audit services to Carillion for the previous 19 years and was charging fees of up to £29 million annually. However, in the last annual report released by Carillion, KPMG declared that this company has sufficient strength and capability to" live at least three years." (Wren-Lewis, 2018) In fact, in addition to KPMG the other three of the Big Four all have had serious audit errors due to interest issues:

PwC was investigated for negligence during the audit – they failed to detect large-scale fraudulent activity in key clients of the Colonial Bank of Alabama. As a result, the bank declared bankruptcy in 2009 and the plaintiff, the US Federal Deposit Insurance Corporation, suffered a loss of billions of dollars. US District Court Judge Barbara Rothstein fined PwC $625 million, setting a record for the highest fine of an accounting firm in history (Duke, 1990) .

In 2011, Deloitte, as the auditor of the Bankia Bank Group in Spain, was also responsible for the development of accounting accounts, completely deviating from the basic principles of audit independence. Deloitte also announced in Bankia's initial public offering (IPO) prospectus that the bank was profitable and had a sound financial system (Frunza, 2013) . However, the bank was almost closed down due to financial problems less than a year after the IPO.

In 2010, Ernst and Young was sued by New York Attorney General Andrew Cuomo, accusing them of helping Lehman Brothers who they oversaw as auditors for more than seven years to use the "Repurchase 105" to temporarily transfer $10 billion to Lehman Brothers. This is the largest lawsuit filed by US officials against any accounting firm in the previous decade. The reports show that Ernst and Young earned more than $185 million from Lehman in the decade before Lehman's collapse

(Jiang et al., 2018) It is undeniable that improper auditing will aggravate the negative impacts and losses caused by financial risks. and it is considered that presently, there is a crisis of confidence in auditing industry (Kend et al., 2014; White, 2014)

Faced with the scandals of large multinational accounting firms, regulators have implemented some antitrust measures, such as forcing the Big Four to spin off their audit practice from their consulting businesses. The pressure of being broken up has increased following high-profile corporate collapses that have called into question the quality of their work as both auditors and consultant services for these largest accounting companies (Madison, 2018)

What Organizations are Responsible for Developing/ Implementing the Proposed Changes?

Although the Big Four firms are directly responsible for causing the proposed change of relative auditing standards, they should not be the only group who are responsible to actually develop the proposed change. The Big Four, as the most influential group in the auditing area, are closely related with a large number of companies, government departments and individuals. Therefore, it is not realistic for the Big Four to merely monitor themselves in implementing the proposed change. Every stakeholder of the Big Four should put effort into the process to make the whole auditing environment healthier.

Government, as the regulatory source of a nation, plays an essential role in improving the auditing environment. Combing the factors mentioned above, it is clear that stakeholders cannot be assured of a high quality of assessment and security when they are engaging with their auditors. Moreover, according to Weber et al. (2008), the lack of legal restriction is responsible for the Big Four's monopoly as they are less influenced than small companies. KPMG, as one of the Big Four, experienced a sharp decrease in its reputation, this according to the feedback of investors (Weber et al., 2008). Since the German government does not provide an effective statutory method for customers to protect their own legitimate interests, they choose to release their negative emotion directly on KPMG, which in turn lead to the declining stock price of the firm. It can be inferred that the Big Four auditing firms' reputation is getting worse, and German law is one of the reasons driving this situation. In conclusion, government must play a key role in the establishment of regulatory requirements, and modification of existing law and standards with the aim of effectively changing the existing unhealthy environment of Big Four auditing firms.

Regulators in the auditing field such as Public Company Accounting Oversight Board (PCAOB) are also responsible for changing the situation in the auditing field. Based on the research of Lennox and Pittman (2010), SOX (Sarbanes-Oxley

Act of 2002) started the journey of PCAOB's supervision of auditing companies. The enactment of SOX indeed has proven to be a significant step in improving the situation as peer view is no longer the only investigation method accepted in the review of the compliance of auditing firms. However, whether PCAOB executes its duties effectively remains uncertain. The Big Four's market share does not seem to have close relationship with the reports provided by PCAOB (Lennox and Pittman, 2010.) PCAOB's report do not reveal the quality control findings to the public, which has a negative impact on the Big Four firms reputation as their performance in quality control is not perceived to be as good as they had experienced in the previous reporting structure. Additionally, the peer review practice is no longer accepted in many auditing companies, especially since the beginning of the PCAOB's investigation (Lennox and Pittman, 2010).

There is a view that a useful evaluative summary in the peer review report, which can, within some limitations, reflect auditing companies' performance objectively and efficiently. According to Lennox and Pittman (2010), it is a detriment to delete the evaluation part of the peer review, and by doing so, adding the evaluation to PCAOB's report can be effective to inspection. Moreover, it is confirmed that PCAOB's punishment towards large auditing firms due to their negative performance in quality control will cause a declining trend in their stock price (Dee et al., 2010; Weber et al., 2008). Therefore, PCAOB has significant influence, but the precondition to application of that influence that should use rights properly, prudently, and maximize the potential for positive influence. If the PCAOB can demonstrate its fairness as the main regulator, the Big Four's monopoly situation may be mitigated.

Legal institutions also play important roles in creating a healthier auditing market. Many large global firms believe that the Big Four take advantage of the price advantage of leveraging financing in the US financial markets (El Ghoul et al., 2016). Compared to auditing firms in other countries where the requirement of litigation is not as strict as the U.S., equity pricing is relatively higher. The reason is that in those countries, stakeholders of Big Four companies find it difficult to use law as weapons to compensate for their own (El Ghoul et al., 2016). Consequently, the Big Four in America benefit from the related legislation and as a result, find that legal institutions have made a protective market condition which benefits the Big Four albeit unconsciously.

To remedy the situation, it would be necessary to modify the relevant legal framework and attempt to establish a level playing field for audit firms of all sizes. The role of legal institutions in forming a competitive, and effective audit process is essential as only they can change the background of the market conditions.

In addition to external factors, internal factors should also be considered. Managers, as the management level in companies, deal with all activities occurring inside firms every day. According to Kornberger et al. (2011), experience and exposure in dealing with various activities play an important role in helping to develop managers' abilities. Consequently, their ability to anticipate likely problems will also be strengthened gradually. Managers in auditing companies should keep comparing Big Four and Non-Big Four's performance regularly and using their professional skills to improve companies' internal control. Moreover, it is also useful for managers to adjust strategies based on direction of public opinion so that Big Four can establish and maintain good perception of the general public and keep their strategies consistent with industry regulations (Kornberger et al., 2011).

In conclusion, government, PCAOB, legal institutions and managers of Big Four are responsible for developing change. With the effort of these four groups, it is likely to weaken the situation of Big Four auditing firms' monopoly.

What are the Expected Benefits/Costs of the Proposed Change and who is Expected to be Impacted?

Whenever people decide whether the advantages of a particular action are likely to outweigh the disadvantages, they use a form of benefit-cost analysis (BCA). In the public domain, the formal BCA is a sometimes-controversial technique for a thorough and consistent assessment of the pros and cons associated with expected policy changes. When the market environment changes, there are fewer monopolies and more choices for customers. There will be changes in both Big Four and non-Big Four. As mentioned above, Big Four have in some sense, an industry monopoly, and as such, their audit fees are higher than the non-Big Four.

According to Hsu et al. (2015), supervision does not necessarily strengthen auditors' effectiveness, however, in insurance companies, supervision can at least partially fulfill the role filled by auditors in other industries. In situations when customers believe that that auditor's work is possibly redundant, it may be that they are not motivated to hire the four major accounting firms. Auditors may be able to expend less resources which could result in lower audit costs.

In addition, the selection of Auditors and the subsequent charging of fees may depend on industry-specific customer characteristics (Hsu et al., 2015). Alali et al. (2019) found that when the competition was fierce, the four companies would not charge extra fees to small customers. Consequently, once non-Big Four have more competition in the marketplace, extra fees to small customers will be likely be reduced. Thus, the audit fees of Big-Four will decline and the revenue of non-Big Four would incrcasc.

These series of changes if realized, could have a deep impact on a wide range of stakeholders, internal as well as external, people, corporations and organizations; for the Big Four, the breakdown of monopolistic market conditions would lead to an open market in the auditing industry. As a result, the market share of the Big

Four would decline, and the revenue of the Big four would also drop accordingly. This situation would not be conducive to the expansion or strengthening of the monopolistic market conditions. More stringent regulation would ultimately force the Big Four, and auditor services providers in general, to provide more professional and normative auditing service to their clients.

For non-Big Four audit firms, the barrier of entering into the auditing market would be reduced, and the special characteristics and strengths of the small companies would be much more attractive and competitive to specific clients who prefer to have unique service. (Hsu, Troy, and Huang, 2015) As a consequence, the market share of the small audit firms would increase. Should this occur, one challenge that would need to be addressed would be for the small audit companies to ensure that they have enough professionally qualified staff to provide high quality services to their clients.

For governmental agencies and regulatory bodies, in particular for officers in relevant bodies such as the Public Company Accounting Oversight Board (PCAOB) doing the regulatory work required to better control the quality of auditing service provided in the market is essential.

For the auditing market, more auditing firms competing in the market would lower the prices of auditing services and would make them more reasonable. With enhanced regulation and benign market competition, a healthy audit market would be created and sustained.

THEORETICAL CONTRIBUTION

This research attempts to address a gap in the previous research, by aiming to investigate the reasons for the market share change of Big Four. From the FTSE 350 report when the Big Four changed from 95% in the last survey of the Competition Commission in 2012/13 to 97% in 2018. The 2% increase means the presence of competition in the auditing market has decreased rather than increased during those years. Additionally, this research points out the disadvantages of monopolization of audit services by the Big Four and explores and attracts attention to the phenomenon of monopolies. This research encourages all stakeholders in auditing market to pay attention to the phenomenon of monopolization of Audit services of the Big Four, the existing potential issues, and also the steps that could be taken to encourage active change in the mitigation of monopolistic market conditions. This study also aims to give specific suggestions to related institutions, including PCAOB and other legal and regulatory institutions, that may be able to play a role in addressing the vacancies in the existing processes and policies, which can be generalized as a part of causation of monopoly of the Big Four.

CONCLUSION

While the topic of this paper is very narrowly defined with a focus on the audit and accounting professional services sector, from a broader perspective, it can be inferred that there are opportunities for smaller firms the enter the market and compete with the Big Four, especially in the niche markets where specific and knowledge and expertise is required, and especially if the expense associate with transition to a new audit from can be minimized. The objective of this paper is twofold, firstly, to find out the reasons and effects of Big Four auditing companies' monopoly and secondly, in doing so, to contribute to the body of knowledge that could serve to enable and encourage new ventures to successfully engage in competition with established monopolies.

The integrated literature review approach is applied is this paper, using replying on research conducted by other scholars as evidence on which to base findings. As discussed above, there are three main reasons. The first one is partner's compensation, which means the large amount of compensation earned by partner. The second one is revenue-generating purpose, which means Big Four can generate more revenue through the process of monopoly. The last one is better auditing service and disclosure advice compared to other companies, which give customers a more convincing reason to choose Big Four companies. As for influences, raising prices of auditing industry and frauds are quite severe. Government, PCAOB, legal institutions and Big Four themselves should all participate in changing the industry's environment.

In conclusion, this paper discusses causes of, and solutions for the Big Four's monopoly providing a possibility to attract related departments and society's attention and urging the Big Four to improve their internal control processes. In doing so, it is hope that this paper will contribute to a larger body of knowledge on the causes of monopolistic business practices, the situation and circumstances that all such business practices to flourish, and how new ventures and SMEs can enter into large markets that are dominated by one or more large firms.

REFERENCES

Alali, F., Elder, R., & Zhou, J. (2019). An Analysis of Big 4 Pricing and Firm Size: The Differential Impact of Demand and Supply Shocks on Large and Small Clients. *Journal of Accounting, Auditing & Finance*, *34*(2), 204 230. doi:10.1177/0148558X17704555

Balsam, S., Krishnan, J., & Yang, J. S. (2003). Auditor industry specialization and earnings quality. *Auditing*, *22*(2), 71–97. doi:10.2308/aud.2003.22.2.71

Bertoletti, P., & Etro, F. (2017). Monopolistic Competition When Income Matters. *Economic Journal (London)*, *127*(603), 1217–1243. doi:10.1111/ecoj.12329

Bloom, R., & Schirm, D. (2008). An analysis of the GAO study on audit market concentration. *The CPA Journal*, *78*(4), 6.

Cassagnard, P., & Regibeau, P. (2018). *Collective Entry Deterrence and Free Riding: Airbus and Boeing in China*. https://hal-univ-pau.archives-ouvertes.fr/hal-02141056

Cheng, Y.-L., & Tabuchi, T. (2019). First mover advantage by product proliferation in multiproduct duopoly. *International Journal of Economic Theory*. doi:10.1111/ijet.12242

Chu, L., Simunic, D. A., Ye, M., & Zhang, P. (2018). Transaction costs and competition among audit firms in local markets. *Journal of Accounting and Economics*, *65*(1), 129–147. doi:10.1016/j.jacceco.2017.11.004

Craswell, A. T., Francis, J. R., & Taylor, S. L. (1995). Auditor brand name reputations and industry specializations. *Journal of Accounting and Economics*, *20*(3), 297–322. doi:10.1016/0165-4101(95)00403-3

Curwen, P., & Whalley, J. (2017). The evolution of US mobile operators within a multi-play world. *Digital Policy, Regulation and Governance*.

Dee, C. C., Lulseged, A. A., & Zhang, T. (2010). *Client Stock Market Reaction to PCAOB Sanctions Against a Big Four Auditor* (SSRN Scholarly Paper ID 1598401). Social Science Research Network. https://papers.ssrn.com/abstract=1598401

Duke, J. D. (1990). Accountants' Liability to Third Parties for Negligent Misrepresentation: Should There Be a Uniform Standard. *The American Journal of Trial Advocacy*, *14*, 133.

Dunn, K. A., & Mayhew, B. W. (2004). Audit Firm Industry Specialization and Client Disclosure Quality. *Review of Accounting Studies*, *9*(1), 35–58. doi:10.1023/B:RAST.0000013628.49401.69

El Ghoul, S., Guedhami, O., & Pittman, J. (2016). Cross-country evidence on the importance of Big Four auditors to equity pricing: The mediating role of legal institutions. *Accounting, Organizations and Society*, *54*, 60–81. doi:10.1016/j.aos.2016.03.002

Elert, N., & Henrekson, M. (2016). Evasive entrepreneurship. *Small Business Economics*, *47*(1), 95–113. doi:10.100711187-016-9725-x

Esty, B., & Fisher, D. (2019). *Gillette: Cutting Prices to Regain Share* (SSRN Scholarly Paper ID 3481513). Social Science Research Network. https://papers.ssrn.com/abstract=3481513

Fischer, C., & Normann, H.-T. (2019). Collusion and bargaining in asymmetric Cournot duopoly—An experiment. *European Economic Review, 111*, 360–379. doi:10.1016/j.euroecorev.2018.10.005

Francis, J. R., & Michas, P. N. (2012). The Contagion Effect of Low-Quality Audits. *The Accounting Review, 88*(2), 521–552. doi:10.2308/accr-50322

Frunza, M. (2013). *Market Manipulation and Moral Hazard: Can the LIBOR be Fixed?* (SSRN Scholarly Paper ID 2207703). Social Science Research Network. https://papers.ssrn.com/abstract=2207703

Guo, Q., Koch, C., & Zhu, A. (2017). Joint audit, audit market structure, and consumer surplus. *Review of Accounting Studies, 22*(4), 1595–1627. doi:10.100711142-017-9429-8

He, S., Hipel, K. W., & Kilgour, D. M. (2017). Analyzing market competition between Airbus and Boeing using a duo hierarchical graph model for conflict resolution. *Journal of Systems Science and Systems Engineering, 26*(6), 683–710. doi:10.100711518-017-5351-7

Heß, B., & Stefani, U. (2012). *Audit market regulation and supplier concentration around the world: Empirical evidence*. Academic Press.

Hsu, W.-Y., Troy, C., & Huang, Y. (2015). The determinants of auditor choice and audit pricing among property-liability insurers. *Journal of Accounting and Public Policy, 34*(1), 95–124. doi:10.1016/j.jaccpubpol.2014.09.001

Huddart, S. (2013). Discussion of Empirical Evidence on the Implicit Determinants of Compensation in Big 4 Audit Partnerships. *Journal of Accounting Research, 51*(2), 389–397. doi:10.1111/1475-679X.12010

Jiang, J., Wang, I. Y., & Wang, K. P. (2018). Big N Auditors and Audit Quality: New Evidence from Quasi-Experiments. *The Accounting Review, 94*(1), 205–227. doi:10.2308/accr-52106

Kend, M., Houghton, K. A., & Jubb, C. (2014). Competition issues in the market for audit and assurance services: Are the concerns justified? *Australian Accounting Review, 24*(4), 313–320. doi:10.1111/auar.12063

Knechel, W. R., Niemi, L., & Zerni, M. (2013). Empirical Evidence on the Implicit Determinants of Compensation in Big 4 Audit Partnerships. *Journal of Accounting Research, 51*(2), 349–387. doi:10.1111/1475-679X.12009

Kornberger, M., Justesen, L., & Mouritsen, J. (2011). "When you make manager, we put a big mountain in front of you": An ethnography of managers in a Big 4 Accounting Firm. *Accounting, Organizations and Society, 36*(8), 514–533. doi:10.1016/j.aos.2011.07.007

Lennox, C., & Pittman, J. (2010). Auditing the auditors: Evidence on the recent reforms to the external monitoring of audit firms. *Journal of Accounting and Economics, 49*(1), 84–103. doi:10.1016/j.jacceco.2009.04.002

Louis, H. (2005). Acquirers' abnormal returns and the non-Big 4 auditor clientele effect. *Journal of Accounting and Economics, 40*(1–3), 75–99. doi:10.1016/j.jacceco.2005.03.001

Martins, P. M. M. da S. (2019). *Shaving as a subscription: Analysis of Portuguese male consumers interest on buying razors and blades by subscription.* https://repositorio.ucp.pt/handle/10400.14/26910

Mueller, F., Carter, C., & Whittle, A. (2015). Can audit (still) be trusted? *Organization Studies, 36*(9), 1171–1203. doi:10.1177/0170840615585336

Parenti, M., Ushchev, P., & Thisse, J.-F. (2017). Toward a theory of monopolistic competition. *Journal of Economic Theory, 167*, 86–115. doi:10.1016/j.jet.2016.10.005

Robertson, H. (2018). *No Sign of Landing: Airbus, Boeing, the WTO, and the Expanding Large Civil Aircraft Battle* (SSRN Scholarly Paper ID 3114942). Social Science Research Network. https://papers.ssrn.com/abstract=3114942

Salop, S. C. (1979). Monopolistic Competition with Outside Goods. *The Bell Journal of Economics, 10*(1), 141–156. JSTOR. doi:10.2307/3003323

Siegel, P. H., Naser-Tavakolian, M., & O'Shaughnessy, J. J. (2008). *Factors Influencing Auditor Switching in the European Union* (SSRN Scholarly Paper ID 1612540). Social Science Research Network. https://papers.ssrn.com/abstract=1612540

Vorobiyenko, P., Tikhonov, V., & Taher, A. (2015). The LTE technology perspectives in multimedia applications. *Цифрові Технології, 17*, 7–14.

Weber, J., Willenborg, M., & Zhang, J. (2008). Does Auditor Reputation Matter? The Case of KPMG Germany and ComROAD AG. *Journal of Accounting Research, 46*(4), 941–972. doi:10.1111/j.1475-679X.2008.00298.x

White, P. (2014). An assessment of the Competition Commission report and subsequent outcomes. *Research in Transportation Economics, 48*, 277–285. doi:10.1016/j.retrec.2014.09.053

Whittle, A., Carter, C., & Mueller, F. (2014). 'Above the fray': Interests, discourse and legitimacy in the audit field. *Critical Perspectives on Accounting, 25*(8), 783–802. doi:10.1016/j.cpa.2013.09.001

Wren-Lewis, S. (2018, January 20). *What Carillion's collapse tells us about public sector outsourcing*. British Politics and Policy at LSE. https://blogs.lse.ac.uk/politicsandpolicy

Zhou, S., Song, B., & Gavirneni, S. (2020). Bundling Decisions in a Two-Product Duopoly—Lead or Follow? *European Journal of Operational Research, 284*(3), 980–989. Advance online publication. doi:10.1016/j.ejor.2020.01.030

Zhu, L., Zhang, L., & Zhao, J. (2019). The study on China civil aviation manufacturing industry's development Strategy facing international industrial transfer. *2019 3rd International Seminar on Education, Management and Social Sciences (ISEMSS 2019).* 10.2991/isemss-19.2019.2

KEY TERMS AND DEFINITIONS

Big Four: Term used to define the business influence in the market of four accounting firms; Deloitte, Ernst and Young, KPMG, and PricewaterhouseCoopers.

FTSE 350: Acronym of Financial Times Stock Exchange, it includes the 350 stocks with the highest market capitalization.

Initial Public Offering (IPO): It is the process by which a private firm sale its stocks to private investors.

Monopolistic Business Practices (MBPs): They consist of common, especially in the era of globalization and multinational corporations, strategies to create market conditions that are unique and often difficult for Small and Medium-Sized Businesses (SMEs), and new ventures.

Public Company Accounting Oversight Board (PCAOB): It is a nonprofit public corporation established by the U.S. Congress to oversee the audits of public companies to protect investors and the public interest.

Sarbanes-Oxley Act: A legal act approved in 2002 by the U.S. Congress to help protect investors from fraudulent financial reporting by corporations.

Chapter 3
Chamber of Popular Micro-Businesses, Popular Brands, and Multi-Place Fairs:
Entrepreneurial Association in Monte Sinai (Guayaquil, Ecuador)

Uriel Hitamar Castillo-Nazareno
Universidad Católica de Santiago de Guayaquil, Ecuador

Jessica Silvana Matute-Petroche
Universidad Católica de Santiago de Guayaquil, Ecuador

María-Teresa Alcívar-Avilés
Universidad Católica de Santiago de Guayaquil, Ecuador

ABSTRACT

Monte Sinai is a town located in the northwest of the city of Guayaquil, Ecuador, and has about 99,325 hectares. There are some signs that this population is in the process of being transformed into a satellite city, given the increasing number of startups and the formation of small markets to buy and sell raw materials. Also, extreme poverty has increased from 7.9% to 15% from 2010 to 2020. There are approximately 12,152 businesses: cyber shops (spaces for renting internet services by the hour or fraction thereof), grocery stores, canteens, pharmacies, bazaars, hairdressers, chicken restaurants, creative entertainment services, among others. This fact implies an economically active population of 34,584 (there are no rigorous statistics on the population), which means a possibility of a very varied supply at the retail level. The objective of this chapter is to propose a Chamber of Popular Entrepreneurs that will lead to the continuous creation of popular brands. For this goal, the authors analyze the Multiplazas Itinerant Fairs as a strategy for popular micro businesses.

DOI: 10.4018/978-1-7998-3568-4.ch003

INTRODUCTION

This part of the city of Guayaquil began in the mid-80s with the construction of small villages. A situation finished in the 1990s. From this date onwards, housing cooperatives appeared that allowed the acquisition of houses or land in that area at a low cost. The cooperatives were around the number of five at that time. The expansion of cooperatives, which at the end of the 1990s reached approximately 20, caused the population to multiply (MIDUVI, 2011). Today, in 2020, Monte Sinaí is made up of roughly 40 cooperatives (INEC, 2019). Social groups without housing in Guayaquil and other cantons (mainly in Manabí) decided to turn it into a micro-city formed by a large area of valleys and hills covered by the dry forest of the coast, and cattle ranches, to be the most extensive popular sector of Guayaquil.

Monte Sinaí represents a *classic popular society* in which, when it comes to business, it does not differentiate any ethnic, religious, or educational situation. From this, an original and proper life dynamic is born based on solving the family economy. Thus, the great majority in these popular communities live the same socio-economic concerns in a horizontal way (Tabara, 2017). In this micro-society, the critical aspect of the circumstance can be observed in the precarious essential services, the rudimentary housing, the trivial education, the inefficient health care, the informal sources of monetary income, and the low level of employment (Hernández, 2016).

In that sense, the popular must pass, in the process of its construction, through formal criteria of legalization. The National Institute of Agrarian Development (INDA) grants notifications to the cooperatives, which facilitated the distribution of legal land parcels (MIDUVI, 2018); thus, the land began to fragment more rapidly, which was later formalized before the Municipality of the city of Guayaquil. The sale of land became a very lucrative business since 1996 when it began to offer illegal and cheap land to poor migrants from around the country, which caused the arrival of a mass of migrants. Precariousness was so great that, in some cases, this land was reached only after having crossed a river and ravines, with a rope tied around his waist (Tabara, 2017). Under these conditions, people earned a living even though they were selling products on the street. This idea becomes the breeding ground for entrepreneurship due to necessity and precariousness of life.

By 2010, Monte Sinaí had expanded to 38 cooperatives (99,000 hectares), housing approximately 45,667 families, about 274,000 inhabitants, and this dynamic growth continued. Given this reality of chaotic change, a decree was issued (Reform Law 88 to regularize the human settlements registered in Monte Sinaí) that tried to stop its expansion (MIDUVI, 2018).

The evictions of the invaders (those who do not have title to the land) multiplied, some families were relocated, but the growth of Monte Sinaí did not stop. Only faith accompanied them during this social journey. Many temples of many religions were built. Even the names of their 40 housing cooperatives speak of the religiosity of the population. The most important ones, because of their size, are Will of God, New Life, Ebenezer, Trinity of God, Will of God, Gift of God, among others (Hernandez, 2016). All of them form the extensive area of Monte Sinaí. It is a territory that continues to enlarge towards the northwest of the Perimeter Road of Guayaquil.

This is how the popular areas of Guayaquil are born, with some nuances. There are many improvisations in all economic and social aspects: schools are made by improvising premises and teachers, markets, as well as work, are informal, health and sanitation are extremely precarious, and housing is in minimum conditions for life (Sánchez, 2014). But with the stability of having a house, precarious startups emerge to earn urgent income.

Startups, which include precarious micro-businesses out of necessity, is known as a marginal area with a large and growing population density (Abramo, 2012). In this area, poverty is the inheritance that is reproduced among its extremely vulnerable inhabitants and in a state of defenselessness that prevents them from demanding their rights and assuming their duties as citizens. This fact mainly affects the daily lives of the families that have to solve the problem of survival. In this circumstance, it is necessary to generate income that eliminates or reduces the precariousness of life, and housing is the only one that provides the security to undertake business at the lowest possible costs and risks.

PRIVATE HOMES AS A SOURCE OF BUSINESS

In these circumstances, each of the homes becomes a potential place of business; you can sell anything that looks interchangeable (notebooks, candy, cigarettes, cell phone cards, ice creams, food, others) what is understood as necessary. The characteristics of the family provide a lot of labor at a low cost. They are generally huge families, made up of an average of six members: father, mother, and four children. In these, 64% of women do not have any fixed income, compared to 36% of men. Women have been mothers since adolescence, which is why there is a large young population, approximately 60% of whom are under 18 years of age and who are looking for an income in any form (INEC, 2019). Everything indicates that something must be done to get a job; therefore, economic informality is at the doors of every family.

Also, it is essential to note that these families do not have a piped drinking water network in their homes, so they must be supplied with 86.6% of the vital liquid employing delivery trucks or "tankers." These offer them service at a value of $1.00 per 55-gallon tank, with an average family of four consuming two to three tanks a day, which represents approximately $80 a month, constituting 20% of the basic unified salary, only in water (INEC, 2017). The precariousness of the population means that spending is higher than usual in the rest of the city, which adjusts upward the prices of goods and services that can be bought or sold. All prices carry this burden of high costs in businesses or degradation in the quality of the sale.

Hence, 13.4% are supplied through underground wells, which shows the high vulnerability of these families, also caused by the need to reduce costs. This fact is generated, above all, when there is speculation about the value of this service. Besides, there are health and sanitation problems caused by the consumption of undrinkable water. In the same line, Monte Sinai does not have sewage networks, the families of the sector use latrines, built in a rustic way and without sanitary care. The popular culture hides in this base of deep demand for life improvement and vulnerability.

There are approximately 28,000 families that need electricity service, of which 90% are in a non-legal area, according to figures from the Guayaquil Electricity Company (2019). In Monte Sinai, 6,825 families connect to septic tanks, 6,577 to cesspits, 4,255 to latrines, and 1,988 to streams or rivers (INEC, 2017). They seek to change this reality from a non-conscious vision and with self-built entrepreneurial impulse. We are talking about the poverty and extreme poverty of a population that, through its creativity, can face and build a reality of opportunities. Everything is developed from the lived circumstance; they give themselves their opportunities for change.

Likewise, these families lack fixed telephone coverage through state networks. To communicate, their inhabitants use mobile telephony, so they have two repeater antennas installed in the sector by a private company. As for the Internet, there are telephone booths and cyber-cafés, which are the only ones that have access provided by the same mobile phone service provider. The following table shows an approximation of the situation in this social area.

Table 1. Cell Phone Use in the Family (Last Six Months)

	Family members	%
Yes	18,777	54
No	13,382	39
Ignored	2,425	7
Total	34,584	100

Source: INEC - Censo de Población y Vivienda - Monte Sinaí Sector, 2010

According to data provided by the National Institute of Statistics and Censuses (2018), 56.5% of inhabitants at Monte Sinaí use cell phones, as it is the primary means of contact with friends and family. Due to a lack of resources, between 4.3% and 3.2% of citizens do not have one. Additionally, 78.5% of the inhabitants of Monte Sinaí, according to INEC (2010), have not used a computer in the last six months. On the other hand, only 15.6% use a computer regularly, which, concerning the total population of the sector, is small.

These two aspects, cell phones, and computers are strategic when thinking about business in a popular area like Monte Sinaí. The growing use of cell phones indicates that this factor is within the culture of the everyday life of families, which allows ease of communication. On the other hand, the tendency to use computers, although not in the same amount as cell phones, shows that it is increasing. It is possible to consider that in a business project involving these two tools, the micro-entrepreneurs would tend to adapt.

The possibility of generating goods and services from this area of the popular, in an area that from its beginnings has serious economic deficiencies, is anchored to undertake as a channel to have family income. The challenge now is to achieve a capital-generating model that fits this reality of mass mentality and diverse culture in consumption and, at the same time, performs competitiveness in local and regional markets. In this line, we seek to achieve that entrepreneurs stop making homemade products, improvised micro-businesses, and move, giving a qualitative leap, to the markets using what is called, in this article, *popular brands*.

THE BUSINESS CONTEXT IN GUAYAQUIL (CITY AND REGION)

Ecuador's business economy is made up of formal and informal business activities, with the former accounting for 40% of business activity and the latter accounting for 60%. The formal economy contains approximately 880,000 firms, 99.5% MSMEs (around 875,000), and only 0.5% are classified as large enterprises (SEPyS, 2019). An important fact is that 90% of these companies are micro (about 795,000), and 40% of them are businesses, while the remaining 60% of the companies operate informally. In other words, the economy of these regions, and particularly in Ecuador, is profoundly informal and micro. Therefore, it can be understood that the possibility of doing business is possible from the criteria found in Monte Sinai. The first element to consider.

On the other hand, according to the IEPS (2018), 81.97% of sales correspond to large companies, which account for 0.5% of total companies; 11.29% are small companies, and 0.93% are micro-companies, which account for 90% of the entire companies. This data shows the extreme centralization of markets and, therefore, of capital. There is an urgent need to find a formula that allows for more equitable participation in markets so that an economy with fewer poor people can be built—the second element to consider.

In the same vein, it is common to find in every corner of large cities all kinds of sellers of products with or without brands, national or international. The citizens demand these products without any further questions about their quality, but they do look at the price. The important thing to emphasize here is that to initiate businesses, the market is not very demanding in quality, but if it is possible to grant products to him to *relatively low prices*. Therefore, it is necessary to find a criterion to organize brands of products at low prices and mass consumption, so that it is possible to enter local and then regional markets. The third element to be considered.

Besides, it should be considered that this Ecuadorian economy is the most expensive one in the region. The cost of credit for micro-entrepreneurs is between 25 and 30.5% in dollars, which represents an announced bankruptcy since it forces the micro and small producers to incorporate margins above 30%. The costs of production border on 60% of income, and the intrinsic risks are considered to be 9% on average (SEPyS, 2019). The total cost is very close to 100%, generating prices for goods and services 40 to 50% higher than in other counties of the region.

Approximately 95% of micro and small businesses, formal and informal in Ecuador, grow slowly, or they fail. Very often, they go bankrupt. The rotation is approximately 55%; this is due to improvisation in the organization of the business. Inefficiency is one of the highest challenges to achieve because the entrepreneur considers that it is only about risking without considering the aspects of the processes belonging to the structure of the business system. There is a basic level of training that must be applied in this economic sector; also, a set of efficient strategies must be designed to lower costs and reduce the weaknesses that cause growth to be nullified.

Informality is the most recurrent because it is the cheapest way to start a business. Cost avoidance is the first thing this entrepreneur achieves; therefore, *business indigence* is a tactical advantage in the face of the cost framework offered by this Ecuadorian economy. Consequently, understanding business organizations at this level may be the greatest challenge.

POPULAR BRANDS

These refer to the systematization and standardization of brands based on products and services born from popular business networks. Popular businesses are organizations created to sell and/or produce products, mainly taken from low urban cultures, and are directed to the consumption of massive urban sectors with scarce resources; the design of the merchandise is usually the result of the culture of this human mass.

Popular brands are born from the association of multiple businesses, micro and small, that support a brand that is born from that association.

The key is in the criteria with which these businesses share the production and marketing processes in such a way that they leverage the brand that has a collective structure. "All for one, and one for all" is the central criterion, since the brand is born from the collaboration among micro-entrepreneurs. Its purpose is to distribute capital collectively so that the strategic alliance is continually being extended to new popular entrepreneurs and, at the same time, to promote new brands. His popular brand, in its central character, by its nature, has that of mass consumption, therefore, continuously seeks to expand the market. From this perspective, the internationalist spirit of the popular brand concept is born. This means that its sense of success implies a sophisticated (competitive) organization of its business processes that makes possible the penetration of foreign markets in a sustained way, it is necessary the production at a growing scale.

Some examples of popular brands are Don Morocho (hot drink accompanied by yucca bread), Ceviches de 4 de Noviembre (food popular on the coast of Ecuador), Empanadas de Celia (Ecuador has more than 30 types of empanadas), products generated from small farmers (derived from quinoa, oats, corn), and other products born from university research. All this is part of the possibility of a business organization in Monte Sinai. Right there, there are many business styles, and approaches that could develop popular brands like the one pointed out here.

Based on the above, the following table shows some of the current undertakings in Guayaquil that could be treated as popular brands.

These products can be categorized as popular products (even if their birth is not of that social reference). Still, they have been successfully incorporated to solve the central problems of income that Monte Sinaí. From any of them, a strategic association could be worked out that would lead to the creation of popular brands.

Association Criteria: Chamber of Popular Micro-Businesses

Given the complexity of the reality of popular business, an organizational criterion is sought that will sustain in the long term the ways of creating brands and generating market entry strategies by maintaining the relevant business process organizations. This is why we present the *Chamber of Popular Micro-Businesses,* whose mission is to create the necessary popular brands under the strategic criteria of association demanded by the target market.

This Chamber must contain at least these four elements: i) Training, which is responsible for generating all relevant updates in knowledge for popular entrepreneurs (courses, seminars, forums, conferences, diplomas, among others), this can even be in partnership with universities; ii) Technical Assistance, this has the function of ensuring that businesses have the minimum management structure essential to generate value; iii) Creation and Promotion of Brands, this is an area specialized in creating brands from the companies that want to start; iv) Market Intelligence, this studies the markets and determines the partnership strategy for the brand to be successful.

For the business culture and popular sectors being studied, this can be considered a mechanism that overcomes bottlenecks in participation. The business culture is best enhanced in an environment where power remains in the hands of entrepreneurs but with organizational criteria that everyone must respect based on results. Therefore, management must be resolved based on equal participation of all members in assemblies, which define the President of the Chamber and the Council members.

Table 2. Products and service in the perspective of Popular Brands

Product or Service	Feature	Comments
Morocho	Hot sweet drink	Origin of the Sierra
Casting	Hot sweet drink	Coastal origin
Cassava Bread	Small round bread made with Yucca	Origin of the Sierra
Cassava strips	Yucca cut into strips and cooked	Origin of the Sierra
Empanadas	Fast food	More than 30 varieties
Artisan Tea	Casual energy drink	Popular creation
Homemade candies	Different flavors	Popular creation
Homemade ice cream	Various flavors	Popular creation
Shoe Design and Arrangement	Exclusive editions	Popular creation
Custom sewing	Exclusive editions	Popular creation
custom tailors	Exclusive editions	Popular creation
Coastal Ceviches	Typical fish meal	Popular creation
Hairdressers	Exclusive attention	
Handicrafts Woodworking Retail trade	Products of cultures Exclusive and massive designs trade in finished goods	Cultures of the Coast Popular creation Popular creation

Source: own elaboration

Multiplatform Traveling Fairs

From having the two strategies elaborated, *the popular brands, and the Chamber of Micro Businesses,* one must move on to analyze how to sell, how to make the brands enter the markets to minimize resistance and market competition. It is necessary to generate marketing levers to make the brand known at low costs.

In that perspective, an organization of fairs that are articulated from multiple products, which are offered under *popular brands* created, which are installed in different popular sectors and then move to other economic spaces of the city and the country, from that comes its name of *Multiple Traveling Fairs*. Organize fairs that allow not to sell products but to sell brands permanently. The channels of sale are the multiple squares in all the places of the country where the fair is installed, and then it rotates towards other sectors of the city, even towards other cantons. The same logic applies to the rest of the country and eventually can be taken to other countries (Colombia, Peru, Brazil, Argentina, among others). This is a competitive strategy to penetrate the market since it leverages all the power of the associations of micro and small enterprises.

In this proposed organization, the technical requirement is in the logistics of supplies and installation of the *multi-site fair*. Choosing the place and doing the corresponding advertising, so that the attendees internalize brands that are not in the style of those manufactured in the game of global corporate supply and demand that seek pure accumulation, requires a lot of motivating power. Getting used to demanding brands that aim to invest and reinvest in the living conditions of the territories (communities and neighborhoods) surrounds the call for buyers with special needs. This requires the existence of trained management that can successfully navigate this logic of market behavior.

This structure can be promoted in the area of Monte Sinaí in a population of approximately 200,000 inhabitants with profoundly popular characteristics (massive), as an example of something that can be replicated in other sectors and cities. In a preliminary approach, it can be said that this business criterion can be perfectly executed in this part of the town. Although the income is low, internal consumption can be motivated with this *multi-plaza fair* (moving demand inwards), making the expenditure out of the territory progressively decrease. A population in which more than 60% of the EAP undertake some business shows the great spirit linked to this business area.

ANALYSIS OF RESULTS OF THE SURVEY CARRIED OUT IN MONTE SINAÍ

In a detailed review of the possibilities of setting up an organization of this level of strategic socio-business coordination, a survey was carried out in this sector of Guayaquil (Monte Sinai). This survey reports in general terms a great possibility of the acceptability of the organization that demands the *Popular Brands*. Based on 12,192 businesses, a sample of 374 was chosen, assuming a risk of 5%, and a z coefficient of 1.96.

This research is based on economically busy inhabitants who are business owners, entrepreneurs in the same sector. The survey was conducted to determine the perception and cultural affinity of those involved in a business, given the urban conditions they face. The first question has to do with the level of study and academic specialization shown in Figure 1, a critical aspect to access the business model proposed in this chapter.

Figure 1.

Graph 1 (pp12)

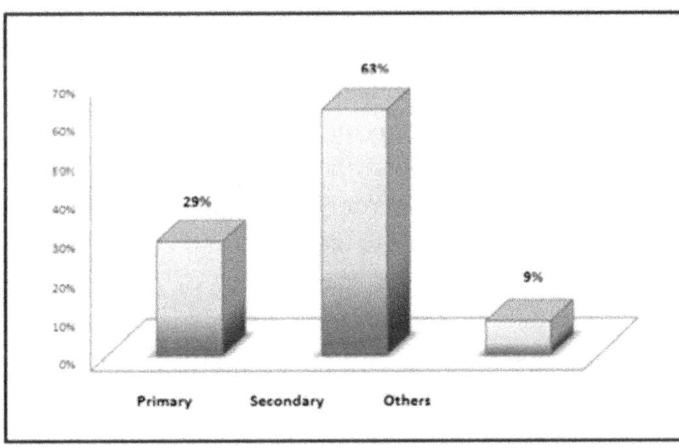

As can be verified in Figure 1, of the 374 people who were surveyed, 63% indicated that they had completed secondary school, 29% stated that they had only reached primary school and 9% that their studies had been higher than primary school. This is an essential factor to know to determine the associative criteria of the business model and that the Chamber of Microentrepreneurs should give much importance to the training and technical advice.

On the other hand, 72% (269) of the respondents said that they did not have any internet service, while 28% (105) did. This is an important indicator to determine the intensity of the use of technology to which they can be submitted and also indicates that the *Chamber of Micro Businesses* should implement strategies aimed at incorporating technology to those involved. Deepening in the situation of the use of the internet, 22% purchase consumer products or services, 14% purchase technology products, and 3% buy clothing. All this is having in mind that 15% responded that they purchase a little of all.

In another question, complementary to the previous one, we sought to know the ease and responsibility they have to pay for their basic needs. The answers were as follows: 66% (245) have not been late in paying for water, electricity, or telephone, while 34% (129) said they had been late. This data indicates the precariousness of income, but it is also vital since it determines whether they are reliable and responsible for meeting their payment obligations if some type of credit is assumed.

In turn, a significant issue is that of the 374, only 10% (38 entrepreneurs) indicated that they would not like to apply for a job in a private company, compared to 90% (336 entrepreneurs) who said they would. In some way, this response indicates the true entrepreneurial spirit; it allows the possibility of discriminating between those who are only for an income and those who are willing to risk with a business; this could be the first filter. In another perspective of questions, it was investigated the companies with more potential to focus interest and cross with financial feasibility. Along these lines, the 374 entrepreneurs were asked which businesses would be the most productive in economic terms. From this, the highest performance is located between 10 and 11% and corresponds to the Stores and Dining rooms, respectively. Here we have a clue of where to start the creation of *popular brands* since this perception clarifies a culture that allows massification and places us in the margin that would be looking for the entrepreneur. Then, with 8%, the hardware business is located; additionally, the criteria that the most demanded hardware materials are those to build houses or to fix some aspect related to it. In fourth place are Lubricators with 7%. Then, with 6%, there are the meatpacking plants or butcher's shops and, finally, each one with 5%, there are the Cyber and Beauty Cabinets, the latter being the determining factors for the proposal of this research.

We must not rule out the possibility of combining two, or more than two, of the proposed businesses, that is, for example, joining: *Store - Refrigerator* or *Dining Room - Lube machine or* three of them or all four in a single criterion, *it* can also be *Hardware Store, or it* can be organized Store - *Refrigerator - Dining Room,* among other options; this implies applying the corresponding marketing, designing a characteristic service and developing the *popular brand* as indicated. This does not obviate the fact that products can be generated that are marketed separately from it.

In that line of business structure and performance, the question "Is the business enough to live on? The answers are presented in table 3 below.

Table 3. Firms as a Good Source of Living in Monte Sinaí

Level	Absolute Frequency	Relative Frequency
Very good	0	0%
Well	107	29%
Regular	235	63%
Insufficient	32	9%
TOTAL	374	100%

Source: own elaboration

In this question, the 374 respondents express their discomfort, respond negatively, because in the business they have they are doing "regular" in 63%; another group of 29% is doing "well" while 9% are doing "insufficient," no one expresses that they are doing "very well." This is another critical factor in determining the type of inclusive entrepreneurial business they could be helped with; in other words, they say, "I am doing regular and well," but I would like it to be better or very well. In other words, the proposal must go beyond this framework of returns in the short term to gain sustainability.

Based on the above, research is carried out on the sources of financing chosen by entrepreneurs of *Monte Sinaí.* The results are shown in Figure 2.

In response to this question, 68% of the 374 small entrepreneurs surveyed answered that their primary source is self-financing. In other words, startup involves personal funds and then working capital and extensions are made with what the business generates; 25% do so with bank loans (public and private), and 7% do so through loans to "chulqueros" and other people, respectively. Making it clear that this is an austere and very disciplined group of people with which the risk (moral, adverse selection, market) is reduced to a minimum, they are people used to paying and working very hard in scarcity.

In turn, when asked about the presence of State policies aimed at entrepreneurship, only 2% said that they had received aid from the Government. In comparison, 98% indicated that they had not received support or were not aware of relevant public policies. This fact leads us to evidence that these people have self-management as the axis of microenterprise life, so there is a great spirit to move forward with their businesses. This result raises one of the critical questions: Do you think that partnerships with other similar companies would be useful? The answers are presented in Table 4.

Results show that 301 (80%) affirm that it would be suitable for everyone to associate with other similar businesses, a primary factor in determining the proposal that will be presented later.

Figure 2.

Graph 2 (pp14)

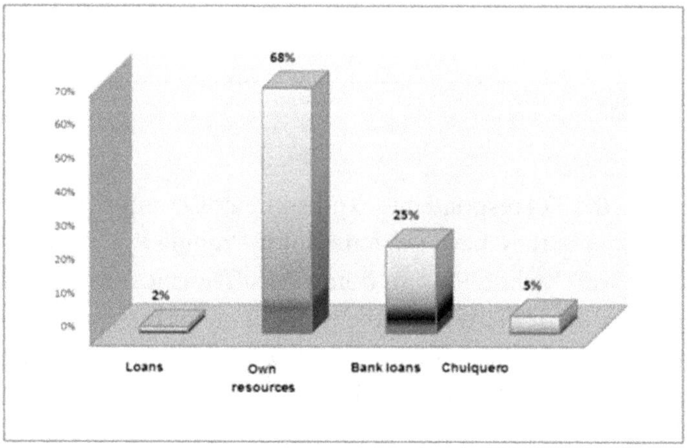

Table 4. Business Partnerships

Response	Absolute Frequency	Relative Frequency
YES	88	24%
NO	73	20%
Maybe.	67	18%
Yes, with conditions	146	39%
TOTAL	374	100%

Source: own elaboration

Along these lines, it is essential to ask the orientation of the organization *Chamber of Popular Micro Businesses* a question that gives the perspective of the problem to be overcome: Which of the following elements do you think you need most? (Table 5)

These answers clarify the components of the Chamber, since the 374 respondents chose, in order of priority, the five most essential elements to undertake some type of business and/or implement it in their own business: financial support (82%), advertising (68%); opportunity to compete (60%), and training (44%). Competition links with *Popular Brands* and the market penetration strategy.

Table 5. Entrepreneurs' Needs

Element	Absolute Frequency	Relative Frequency
Financial support	305	82%
Technical advice	111	30%
Training	166	44%
Accountant	0	0%
Organization	61	16%
Advertising	254	68%
Give them a chance to compete	225	60%
TOTAL	1122	156%

Source: own elaboration

It can be concluded that the micro and small informal entrepreneurs have a clear vision that in autarchy with their businesses is not doing well. Still, they consider that they could improve if there were support from the Government to receive some type of credit where the financing interests are minimal. However, this is not something that stops them as they are urged by the need to live.

They need to be trained to broaden their understanding of their business context and what the world is saying about innovation and accumulation in their business value chains. It is essential to understand that the management of a company is not achieved outside of academia because of the complex structure of capital that must build *collective accumulation,* through the *Chamber of Popular Micro-Businesses*, in the absence of financing and public policies.

Also, it is worth noting that there are aspects that need to be taken into account when including them among the projects for strengthening popular microenterprises, even though they were not specified favorably in the survey. One of the most delicate of these is the accounting organization of the business and general management. Although accounting and management have not been declared as urgent, an available format needs to be applied to have clarity on business growth.

Finally, popular firms need to be supported by advertising to increase sales. Their resurgence as an entity increases and thickens the economy's GDP without begging and without feeling vulnerable because they lack resources to complete their basic basket.

CONCLUSION

There is no experience in creating a business model based on *popular global micro-firms and brands,* and *Multiplazas Itinerant Fairs* as a strategy of market penetration, but we have shown that conditions exist to initiate pilot plans in Monte Sinai in Guayaquil.

In the reality of business in Monte Sinaí, it is possible to design an organizational business structure that allows entrepreneurs to accumulate levels of wealth to overcome the social precariousness and economic vulnerability in which they live. The association of entrepreneurs align processes and must create brands that can trade throughout the economy, and eventually can push for an expansion of their markets internationally. Neighboring countries have systemic gaps that could accept a model like this one if logistics are resolved. This proposal is structured from two macro elements: first, the organization that generates the *Popular Brands* and, second, the structure of the *Multiplaza Itinerant Fair*. These two strategies, linked in a single macro-strategy executed from the *Chamber of Popular Micro-Businesses,* can compensate for the competitiveness in the markets. With the popular brands, it is possible to focus the niche (or niches) to be penetrated, while the fair is a mechanism to possess products, brands, and patents. The measurement of the perception of the popular microentrepreneurs carried out leaves us with great possibilities of the feasibility of a model like the one presented.

REFERENCES

Abramo, P. (2012). La ciudad confusa: Mercado y producción de la estructura urbana en las grandes metrópolis latinoamericanas. *EURE. Revista Latinoamericana de Estudios Urbano Regionales*, *38*(114), 35–69. doi:10.4067/S0250-71612012000200002

Hernández, J. C. (2016). *Hogar de Cristo en Monte Sinaí: La herencia de los Vulnerados*. Guayaquil.

INEC. (2017). *Encuesta de Superficie y Producción Agropecuaria Continua ESPAC 2016*. Quito.

INEC. (2019). Reporte de Pobreza - Marzo 2019. Quito.

INEC. (2019). Reporte de Pobreza y Desigualdad- Junio 2019. Quito.

Instituto Nacional de Economía Popular y Solidaria (IEPyS). (2017). http://www.socioeco.org/bdf_organisme-558_es.html

MIDUVI. (2011). *Intervención Urbana Integral en la Zona de Expansión del Noroeste de la Ciudad de Guayaquil*. Subsecretaría de Hábitat y Asentamientos Humanos.

Sánchez, P. (2014). *Mercado de suelo informal y políticas públicas de habitat urbano en la ciudad de Guayaquil*. Quito: Flacso.

Távara, L. (2017). Director Social Hogar de Cristo. In Informalidad Urbana: Comprendiendo el Problema de la Tenencia de la Tierra en Promesa de Dios, Monte Sinai, Guayaquil. Tesis de Grado. Universidad Católica del Ecuador.

KEY TERMS AND DEFINITIONS

Chamber of Popular Micro Businesses: The Ecuadorian governmental office focused on supporting popular firms with tax exemptions and low-interest financing.

***Chulqueros*:** A person dedicated to giving money loans with high-interest rates characteristic of usury.

Invaders: People who do not have any title of the property to occupy land legally (urban or rural).

Monte Sinai: It is one of the poorest neighborhoods in Guayaquil and Ecuador.

National Institute of Agrarian Development (INDA): The official Ecuadorian organization that grants notifications to the cooperatives, which legalize the distribution of land.

Popular Business: Type of business defined by its precariousness, low income-generating capacity and, in many cases, by its illegality.

Tanker: Type of truck designed to bring water towards urban and rural poor areas without water.

Chapter 4
A Proposal for the Transformation of Fossil Fuel Energy Economies to Hydrogen Economies Through Social Entrepreneurship

Jossie Esteban Garzón Baquero
https://orcid.org/0000-0001-9470-7581
Facultad de Ingenierías, Grupo de Investigación Nuevas Tecnologías, Universidad de Santander, Bucaramanga, Colombia

Daniela Bellon Monsalve
Facultad de Ingenierías, Grupo de Investigación Nuevas Tecnologías, Universidad de Santander, Bucaramanga, Colombia

ABSTRACT

The world is growing at an ever-increasing rate, but this growth has occurred alongside an energy model based on fossil fuels, which presents serious sustainability problems. The current study seeks to illustrate one of the new alternative energy schemes which could replace fossil fuels in the future: hydrogen. The promise of hydrogen fuel has led large nations to invest in transitioning their fossil fuel economies to a hydrogen-based model. This will result in significant social impacts, leading to the question, How should it be done? Social entrepreneurship can integrate socio-economic actors and agents and help them to devise and implement new forms of energy innovation, which will open spaces for new business models. The current study conceptualizes within a present-day context the connotations of

DOI: 10.4018/978-1-7998-3568-4.ch004

the hydrogen economy at an international level, its implications to society, and its synergy with social entrepreneurship. The authors observed the rapid growth that these entrepreneurship initiatives are generating and how the models used to manage these undertakings play a vital role.

INTRODUCTION

The generation of energy has been essential to humanity for centuries, and Valero (2010) notes that for the last several decades, there has been a focus upon finding suitable alternative energy sources to reduce dependency on fossil fuels and curtail greenhouse gas emissions.

For Roberts (2004), this effort to find sustainable energy sources is driven by various factors; i) political stimuli from net energy importing nations, ii) environmental concerns as expressed by the Kyoto Protocol[1], and iii) diminishing hydrocarbon reserves, especially of petroleum. In this context, and based upon the research of Solano (2004), the development of hydrogen-based energy is logical. Hydrogen does not release carbon to the atmosphere, and the required technologies already exist and are experiencing gradual cost reductions. In contrast, the costs of discovering and extracting hydrocarbons continue to increase.

The factors, as mentioned earlier, support the concept of a "Hydrogen Economy" which has been theorized since the 19th century. In the novel "The Mysterious Island" penned by author Jules Verne in 1874 (Verne, 1874), the author proposes separating the constituent elements of water through electricity and using them as fuel[2]. Naturally, the concept has continued to evolve since then, but the basic transformation was envisioned long ago as humanity has sought to shift its energy matrix (Berry and Aceves, 2006). The term "hydrogen economy" can thus be taken to include the new business structure and system of socio-economic relationships that would be engendered by a move from fossil fuels to hydrogen. The question, therefore, arises as to how these socio-economic relationships can be created in a new business structure that is not only profitable but also promotes projects of community interest that may encompass public works, volunteer involvement, or an array of other types.

To answer this question, it is crucial to understand that the world is currently on the verge of energy and environmental crisis. In recent years, every crisis which has arisen has required humans to look beyond the present, leading to a vision of entrepreneurship as being the natural solution to such problems. Nevertheless, in the current crisis, it is not possible to simply apply the traditional definition of entrepreneurship, "the engine of nations' economic growth" (Audretsch and

Keilbach, 2004). Instead, a new and more in-depth explanation is required, which better suits the present time. To this end, Acosta Véliz, Coronel Pérez, and Jiménez Cercado (2018) define social entrepreneurship as an innovative form of approaching a social problem where the market economy cannot, where there is an insufficient or non-existent public administrative action, or where there is room in the market for intensification or improvement of services to achieve social goals.

Concerning the hydrogen economy, Sanabria, Pedraza, and Hurtado (2014) propose that social entrepreneurship is the way to take advantage of the potential of clean energy3 sources existing in a territory, in this case, hydrogen; furthermore, it allows to raise the economic value of renewable energies, which as a new pattern, generates jobs and promotes the reactivation of other industries of local nature, which can act as suppliers of this.

In this context, the present study proposes a transformation of fossil fuel economies to a new model that uses hydrogen as an energy vector. It suggests that this transformation can best be undertaken through synergy with social entrepreneurship[4], which aims for social and environmental development and the resolution of socio-economic problems employing sustainable strategies (Acosta Véliz et al., 2018).

THEORETICAL FRAMEWORK

Hydrogen is one of the most abundant elements in the universe, generally being found in its gas phase. The total amount of energy available in hydrogen is practically unlimited. Still, because it is rarely found in a free state (Valero, 2010), it is typically used as an energy vector rather than a primary energy source; and therefore requires an efficient means of production. Also, according to Solano (2004), since the era of fossil fuels is coming to an end, and at the same time, new energy systems are appearing which have the potential to change our civilization radically, it is necessary to comprehend the benefits of a major one of these; hydrogen. (Nicoletti, Arcuri, Nicoletti, and Bruno, 2015) develop a comparison of the most important physical and chemical properties that must be considered in an energy supply system, taking gasoline, methane, and hydrogen as a reference; this is presented in Table 1. Table 2 shows a comparison of the safety aspects, highlighting that, in eight of eleven parameters analyzed, hydrogen is the safest among the investigated fuels.

In this sense, Rifkin (2010) posits that as hydrogen is the most basic and ubiquitous element in the universe, it meets the conditions to be an endless and clean fuel, since it can neither be used up nor does it produce harmful CO_2 emissions when burned. These characteristics make hydrogen a perfect fuel upon which to base a new economy, an economy with markets and institutions that are sustainable[5], and avoid the errors of "The Industrial Era."

Table 1. Physics and chemical properties of three fuels

Property	Gasoline	Methane	Hydrogen
Density (kg/m^3)	4.40	0.65	0.84
Diffusion coefficient in air (cm^2/s)	0.05	0.16	0.610
Specific heat at constant pressure (J/ kg K)	1.20	2.22	14.89
Flammable limit in air (vol%)	1.0-7.6	5.3-15.0	4.0-75.0
Flammable energy in air (MJ)	0.24	0.29	0.02
Flammable temperature (K)	501-744	813	858
Flammable temperature in air (K)	2470	2148	2318
Explosion limit in air (vol%)	1.1-3.3	6.3-14.0	13.0-59.0

Source: (Nicoletti et al., 2015)

Table 2. Safety levels reached in the combustion processes

Characteristic	Safety level [a]		
	Gasoline	Methane	Hydrogen
Fuel toxicity	*	**	***
Combustion products toxicity	*	**	***
Density	*	**	***
Diffusion coefficient	*	**	***
Specific heat	*	**	***
Flammable	***	**	*
Flammable energy	**	***	*
Flammable temperature	*	**	***
Flame temperature	*	***	**
Explosion energy	*	**	***
Flame emissivity	*	**	***
[a] ***Safest, **Intermediate safety, *low safety			

Source: Nicoletti et al. (2015)

This new "hydrogen economy" must be supported by a social base. Per Hoffmann and Mirza (2002), hydrogen technologies will be applied to transportation, as well as the independent generation and domestic use of electricity. There will be a redistribution of global power. Emissions of carbon dioxide will be reduced, and the effects of climate change will be mitigated. The dependence of the developed nations on imported petroleum will disappear, producing new geopolitical realities. Also, Koppel, cited by Solano (2004), adds that the hydrogen economy will supply poor populations with the energy required to agricultural power equipment, small factories, and workshops, in addition to homes, schools, and hospitals.

The hydrogen economy will involve a systematic infrastructure, including the production, storage, transport, and usage of energy from hydrogen; and using fuel cells to transform hydrogen into electricity and heat (Chen and Hsu, 2018; Pudukudy, Yaakob, Mohammad, Narayanan, and Sopian, 2014).

The conceptual birth of the hydrogen economy resulted from a scientific meeting in Stockholm in 1968, which inspired chemist John Bockris to join research efforts in the field. The results of this work were published in 1972 as the first article using the name "A Hydrogen Economy" (Bockris, 1972, 2013). In this paper, the author bases his premise of using hydrogen as an energy vector upon three fundamental factors: i) The imminent increase in demand for energy resources in the coming years, which would require, in turn, mechanisms to reduce atmospheric contamination levels and in the amount of heat which would have to be produced to meet these requirements; ii) the generation of electricity far more cheaply than by using conventional methods, and iii) the potential to revolutionize transportation systems, leveraging the high performance of the hydrogen conversion process to reduce operating costs and create silent and non-polluting vehicles (Bockris, 1972).

Later, in 1976, the first "World Hydrogen Energy Conference" was convened, where hydrogen was promoted as a clean and promising energy vector for the future (Moliner, Lázaro, and Suelves, 2016). Finally, in 2003, the first government support appeared for the hydrogen economy, under US president George Bush, Romano Prodi in the European Union, and with Arnold Schwarzenegger as the governor of California (Sperling and Cannon, 2004b).

The same historical evolution which characterizes the concept of the hydrogen economy urges its implementation as a response to the environmental and social worries generated by the current fossil fuel economy (Moliner et al., 2016), basing this on two reasons. The first is associated with the limitations of the petroleum supply in the medium and long terms, and the second relates to the fears concerning global warming due to pollution and the generation of greenhouse gases (Moliner et al., 2016). As such, the concept has received a great deal of attention from various entities, both governmental and the private sector around the world. These bodies recognize the promise of hydrogen to de-carbonize transportation, reduce the generation of greenhouse gases, and guarantee the energy supply (Scipioni, Manzardo, and Ren, 2017).

Additionally, it is becoming evident that the hydrogen economy presents a set of challenges that are being gradually overcome in each of the critical links towards its implementation. These challenges relate to the production, conversion, and final use of hydrogen, as illustrated in Figure 1. Nevertheless, there remain essential barriers, within which two stand out. The first challenge is the tendency towards investment in fossil fuels, and the lack of policies that promote and facilitate the research, development, and implementation of new technologies for clean energy, which would help make hydrogen a competitive option. The second challenge has to do with the transportation and distribution of hydrogen from its place of production to points of consumption. Currently, these costs exceed production costs. In order to ameliorate this situation, the decentralized production of hydrogen has been proposed, which would bring about a broad expansion in its possible applications, both in mobile and stationary roles and result in a much broader number of people being able to benefit from the technology (Sperling and Cannon, 2004a).

In this context, the strategy that would allow for a reduction in the gap between the fossil fuel economy and the hydrogen economy must deal with one of the key links mentioned above, and must integrate the triple helix of the state (in terms of the creation of policies that facilitate its integration into various social processes); private industry (the creation of new business models that involve energy innovation processes); and finally academia (through the different educational and research methods that bring not only an improvement of the concept, itself, but also the creation of social and environmental awareness).

Figure 1. Links in the hydrogen economy
Source: Authors, adapted from (Pudukudy et al., 2014)

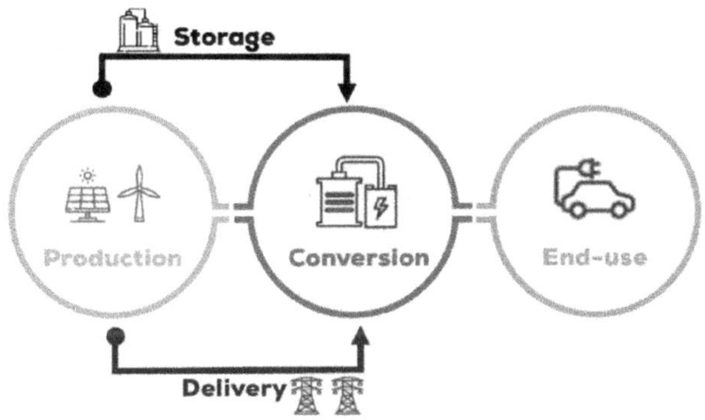

Within this triple helix, a common denominator appears that connects and facilitates work among the players, the concept of entrepreneurship. According to Escamilla, Alonso, and Plaza (2017), entrepreneurship has been studied from an academic perspective from many different angles[6]. From an economic perspective (this being the most commonly used), for example, entrepreneurship has always sought a relationship between economic development and the profit motive. However, if one looks at the concept chronologically, Cantillon and Higgs (1932) define entrepreneurship as a commercial activity arising from uncertainty. Say (1821) describes the concept as an intermediary between capital and labor, and Fritsch (2017) ties it to innovation and considers it the basis of the economy. In the same sense, since the 1990s, authors such as Varela (1998) define entrepreneurship as opportunities that require inputs such as financial and human resources. A definition which is broadened by Formichella (2015) to describe the concept as the act of creating or improving a product or service. Additionally, the social and human sciences have provided their point of view upon entrepreneurship (Guzmán and Trujillo, 2008), from which the illustration in Figure 2 has been created.

Figure 2. Evolution of the concept of entrepreneurship
Source: Authors, adapted from Bertelsmann (2019)

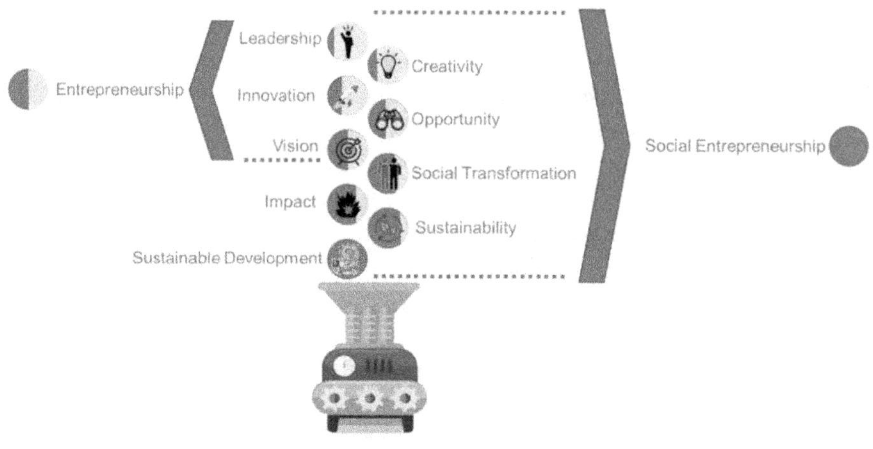

Social entrepreneurship is a new term with roots tracing back to the 1980s. According to Escamilla, Alonso, and Plaza (2017), it first appeared as a concept of obtaining resources for non-profit organizations. In greater detail, Shane and Venkataraman (2000) describe it as a sequential process, in which the entrepreneur creates, detects, and exploits an opportunity. This definition is seconded and expanded by Roberts and Woods (2005), who characterize the sequential process as the construction, evaluation, and pursuit of opportunities; but through a lens of transformative vision and social change. Austin, Stevenson, and Wei-Skillern

(2012) go further, considering social entrepreneurship as a weapon against market failures. As such, the concept involves innovative ideas aimed at sustainable change on a grand scale. This argument is also adopted by Simón Moya, Sastre Sánchez, and Revuelto Taboada (2015), in positing that the social entrepreneur fights for a truly lasting impact that has nothing to do with profit, but rather with producing significant changes in real communities.

Supported by all the theoretical, conceptual, and historical backing detailed above, and taking the economy as social science, the authors propose a transformation of the current fossil fuel economy to a future hydrogen economy in a triangular fashion, which places the social entrepreneur at its center. In our study, the entrepreneur is defined as the individual who takes advantage of opportunities and puts them into practice, with an impact upon society in the creation of jobs and income. It is also a person who demonstrates a desire to make a positive social change in society, exhibits high work performance and dedication, and whose contributions are aimed towards the construction of a denser social fabric and society in harmony with the state and the environment.

HOW TO BE AN ENTREPRENEUR IN THE NEW HYDROGEN ECONOMY

Capitalism and its logic of competition allow for the entrepreneur to play a significant role, understanding entrepreneurship as an activity that any individual can undertake upon their own initiative. However, from an economic viewpoint, Shane and Venkataraman (2000) suggest that entrepreneurship is the creation and consolidation of firms that detect and exploit market opportunities. Even then, to be an entrepreneur in this new hydrogen economy requires a form of entrepreneurship that distances itself from competitive capitalism, and which, according to Dees (1998), can contribute to resolving some of the social problems generated by the capitalist economic system.

Also, social entrepreneurship can be considered an economic activity that tends to create value in its approach to social challenges, such as the need to provide energy to the majority of the population and to mitigate the effects of anthropogenic climate change (Becker, Kunze, and Vancea, 2017; Surie, 2017).

However, according to Linares (2013), a social entrepreneurship initiative cannot only solve a social demand but must also do so by using resources responsibly with society and the environment; for this reason, the choice of appropriate technology is essential in this aspect. In this sense, and understanding that technology isn't neutral, but through its selection, the use of natural resources is conditioned, energy technologies must be prioritized.

In the specific case of initiatives entrepreneurship related to the diffusion of renewable energy technologies, which include the implementation of the hydrogen economy, it has been noted that developing economies possess specific shared characteristics. They tend to exhibit a deficiency or lack of incentive for innovation on the part of government entities. They also demonstrate low demand for renewables given the lack of knowledge in the market, which makes new projects considerably riskier, and slows the adoption of solutions (Walsh, 2012). In these cases, the role of social entrepreneurship assumed by NGOs or by academia becomes fundamental in the success of the diffusion of this kind of innovation (Balachandra, Kristle Nathan, and Reddy, 2010).

As well, one problem of the current economic system, which also affects this new economy is the type of entrepreneurship that is being created. On the one hand, there is destructive entrepreneurship of speculative activities that do not generate value. Their final goal is only a drive for profit on the part of the entrepreneur. On the other hand, there is also unproductive entrepreneurship, which does maximize benefits in the short term and generates a specific added value, but only through imitation (Santos, Barroso, and Guzmán, 2013).

What, then, would be a common starting point for social entrepreneurship in today's world? It is clear that the profit motive is a common feature of entrepreneurship under the present economic system, and more so in the fossil fuel energy model, a model with a highly destructive and unproductive basis driven by greed and the competition paradigm. For the new hydrogen economy, the entrepreneurial activity must exhibit a philosophy based on producing goods and services that serve the goals of the population. According to Cuevas (1994), a social businessperson or entrepreneur must be proactive and creative, as well as continually working to reduce uncertainty, and being open to new opportunities. Thus, if the social entrepreneur understands that their work drives and dynamizes their economy, they will be a key player in economic development. To be an entrepreneur in this new hydrogen economy, one must not focus on the model in itself, but rather upon their underlying motivation and the result that they want to achieve with it.

FROM THEORY TO PRACTICE

Various countries around the world have begun to explore the hydrogen economy, implementing an array of strategies to do so. In this regard, within the international political context, several countries have distinguished themselves by their implementation policies: including Japan, Germany, China, the United States, South Korea, and the United Kingdom. Each of these countries has different national priorities and reasons to pursue hydrogen technology, such as the desire to improve urban air quality, drive economic growth, guarantee energy security, revitalize regional economies, and reduce greenhouse gas emissions (Staffell et al., 2019).

Entrepreneurship associated with the hydrogen economy in these countries tends to be made tangible through experiences such as that of Hyundai Motor, one of the pioneering companies at a global level in producing fuel-cell-powered vehicles. This is an example of a firm that is not only profitable but also looking to expand its social role by implementing its philosophy for the future and supporting the transition to clean hydrogen energy[7] (Hyundai Motor, 2009). Also, in the field of hydrogen entrepreneurship, it is worth highlighting Hbank Technology, which is a Taiwanese company known for its consulting and production of systems for the purification and storage of hydrogen. The firm excels in storage using metal hydrides and has secured about 13 patents in this field since 1999. Among their products, they are recognized for analytical instruments, fuel cells, and mixed-fuel and fuel-saving burners.

At the international level, the number of ventures supporting aspects of the hydrogen economy has been growing considerably, such that these companies have positioned themselves in the market and even become publicly traded, as in the case of Ballard Power Systems, Plug Power, Hydrogenics, and FuelCell Energy, among others. Colombia, for its part, has seen the participation of firms, such as EcoWill Engineering Group, a Spanish company that operates in the country and is dedicated to the generation of sustainable energy solutions, including hydrogen products such as solid storage, fuel cells, and electrolyzers. Another firm working in Colombia is McPhy Energy, a French company focused on the creation of hydrogen energy solutions, with products such as electrolyzers, hydrogen fueling stations, industrial hydrogen, energy storage, and hydrogen for local communities, among others.

The actors mentioned above illustrate social entrepreneurship through the experience of each of the companies and countries above, from their usage of hydrogen as an energy vector to setting up an energy system able to reduce carbon emissions, guarantee the energy supply, strengthen their economies, and support the production and implementation of renewable energy through hybrid systems to integrate solar, wind, and biomass, among others, depending on the characteristics of each region, and leading to solutions for social problems.

METHODOLOGY

The present study is descriptive and of qualitative analysis. It answers the question, "how can fossil fuel economies be transformed into hydrogen economies through social entrepreneurship? An in-depth examination has been made of the concepts of "social entrepreneurship" and "hydrogen economy" through secondary sources. The study concludes with a proposal based upon national and international entrepreneurship that demonstrates cooperative work between social entrepreneurship and the hydrogen economy to move beyond fossil fuel economies.

ANALYSIS

Hydrogen power and entrepreneurship have become topics in the public eye, as well as the business and academic communities, given their influence on the world economy. The behavior of these sectors depends on the incentives that create aggregate demand, competition, and, finally, the need for continuous innovation. Around the world, we see a proportional relationship between the level of economic development and a high level of innovative entrepreneurship (Rodríguez Moreno, 2016); nevertheless, entrepreneurship can also produce positive or negative externalities. The hydrogen economy needs to have as its base social entrepreneurship that creates positive externalities such as new jobs and an increase of the per capita GDP. Additionally, and according to Cohen and Winn (2007), if commercial action leads to the generation of negative externalities such as the exploitation of natural resources for the maximization of shareholder profits, then the implementation of a hydrogen economy can be used to reduce air and water pollution, diminish the depletion of the ozone layer, and eliminate industrial pollution and nuclear radiation. In countries such as Colombia, the elimination of additional negative externalities must be emphasized, such as inequality in the distribution of income, poverty, and land concentration; these being vicious cycles as indicated by Martínez Cousinou (2003), which overwhelm the poor population and are perpetuated by generations of business and political families.

Also, moving from externalities to costs, these can be economic, social, and environmental, among others. The relationship between these different costs is easily illustrated by considering the effects of climate change. The meteorological phenomena caused by climate variation can cause incidents that increase the prices of goods and services and reduce the value proposition of the entrepreneur. This, in turn, creates uncertainty in markets and reduces family income, which increases the demand for government support.

For this reason, the society within this new hydrogen economy must demand a radical change across many economic sectors; prioritize sustainable development, and integrate this into its business plans employing social entrepreneurship. In this way, entrepreneurs can create and build value with their ideas, which can improve the use of the scarce resources provided by nature. The current study suggests that, as the center and base of this new economy, the entrepreneur should not focus merely on financial aspects, but rather upon the social and environmental needs of the world.

TRANSFORMING FOSSIL FUEL ECONOMIES INTO HYDROGEN ECONOMIES THROUGH SOCIAL ENTREPRENEURSHIP

Geoffrey Edwin Hall Ballard, the founder of Ballard Power Systems, supported the need for efforts together with the government, academia, and industry, for the transition of a fossil fuel economy to a hydrogen economy to be possible[8] (Ballard, 2008).

In this vision, where the government, academia, and industry are entrusted with the transition of a fossil fuel economy to a hydrogen economy, entrepreneurship must be prioritized as a critical tool in the process, without forgetting that this entrepreneurship must emphasize the social aspect. In today's world, all economic actors pursue their own ends, without considering the environment, and without taking into account the array of different types of companies; much less the previous work, experience, and knowledge provided by academia. Therefore, the current proposal links the hydrogen economy and social entrepreneurship in a manner that is pertinent, timely, and focused on innovative ideas from multidisciplinary sources from around the world. This allows for the structuring of business plans with higher chances of accessing public and/or private resources and converting them into sustainable companies with a more significant impact upon any economy.

The proposal is based on the idea that it is possible to transform current fossil fuel economies using a multidisciplinary array of interdisciplinary ventures, an energy proposal that fits with the conditions of large economies and their ecosystems, the application of new technologies and good management practices, as well as the use of social networks and online learning communities as support strategies for knowledge diffusion between participants. The plan depends on support by the state (both its government and the population that benefits), industry (entrepreneur and intrapreneur), academia, and the environment (both the physical environment, as well as the social one) as a transversal axis. This proposal also takes into account the individual, in addition to corporations and the community.

The ecosystem that is suggested for this hydrogen economy must support the training of entrepreneurs and the creation of knowledge in order to improve the sustainability of start-up businesses over time. For Gómez and Mitchell (2014), scientific and technological strategies must be implemented that revolve around human management, the creation of new knowledge, and dynamic and innovative social entrepreneurship that does not neglect productivity; all supported by robust institutions and the state, and a competitive environment conducive to business development. The current study is based upon this premise, as is shown in Figure 3, where each one of the actors described above plays a fundamental role, as explained below.

Figure 3. Key players in the transition of a fossil fuel economy to a hydrogen economy
Source: Authors

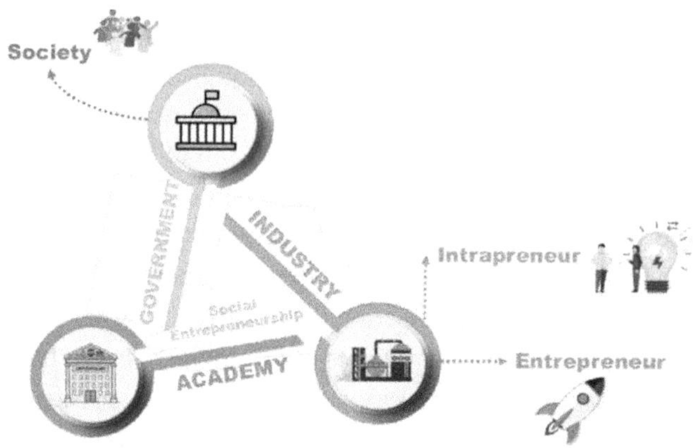

The proposed hydrogen economy, by means of social entrepreneurship, must meet the needs currently covered by the fossil fuel economy. The economy must be oriented towards those who are interested in creating firms with a social impact. According to Gámez and Garzón (2016), entrepreneurs who create firms are key agents of the economy because they drive technological change, wealth generation, and job creation. Entrepreneurship is a way of life and is the ideal basis of the proposal in this study.

THE ROLE OF THE STATE

The state is made up, primarily, of two agents. The first is the government, which, as the principal pillar of the state, must give clear directives towards promoting the use of hydrogen as a fuel. The government must train its institutions – especially its ministries – so that within their spheres of responsibility, they can develop action plans that promote research into, production, and commercialization of hydrogen as a fuel.

The powers of the state must be aimed towards driving decisive action and coordinating all levels of society in the adoption of hydrogen in transportation and electricity production, among other technologies that modernize institutions. These plans must be predicated not only upon national policy, but also the objectives presented in the UN climate change conference of 2020. These objectives should seek to promote the exploration and use of alternative sources of environmentally-friendly energy that are already established in official documents such as the National Development Plan. Finally, the government must work to clear away the barriers that block the development of the hydrogen economy, including raw materials, lack of infrastructure, safety aspects, and price, among others. The current economic reality can be changed by government incentives to stimulate the growth of hydrogen fuel, and the world can indeed leave the fossil fuel economy behind.

The second agent of the state is the society itself. Society is arguably the more important of the two agents since it is ultimately the people who will become the end users of each of the technologies linked to the implementation of the hydrogen economy. Society's role must be dynamic and continually evolve, given that individuals initially act as consumers, but some also become agents of change as members of industry or academia. This reality means that people can move from being mere users to become drivers of change through entrepreneurship or intrapreneurship[9], promoting social consciousness in all of their activities.

THE ROLE OF INDUSTRY

As an institution dedicated to commercial activities to satisfy social needs for goods and services, the industry should work through large multinational companies to strengthen the global initiative known as the Hydrogen Council, which strives to position hydrogen among the solutions for a transition to a clean, low-carbon energy system. New ventures should be aligned with the projects already being led by the firms: Air Liquide, Alstom, Anglo American, BMW Group, Daimler, ENGIE, Honda, Hyundai, Kawasaki, Royal Dutch Shell, The Linde Group, Total, and Toyota.

For its own part, this council must undertake continuous investments to increase the role of hydrogen in the energy mix of the future, through policies and support programs in concert with individual governments. An investment of 1.4 billion Euros is estimated to be necessary. According to Benoît Potier, CEO of Air Liquide, "the 2015 Paris Accord to fight climate change was a considerable step in the right direction, but actions on the part of the business are required to make the commitment a reality" (ONU, 2015).

In this manner, efforts on the part of the state (government and society) must be integrated with those of academia, focusing on the development of strategies that prioritize the resources of each country towards projects dedicated to this transition, especially social entrepreneurship with emphasis on renewable energy, recognizing its value and importance in the development of a sustainable society, and on all of the positive externalities it will bring.

In conclusion, the hydrogen economy depends on constant and robust business activity, supported by governments and academia, all the while encouraging the responsible leadership of social entrepreneurs.

THE ROLE OF ACADEMIA

One of the actors most relevant to the transition from a fossil fuel economy to a hydrogen economy is academia. In general, technologies for the production and distribution of hydrogen have enjoyed tremendous development in recent decades. Still, the role of academia[10] is fundamental in bringing these technologies to Earth in each of the societies where they are to be implemented, taking into account their cultural, technological, social, economic, and political differences. In this sense, the current proposal highlights the role of academia from three fundamental elements, which are: i) Strengthening implementation prospects through the identification of potential and opportunities in each region; ii) Research, development, and innovation, given that academia enjoys the intellectual and human capital and the laboratory infrastructure for systemic and integrated development based on fundamental engineering and economic analysis; and iii) Training and education, taking the first to mean each person learning about the world around them, and the second being about the sociocultural collective that surrounds and affects each of us. Figure 4 illustrates how these elements are articulated and highlight the importance of their progressive and sequential execution, this being a cyclical process towards continuous improvement.

Concerning the first element, strengthening implementation prospects, this includes the identification of potential and opportunities to implement the hydrogen economy in the various regions of the country, taking into account the characteristics of each region in terms of temperature, geographic location, and geological features, among others. This identification makes it possible to find integration opportunities for micro-networks to achieve maximum benefits. This element leads to the establishment of a detailed collective roadmap to follow for the transition of the fossil fuel economy to a hydrogen one. It must be characterized by interdisciplinary work where academia leads collaborative networks with the state and industry to establish the objectives, goals, and priorities for this transition, which should themselves be aligned with the purposes for sustainable development and supported by social entrepreneurship.

With respect to the element of research, development, and innovation, this item aims to improve the development of advanced materials for each of the aspects in the implementation of the hydrogen economy. It also seeks increasing performance in existing aspects, in the development of mobile and stationary applications, and the diversification of the energy matrix due to the integration of micro-networks to take advantage of the resources of each region. It furthermore strives for the development of efficient systems that improve the cost-benefit ratio. In this element, academia must administrate resources for research, prioritizing those projects with more generous social benefits, which in turn help incubate and support social ventures, specifically in the field of renewable energy.

The third and last element is training and education, which seeks not only to increase the intellectual capacity in each aspect of the hydrogen economy, but also to raise awareness and consciousness of the majority of the population. This last element should create a genuine cultural change concerning the importance of the transition, as well as in terms of the implementation and use of each of the components of the hydrogen economy. Finally, it must be highlighted that when the implementation of the hydrogen economy becomes more tangible, it will be necessary to undertake a process of training, which will strengthen the labor force at a technical and technological level.

Figure 4. Fundamental elements of the role of academia
Source: Authors.

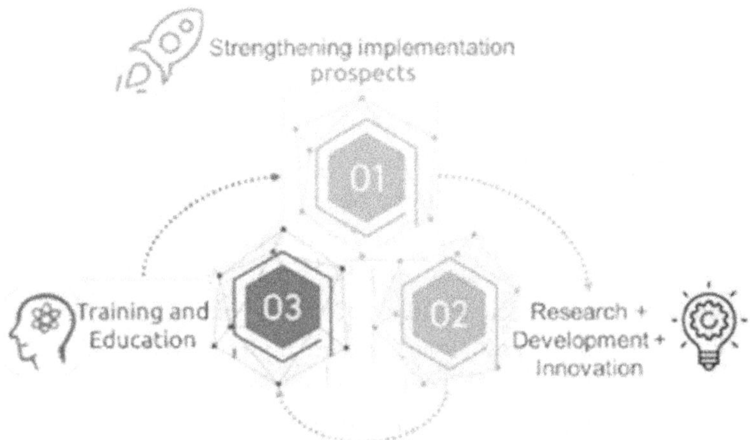

DISCUSSION

The current analysis is based on the transition of fossil fuel economies to hydrogen economies through social entrepreneurship and could be replicated for other types of clean energy. A pilot program remains to be undertaken with various social ventures to identify the factors that support the process of consolidation of business ideas in clean economies around the world, taking into account both growth and sustainability. Evaluation processes for the implementation of these social ventures should be implemented in fossil fuel economies, helping determine how to drive the transition to a hydrogen economy. The depth of the shortcomings detected by the great powers are not well known, nor how they have been corrected. Neither is it yet clear the impact of existing ventures and their relationship with the business fabric of the hydrogen economy posited by the current study. Social entrepreneurship and the hydrogen economy are areas to be explored to determine if a relationship exists. In this chapter, we analyzed the process of building entrepreneurship with a social vision; however, social entrepreneurship can be studied in a world that is still in the process of constructing environmental protection scenarios and requires entrepreneurs who set forth and embody these values and propose new forms of environmental innovation (Gámez Gutiérrez and Garzón Baquero, 2017).

It is to be hoped that, in the medium term, industry and academia will contribute to forming strategies that strengthen the development of new hydrogen economies around the world; without neglecting sustainable development and emphasizing the human being as a critical link in the evolutionary chain (Latorre, 2019).

CONCLUSION

The hydrogen economy represents a viable opportunity to replace that of fossil fuels in the medium to long term. The great powers of the world are showing considerable interest in implementing and enjoying the benefits thereof. Nevertheless, this will only be possible with the support of the three primary axes of each country; the state (including the government and society, as the ultimate end-user), an industry which highlights the social entrepreneur as its principal agent, and of course, academia, to lead and orient the required processes, interdisciplinary work, and collaborative networks.

In proposing such a drastic transition as that of a fossil fuel economy changing to hydrogen, it is necessary to give weight not only to the economic and financial costs of the projects that will make it possible, but also to take into account other social costs, to make it a viable transition. It is in this sense that the role of social entrepreneurship plays a fundamental and essential role, which must be supported by academia, existing industry, and the state, in a joint effort for a sustainable economy that will guarantee the energy supply, decrease wealth inequality, and promote the efficient use of resources and an environment with lower levels of pollution.

REFERENCES

Acosta Véliz, M. M., Coronel Pérez, V., & Jiménez Cercado, M. (2018). Emprendimiento Social Y Su Relación Con La Base De La Pirámide En Latinoamérica. *3C Empresa. Investigación y Pensamiento Crítico*, *7*(4), 50–67. doi:10.17993/3cemp.2018.070436.50-67/

Audretsch, D. B., & Keilbach, M. (2004). Does entrepreneurship capital matter? *Entrepreneurship Theory and Practice*, *28*(5), 419–429. doi:10.1111/j.1540-6520.2004.00055.x

Austin, J., Stevenson, H., & Wei-Skillern, J. (2012). Social and commercial entrepreneurship: Same, different, or both? *Revista ADM*, *47*(3), 370–384. doi:10.5700/rausp1055

B., J., Cantillon, R., & Higgs, H. (1932). Essai sur la Nature du Commerce en General. *Journal of the Royal Statistical Society*, *95*(1), 131. doi:10.2307/2341977

Balachandra, P., Kristle Nathan, H. S., & Reddy, B. S. (2010). Commercialization of sustainable energy technologies. *Renewable Energy*, *35*(8), 1842–1851. doi:10.1016/j.renene.2009.12.020

Ballard, G. (2008). *Our History - Power to Change the World | Ballard Power*. Retrieved January 16, 2020, from https://www.ballard.com/about-ballard/our-history

Becker, S., Kunze, C., & Vancea, M. (2017). Community energy and social entrepreneurship: Addressing purpose, organisation and embeddedness of renewable energy projects. *Journal of Cleaner Production*, *147*, 25–36. doi:10.1016/j.jclepro.2017.01.048

Berry, G., & Aceves, S. (2006). La Economía del Hidrógeno como Solución al Problema de la Estabilización del Clima Mundial. *Acta Universitaria*, *16*(1), 5–14. doi:10.15174/au.2006.192

Bertelsmann, F. (2019). *Emprendimiento Social Juvenil*. Academic Press.

Bockris, J. (1972). *A Hydrogen Economy*. Academic Press.

Bockris, J. (2013). The hydrogen economy: Its history. *International Journal of Hydrogen Energy*, *38*(6), 2579–2588. doi:10.1016/j.ijhydene.2012.12.026

Chandler, G. N., DeTienne, D. R., McKelvie, A., & Mumford, T. V. (2011). Causation and effectuation processes: A validation study. *Journal of Business Venturing*, *26*(3), 375–390. doi:10.1016/j.jbusvent.2009.10.006

Chen, Y. T., & Hsu, C. W. (2018). The key factors affecting the strategy planning of Taiwan's hydrogen economy. *International Journal of Hydrogen Energy*, 3290–3305. doi:10.1016/j.ijhydene.2018.07.159

Cohen, B., & Winn, M. I. (2007). Market imperfections, opportunity and sustainable entrepreneurship. *Journal of Business Venturing, 22*(1), 29–49. doi:10.1016/j.jbusvent.2004.12.001

Cuevas, J. G. (1994). Towards a Taxonomy of Entrepreneurial Theories. *International Small Business Journal, 12*(4), 77–88. Advance online publication. doi:10.1177/0266242694124005

Dees, J. G. (1998). *The Meaning of "Social Entrepreneurship."* Academic Press.

Escamilla, S., Alonso, N., & Plaza, P. (2017). Emprendimiento social. *Revista de Estudios de Juventud, 118*, 240. doi:10.1017/CBO9781107415324.004

Formichella, M. M. (2015, Sept.). "La Administración en un mundo complejo" "La recuperación de la Competitividad, el Crecimiento y el Trabajo." *Monografia.*

Fritsch, M. (2017). The theory of economic development – An inquiry into profits, capital, credit, interest, and the business cycle. *Regional Studies, 51*(4), 654–655. doi:10.1080/00343404.2017.1278975

Gámez G.J., & Garzón, J. (2016). Teaching entrepreneurship: towards a proposal of an educational program in the third level (tertiary) education. *i*, 458.

Gámez Gutiérrez, J., & Garzón Baquero, J. E. (2017). Nueva propuesta transversal de emprendimiento e innovación para programas educativos en el tercer nivel de educación. *Contaduría y Administración, 62*(1), 239–261. doi:10.1016/j.cya.2016.10.005

Gómez R., H. J., & Mitchell, D. (2014). Innovación y emprendimiento en Colombia: alcance, perspectivas y recomendaciones de política, 2014-2018. *Cuadernos de Fedesarrollo*, 82.

Guzmán, A., & Trujillo, M. (2008). Emprendimiento social - revisión de literatura. *Estudios Gerenciales, 24*, 20.

Hoffmann, P., & Mirza, U. K. (2002). Tomorrow's energy: Hydrogen, fuel cells, and the prospects for a cleaner planet. *Electronic Green Journal, 37*(16), 95521. doi:10.2307/20050353

Latorre, J. I. (2019). *Ética para máquinas*. Academic Press.

Linares, P. (2013). Dimensión tecnológica del emprendimiento social. In Guía del emprendedor social: inspiraciones para la creación de empresas al servicio de la sociedad. Academic Press.

Martínez Cousinou, G. (2003). El malestar en la globalización. Madrid, Taurus, 2002. *Revista Internacional de Sociologia*, *61*(34), 216–220.

Moliner, R., Lázaro, M. J., & Suelves, I. (2016). Analysis of the strategies for bridging the gap towards the Hydrogen Economy. *International Journal of Hydrogen Energy*, *41*(43), 19500–19508. doi:10.1016/j.ijhydene.2016.06.202

Hyundai Motor. (2009). *Hyundai motor company I 2009 Annual Report Table of Contents*. Hyundai Motor Company Annual Report.

Nicoletti, G., Arcuri, N., Nicoletti, G., & Bruno, R. (2015). A technical and environmental comparison between hydrogen and some fossil fuels. *Energy Conversion and Management*, *89*, 205–213. doi:10.1016/j.enconman.2014.09.057

ONU. (2015). *Convención Marco sobre el Cambio Climático, 21930*. Retrieved from file:///C:/Users/W7/Desktop/ufc.pdf

Pudukudy, M., Yaakob, Z., Mohammad, M., Narayanan, B., & Sopian, K. (2014). Renewable hydrogen economy in Asia - Opportunities and challenges: An overview. *Renewable & Sustainable Energy Reviews*, *30*, 743–757. doi:10.1016/j.rser.2013.11.015

Rifkin, J. (2010). *La economía del hidrógeno*. Academic Press.

Roberts, P. (2004). The End of Oil: On the Edge of a Perilous New World. *Journal of Ecological Anthropology*, *9*. doi:10.5038/2162-4593.9.1.8

Roberts, R., & Woods, C. (2005). Changing the world on a shoestring: The concept of social entrepreneurship. *University of Auckland Business Review*, *7*(1), 45–51.

Rodríguez Moreno, D. C. (2016). Emprendimiento sostenible, significado y dimensiones. *Katharsis*, (21), 449. doi:10.25057/25005731.775

Sanabria A., S. E., Pedraza, P. A., & Hurtado A., E. (2014). El emprendimiento como fuente de desarrollo y fortalecimiento de las capacidades endógenas para el aprovechamiento de las energías renovables. *Revista EAN*, (77), 152. doi:10.21158/01208160.n77.2014.821

Santos, F. J., Barroso, M. d l O., & Guzmán, C. (2013). *La economía global y los emprendimientos sociales*. Academic Press.

Say, J. B. (1821). *Tratado de Economía Política o Exposición sencilla del modo con que se forman, se distribuyen y se consumen las riquezas*. Academic Press.

Scipioni, A., Manzardo, A., & Ren, J. (2017). Hydrogen Economy: Supply Chain, Life Cycle Analysis and Energy Transition for Sustainability. *The American Historical Review*, *40*. doi:10.1086/ahr/40.1.128

Shane, S., & Venkataraman, S. (2000). Note As the Promise of Entrepreneurship. *Academy of Management Review*, *25*(1), 217–226. doi:10.2307/259271

Simón Moya, V., Sastre Sánchez, O., & Revuelto Taboada, L. (2015). El emprendedor social: Análisis de la alerta social. *Suma de Negocios*, *6*(14), 155–165. doi:10.1016/j.sumneg.2015.07.001

Solano, J. (2004). Hacia una economía basada en el hidrógeno. *Anales de La Universidad Metropolitana*, *4*(1), 165–180.

Sperling, D., & Cannon, J. (2004a). Hydrogen Hope or Hype? In The Hydrogen Economy Transition (Vol. 17, pp. 235–239). doi:10.1016/B978-012656881-3/50017-4

Sperling, D., & Cannon, J. (2004b). *The Hydrogen Energy Transition. Moving toward the post-petroleum age in transportation. Growth*. Lakeland.

Staffell, I., Scamman, D., Velazquez Abad, A., Balcombe, P., Dodds, P. E., Ekins, P., Shah, N., & Ward, K. R. (2019). The role of hydrogen and fuel cells in the global energy system. *Energy & Environmental Science*, *12*(2), 463–491. doi:10.1039/C8EE01157E

Surie, G. (2017). Creating the innovation ecosystem for renewable energy via social entrepreneurship: Insights from India. *Technological Forecasting and Social Change*, *121*, 184–195. doi:10.1016/j.techfore.2017.03.006

Trujillo Dávila, M. A., & Guzmán Vásquez, A. (2008). Intraemprendimiento: una revisión al constructo teórico, sus implicaciones y agenda de investigación futura. *Cuad. Adm. Bogotá (Colombia)*, *21*(2135), 37–63.

Valero, J. A. (2010). El Espejismo De Una Energía Social: La Economía Del Hidrógeno. *Revista Internacional de Sociologia*, *68*(2), 429–452. doi:10.3989/ris.2008.08.13

Varela, R. (1998). El espiritu empresarial y la generación de empleos. *Univalle - ICESI*, 8.

Verne, J. (1874). La Isla Misteriosa. *Historia, 4*(1935), 1–27.

Walsh, P. R. (2012). Innovation Nirvana or Innovation Wasteland? Identifying commercialization strategies for small and medium renewable energy enterprises. *Technovation*, *32*(1), 32–42. doi:10.1016/j.technovation.2011.09.002

Zarta Ávila, P. (2018). La sustentabilidad o sostenibilidad: un concepto poderoso para la humanidad. *Tabula Rasa*, (28), 409–423. doi:10.25058/20112742.n28.18

KEY TERMS AND DEFINITIONS

Biomass: It is defined as an organic matter used as a fuel, especially in a power station for the generation of electricity.

Externalities: Outer economic effects (positive and negative) caused by the economic activity of a firm.

Fossil Fuel: Mainly defined by oil, coal, and natural gas, it is formed in the geological past from the fossilization of living organisms, mainly plants.

Greenhouse Effect: It is a natural process that warms the Earth's surface.

Hydrogen: It is one of the most abundant elements in the universe, generally being found in its gas phase.

Hydrogen Economy: The new business structure and system of socio-economic relationships engendered by a move from fossil fuels to hydrogen.

Intrapreneurship: Sort of an entrepreneurial activity carried out in an already-existing organization.

Kyoto Protocol: Signed in December 1997, in which developed countries committed to reducing carbon dioxide (CO2) emissions between 2008 and 2012, by at least 5% compared to 1990 levels.

ENDNOTES

1 Signed in December 1997, in which developed countries committed to reducing carbon dioxide (CO_2) emissions between 2008 and 2012, by at least 5% compared to 1990 levels.

2 "What will be burned in place of coal if it runs out?" "Water," replied Pencroft, "Water, broken down into its elements by electricity. Yes, my friends, I believe that water will one day be used as fuel, that the hydrogen and oxygen which constitute it, used in isolation or simultaneously, will provide an inexhaustible source of heat and light. Water is the coal of the future."

3 Energy is used to power devices, to produce goods, to transmit information, among other necessary activities to develop tasks of social entrepreneurship, however, society is not aware of the use of this resource (Linares, 2013).

4 In a context of socially responsible entrepreneurship, it's important to be aware of the available alternatives for an appropriate use of energy. Furthermore, facilitating responsible energy use can also be a matter of social entrepreneurship, since providing access to energy to those who don't have it, or facilitating access to sources, are activities that provide a very important space for entrepreneurship (Linares, 2013).

5 Sustainability must be understood as an articulated discipline of knowledge and as a new way of rethinking the human relationship with nature; based on the totality of the economic, social, environmental, and value dimensions; leading to a global revolution in survival with the planet (Zarta Ávila, 2018).

6 Chandler, DeTienne, McKelvie, and Mumford (2011) address only two of the key theories of entrepreneurship: 1) the theory of creation, where the entrepreneur creates his own opportunities, and 2) the theory of discovery, where the entrepreneur does not create opportunities, but only discovers them.

7 "... firms will play a fundamental role in the transition of global societies towards clean energy by helping making hydrogen an economically viable energy source."

8 "It will take a combined effort of academia, government, and industry to bring about the change from a gasoline economy to a hydrogen economy. The forces are building, and progress is being made. It is of major importance that a change of this magnitude not be forced on unwilling participants, but that all of us work together for an economically viable path to change." — Geoffrey Ballard (1932-2008).

9 Intrapreneurship is here defined as an entrepreneurial activity carried out in an already-existing organization (Trujillo, Dávila, and Guzmán Vásquez, 2008).

10 The role of the academy will be played by institutions of higher education that accredit their performance with criteria of universality in the following activities: scientific or technological research; academic training in professions or disciplines, and finally the production, development and construction of knowledge and universal and national culture. These institutions are also empowered to carry out academic training programs in occupations, professions or disciplines, specialization programs, masters, doctorates, and postdocs.

Chapter 5
Scope for Sustainability in the Fashion Industry Supply Chain:
Technology and Its Impact

Kiara Carranza Gudiel
Wenzhou-Kean University, China

Rob Kim Marjerison
https://orcid.org/0000-0003-1181-8695
Wenzhou-Kean University, China

Yuxi Zhao
Wenzhou-Kean University, China

ABSTRACT

This chapter seeks to determine whether entrepreneurial technological innovation can mitigate the intrinsic contradiction between short-term fashion and the long-term fashion industry in the supply chain to achieve environmental, economic, and social sustainability. The current fashion industry is driven by the ephemeral nature of fashion and its associated wastes which are not very sustainable. Although literature has demonstrated that operations research can be used to reduce inventory wastes, whether emerging technologies can reformat the whole mode of production in the fashion industry to be more sustainable remains unknown. Through interviewing professionals who specialize in the three key stages in the supply chain, this chapter concludes that the transition to sustainability is possible if technology is not just regarded as a tool to reduce carbon emissions, but used to materialize the sustainable design philosophy and integrated into the sustainability rebranding process in the whole supply chain from beginning to end.

DOI: 10.4018/978-1-7998-3568-4.ch005

INTRODUCTION

Fashion is a form of short-term social expression which lasts shorter than a season. The fashion industry, however, aims to secure long-term growth through continuous entrepreneurial technological innovation (Kaiser, 2012). This contradiction in timing creates a sustainability conundrum: how can entrepreneurial innovation commercialize a form of short-term social expression into a long-term industry to achieve sustainable growth? The sustainable growth here not only refers to economic sustainability, but more importantly, to both environmental and social sustainability as well. This chapter uses the lens of supply chain to discuss the possibility of using technology to turn short-term social expression-based fashion into a long-term mass production-based fashion industry to achieve sustainability.

The fashion industry is one of the biggest industries in the world. It is currently worth an estimated $2.4 trillion USD and has grown at an annual rate of 5.5 percent (Amed, Berg, Brantberg, and Hedrich, 2016; Brun, Castelli, RayeCarol, and Doris, 2015). The fashion industry's boom is ascribed to the ephemeral characteristics of fashion. Fashion describes the social and temporal system that people are embedded into within a certain time and context (Kaiser, 2012). For example, after events such as New York Fashion Week, Paris Fashion week, and the Met Gala, consumers worldwide often get rid of clothing which, although physically wearable, fail to keep up with the new fashion trends. People use clothes as a form of social expression. When the world trend changes, consumer tastes change quickly as well. In this sense, it is exactly these short-term wastes caused by the ephemeral nature of fashion that enable the growth of the fashion industry.

This mode of development, however, is not sustainable in the long-term. With the increasing mass-production of consumer commodities at cheaper prices, wastes in the fashion industry coming from fabric waste, packaging waste, and gas emissions waste make the fashion industry one of the largest polluters in the world, second only to oil. The fashion industry contributes to 10% of global greenhouse gas emissions due to its energy-intensive production (Edge Fashion Intelligence, 2018). In addition to their environmental impacts, these wastes also increase economic and social costs. Obviously, this short-term fashion-driven mode of development cannot last long.

This contradiction becomes more complicated when the fashion industry's long supply chain is taken into consideration. According to the United States Fashion Industry Association, the fashion industry ranges from high-end luxury brands to fast-fashion retailers, with the millions of companies in between that produce and sell clothing, shoes, and other textile products (United States Fashion Industry

Association, 2019). As a result, in order to mediate the short-term fashion trend and the long-term sustainability of the fashion industry, companies and professionals across the entire supply chain ranging from design and development to manufacturing and packaging and logistics and transportation all need to adjust their current mode of production simultaneously.

This intrinsic contradiction provides entrepreneurs in the fashion industry with a great business opportunity. Following Schumpeter's (1934) classic definition, entrepreneurs are defined as innovators who bring any new problem-solving idea into use. Among the various types of innovations, this chapter mainly focuses on the entrepreneur's technological innovations. The core issue discussed in this chapter is whether the entrepreneur's technological innovation can mitigate the intrinsic contradiction between the short-term characteristics of fashion design and the long-term prospect of the fashion industry alongside the supply chain system to achieve sustainability. To be specific, using Schumpeter's (1934) classic criteria of measuring the entrepreneur's creative destruction strategies, this core research issue can be further developed into the following two research questions:

1. Can the entrepreneur's creative destruction of technological innovation be "destructive" enough to reformat the fashion industry's intrinsically systematic and contradictory mode of development?
2. Can the entrepreneur's creative destruction of technological innovation be "creative" enough to create a new and more sustainable mode of development?

With this purpose in mind, interviews of four professionals alongside the fashion supply chain, including professionals in the design and development stage, manufacturing and packaging stage, and logistics and transportation stage (Figure 1), are conducted in this chapter.

The rest of this chapter is structured as follows: First, the Background section synthesizes the current literature regarding the dichotomy between short-term and long-term fashion industry, the emerging technologies, the supply chain, and the issue of sustainability in the fashion industry. Second, the Objective and Methodology section describes the objective of this study and the methodology applied in the empirical research. Third, the Results section summarizes the results of this study. Third, the Conclusion section draws conclusions based on the results of the study, and finally, the Limitations and Future Research section identifies areas for future research both in the fashion industry as well as other industries.

Figure 1. Three key stages in the supply chain
Source: own elaboration

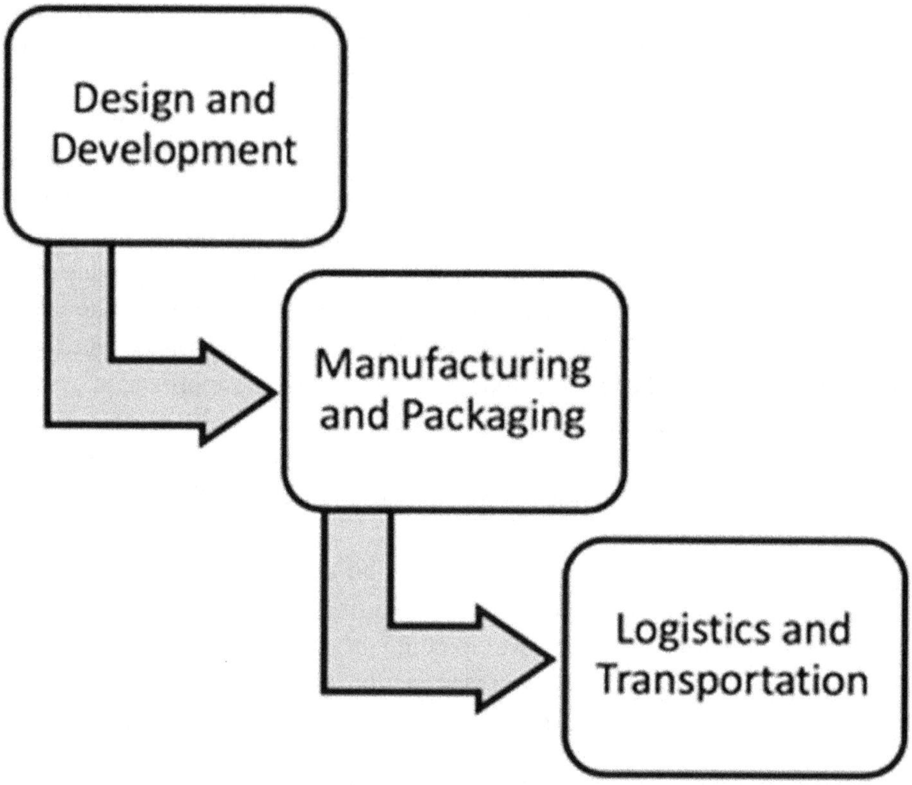

LITERATURE REVIEW

This section summarizes the current literatures which analyze (1) the dichotomy between the artistic aspect of fashion and the mass production-based fashion industry; (2) the supply chain and inventory timing control based on the entire supply chain; (3) emerging technologies such as the Internet of Things (IoT); and (4) the new scope of the sustainability issue in the fashion industry. This collection of literatures prepares the theoretical foundation for this chapter.

Thornquist (2014) focuses on fashion. Fashion comes from many types of academic disciplines, and it has different qualities, materials and shapes. Due to this particular characteristic of fashion, the commodities associated with fashion are often either hand-made, hard to make, limited and/or exclusive. For example, some people carefully choose the fabric of a particular commodity and may even select who handles the materials in person. As a result, the pricing of fashion-associated commodities is often much higher than commodities produced by mass production.

Brun et al. (2015) further analyze luxury brand management and how the philosophy of fashion impacts its target market, operations, and customer experience. Brun et al. (2015) concludes that it is exactly because of the unique characteristics of fashion that luxury brands heavily rely on the symbolic meaning of their logo, which makes customers stay loyal to their brand and willing to splurge thousands of dollars on it.

Unlike fashion and luxury brand management, retail clothing based on mass production heavily relies on its supply chain. Ganeshan, Jack, Magazine, and Stephens (1999) review how the supply chain has developed and grown in the past 20 years and make predictions based on its development and growth. Ganeshan et al. (1999) further emphasize that the distribution function can provide a competitive advantage through channel-wide integration beyond the firm. Wen, Choi, and Chung (2019) also add that customization based on consumer demand can also be a competitive advantage. Due to the challenges experienced by warehouses in facing high demand and supply uncertainties, Wen et al. (2019) explain how customization is superior based on the statistics from different specific areas alongside the supply chain in the fashion industry.

This dichotomy between the artistic aspect of fashion and the mass-production needs of the fashion industry gives rise to a contradiction in terms of timing. Basak, Seddiqe, Islam, and Akanda (2015) explore the timing from the operational level (day to day operations), tactical level (medium term decisions) and strategic level (long term decisions). They use charts and graphs to analyze the four phases of supply management—namely, Generation of Requirements, Sourcing, Pricing, and Post-Award Activities—to shed light on how the different parts of the supply chain respond to timing differently. For example, they analyze how inventory could potentially hide demand, inventory turnover, and the higher cost of goods due to the short-term and long-term dichotomy. Lu (2014) further uses Spanish clothing retailer Zara as an example to illustrate the importance of supply chain timing control. Zara sells 450 million items a year and only has 10% of unsold items. By selling in small batches, there is less inventory to get rid of at the end of the day. The secret behind Zara's retail success is focused around the centralization of its supply chain. They focus on their rhythm and their bi-weekly deliveries to stores. Their distribution strategy allows them to deliver goods within 24-40 hours maximum. It is very coordinated, and they maintain efficient workflow through it as well.

Although timing control and Zara's success through supply chain management do reveal the possibility of waste reduction at the operations level, they fail to mention the role of emerging technologies towards sustainable production. Tu (2018) focuses more on the role of technology in the supply chain—specifically, IoT. The industrial IoT has helped and improved much of supply chains through its logistics and applications. With it, it is now possible to create a global network infrastructure that easily allows the exchange of information. By exploring the factors influencing an enterprise to adopt IoT in its logistics, Tu (2018) has identified how the Internet of Things -IoT- technology makes the whole supply chain different and more effective. Although Tu (2018) doesn't analyze the fashion industry in particular, Aoaeh and Morales-Hellebo (2018) believe that fashion would be the next industry to be taken over by technology. Kazlacheva, Stoykova, Georgieva, and Ilieva (2018) further add that innovative technologies in the fashion industry are welcomed by the younger generation of fashion industry professionals during their education in fashion design. This indicates the potential of emerging technologies applying to the fashion industry in the future.

Sustainability is a somewhat new topic within the fashion industry (Macchion et al., 2018). Because it is so new, it has not realized its highest potential and there is much room for growth and improvement. Macchion et al. (2018) discuss ten cases from product development, delivery and sources. Macchion et al.'s (2018) perspective in analyzing what business practices can promote sustainability focuses more on the business models. Barbosa-Póvoa, da Silva, and Carvalho (2018) also talk about sustainability but focus more on decision-making within the supply chain based on operations research. According to information gathered from the different stages of the supply chain including material collection, descriptive analysis, category selection, and material evaluation, Barbosa-Póvoa et al. (2018) point out a new direction for the fashion industry to transition to the sustainability route based on supply chain analysis.

In summary, current literature has identified the dichotomy between the artistic aspect of fashion and the mass production-based fashion industry. The literature illustrating supply chain analysis based on operations research has been proven to help reduce inventory costs if one is heading towards the direction of more customization. The literature also mentions emerging technologies such as IoT and the new lens of viewing the fashion industry from the perspective of sustainability. However, current literature fails to connect these four domains of literature and to explore whether the entrepreneur's emerging technological innovations can mitigate the intrinsic contradiction between fickle fashion design at the earlier stage of the supply chain and the standard mass production and distribution at the later stage of the supply chain to achieve sustainability on a full scale.

OBJECTIVE AND METHODOLOGY

The aim of this study is to fill in this gap by answering the research questions formulated in the introductory section: (1) Can the entrepreneur's creative destruction of technological innovation be "destructive" enough to reformat the fashion industry's intrinsically systematic and contradictory mode of development? and (2) Can the entrepreneur's creative destruction of technological innovation be "creative" enough to create a new and more sustainable mode of development?

The researchers interviewed four professionals who are either involved in the fashion industry or are experts on supply chain. The first three interviewees are currently leading their own companies in transitioning to the sustainability journey. The last interviewee works in academia and connects the sustainability transition behaviors throughout the supply chain to business theories. To be specific, these four interviewees are:

1. Alessandro Michele
   a. Michele specializes in the design stage of the supply chain.
   b. Michele has been Gucci's new creative director since 2015 and has completely changed the brand for the better since. He has various thoughts on fashion and his vision on fashion is different from that of others (McDean, Shillingford, and Frankel, 2018).
2. Francesca DeBiase
   a. DeBiase specializes in the manufacturing and packaging stage of the supply chain.
   b. DeBiase is the executive vice president of McDonald's who leads the revitalization of McDonald's sustainability vision, which is to be achieved by 2025 (Langert, 2016).
3. Mathilde Dumoulin
   a. Dumoulin specializes in the logistics and transportation stage of the supply chain.
   b. Dumoulin is a Sustainability Development Manager in Bolloré, which is one of the world's leading transport and logistics operators providing services across 106 countries in five continents (Benton, 2018).
4. Yossi Sheffi
   a. Sheffi is from the academia.
   b. Sheffi is a professor at the Massachusetts Institute of Technology. He founded and co-founded five companies, and has authored numerous scientific publications and books regarding supply chain and sustainability (Lacefield, 2018).

All of the four interviewees' interview transcripts are found online. Some interviewees with an expertise in the fashion industry may not necessarily know the supply chain very well, while other interviewees with an expertise in supply chain may not necessarily have a deep understanding of the fashion industry. Through combining these two aspects of expertise with theory, this chapter answers the core question of whether the entrepreneur's technological innovation can mitigate the intrinsic contradiction between the short-term characteristics of fashion design and the long-term prospect of the fashion industry alongside the supply chain system to help the fashion industry achieve full-scale sustainability.

RESULTS

Through framing the data collected from the four interviewees to the theoretical framework, this chapter analyzes the two research questions as follows:

Technology as a Tool is Not Sufficient to Achieve Full-Scale Sustainability

Can the entrepreneur's creative destruction of technological innovation be "destructive" enough to reformat the fashion industry's intrinsically systematic and contradictory mode of development? Through interviewing Alessandro Michele, Francesca DeBiase, and Mathilde Dumoulin alongside the supply chain, it is found that technology alone is not enough because technology serving as a tool often reinforces or even intensifies the existing value creation dichotomy. To be specific, although technology reduces carbon emissions environmentally at certain stages of the supply chain, it fails to be "destructive" enough to deviate from the socioeconomic waste-driven profits generation logic which the fashion industry is rooted in in the first place.

In the design stage, Alessandro Michele believes that fashion is an expression of a way of life; a point of view. It is like a universal language. However, as time changes, this universal language needs to be expressed differently. "We are not in the 80s… you can't keep using the same language." As a result, Alessandro Michele uses new technologies that reflect this change of language. For example, the universal language for Gucci is inclusivity. The contemporary way to express it is to blur the lines between genders, genres, and ages to create culturally diverse clothes. Technology such as chemical effects are used as agents to materially represent this design philosophy. Without the use of new technologies, the contemporary way of expressing inclusivity would become an impossible language. From this perspective, technology reinforces the ephemeral nature of fashion which is where the whole fashion industry originates from.

Although there is not much change in the design stage, technology reveals its efficacy towards sustainability in both the manufacturing and distribution stage. First, in the manufacturing and packaging stage, Francesca DeBiase uses the food industry as an analogy to illustrate how waste reduction through recycling can be achieved with the help of technology. She has particularly mentioned sourcing – for McDonalds, that would be beef, fish, coffee, and palm oil. Based on Francesca Debiase's logic, it can be deduced that in the fashion industry, technology can also help in the quality control of raw materials procurement such as fibers, textiles, leather, and furs. This is not difficult to achieve. For example, for natural fibers such as wool, cotton, silk and linen, stricter eco-criteria have already been imposed. For synthetic fibers, environmentally friendly fibers such as hemp have already gradually taken over the more polluting fiber polyester through the use of high-tech synthetic methods (Steele and Major, 2019). From this perspective, entrepreneurial technological innovations do take the fashion industry towards its sustainability prospect by eliminating the environmental impacts during the manufacturing and packaging stage.

Second, technology also contributes to environmental sustainability in the logistics and transportation stage as well. Mathilde Dumoulin mentions the introduction of the first hybrid shuttle powered by highly efficient diesel and electric motors. The hybrid technology reduces fuel consumption and harmful atmospheric emissions such as CO2 and suspended particles by up to 30%. This technology supports the "Save Program" – an eco-solution program which started in 2011. Since logistics and transportation make up a huge component of the fashion industry, technological improvement in logistics and transportation have the potential to reduce the fashion industry's carbon emissions to a great extent.

The analysis above shows that entrepreneurial technological innovations, as a tool, can be "destructive" to lower the environmental impacts of parts of the supply chain. However, technology by itself is not "destructive" enough to change the ephemeral nature of fashion design which is where the whole fashion industry's supply chain originates from. To a certain extent, technology actually reinforces or even exacerbates the existing short-term and long-term dichotomy. As a result, full-scale sustainability cannot be achieved by technology alone if the socioeconomic waste-driven profit-creation mode remains.

The Prospect to Achieve Full-Scale Sustainability by Integrating Technologies to Create a New Sustainable Business Model

Can the entrepreneur's creative destruction of technological innovation be "creative" enough to create a new and more sustainable mode of development? The short answer is "yes," on the condition that technology is not just viewed as a tool, but rather, must be integrated into and become the backbone of the newly created sustainable business model in the whole supply chain. Two aspects are of particular importance: first, environmental sustainability cannot be separated from the logic of the business model in the first place; second, the whole supply chain must be vertically integrated to create a sustainable branding altogether.

In the design stage, Alessandro Michele claims he uses technologies to speak to the world and make people believe that "you can be exactly what you want to be." Surprisingly, contrary to what people commonly believe, the essence of fashion design according to Alessandro Michele is not creating new styles by abandoning the old, but rather, by "working with empathy towards people." This points to a new way of thinking – if sustainability is exactly what people want to achieve and means giving people the empathy that they need, then sustainable technologies would no longer be regarded just as a tool, but as the exact the driving force which takes fashion design in a new direction. "Gucci Equilibrium," for example, has proved how powerful this new way of thinking is. With the help of technologies in the Gucci ArtLab, emerging technologies are used to help Gucci balance the equilibrium between aesthetics and environmental ethics. This integration of socioenvironmental and economic impacts into design through technology application illustrates that it is not the technology itself, but rather, it is the technology-enabled sustainable design philosophies that enable the ephemeral nature of fashion to adjust to the sustainability route.

Similarly, in the production stage, Francesca DeBiase mentions that technology helps McDonalds enter a new area through integrating a sustainability vision and framework into its new branding. "In the future, there won't be any difference between what we talk about when we say what we stand for as a brand, and what we talk about when we say our sustainably framework. It'll be one and the same. I think that truly means we'll have mainstreamed sustainability into our company at the highest level possible." The fashion industry is kind of like the fast food industry in that there is a potential to rebrand by integrating the idea of sustainability. Although technologies used in the fast food industry and fashion industry differ, general technologies such as IoT used in inventory management, manufacturing automation, and real-time feedback can make this integration and rebranding possible. Like the digitization of the fast food industry wherein customers can easily check McDonald's food's calories, smart clothing technology such as environmental sensors and body sensors can also easily let consumers know of the carbon emissions during the apparel production process and how artificial synthetic clothing materials impact the human body (CB Insights Research, 2019). As a result, these emerging technologies can help rebrand the fashion industry as a whole and make it more sustainably promising.

In the logistics and transportation stage, Mathilde Dumoulin mentions a similar idea. For Bolloré Logistics, sustainability is no longer viewed as something "nice to have," but is recognized as a "must-have". Through integrating sustainability in the entire logistics operation and transportation operation, sustainability now becomes a core pillar which defines Bolloré Logistics. Transportation is a huge component of the fashion industry, especially with the popularity of online shopping. Yossi Sheffi talks about an interesting experiment he did in his class: "I ask my students: 'Who's willing to pay more for sustainability?' Everybody raises their hands. Then I ask,

'Who's willing to stop ordering online because it's not sustainable?' No one raises their hand." If the sustainability of the fashion industry does not require consumers to sacrifice their online shopping convenience through using the entrepreneur's new technologies, then the sustainability transition of the fashion industry can be more promising.

The analysis above shows that entrepreneurial technological innovations can be "creative" enough to create a new and more sustainable mode of development, on the condition that sustainable technology is not just regarded as a tool to serve either the short-term-based fashion design or the long-term-oriented fashion industry separately, but rather, as a driving force behind both fashion design and the fashion industry by being integrated into the whole supply chain's sustainability philosophy and rebranding. Without new technologies, the new fashion design philosophy cannot be materially supported by clothing's new sustainable features. Without new technologies, a new brand image can hardly be vertically integrated alongside the whole supply chain as well.

CONCLUSION

This chapter discusses whether the entrepreneur's technological innovation can mitigate the intrinsic contradiction between the short-term waste-based characteristics of fashion design and the long-term sustainability of the fashion industry using the lens of supply chain. If one just regards technology as a tool to serve the existing mode of development, technology itself is not "destructive" enough to bridge the dichotomy. As a result, in order to achieve full-scale sustainability, sustainable technologies must be viewed as part of the driving force that (1) materially embody the sustainable design philosophy and rebranding, and (2) physically integrate the whole supply chain including the design and development stage, manufacturing and packaging stage, as well as the logistics and transportation stage altogether towards the direction of sustainability.

In terms of materially embodying the sustainable design philosophy and rebranding, the new business model and profit creation must be supported by new technologies. If technology is just used as a tool to serve carbon emission reduction purposes only but has nothing to do with profit generation and customer satisfaction, and if profit generation and customer satisfaction are still based on short-term waste creation, then such kind of environmental sustainability cannot last long.

In terms of physically integrating the whole supply chain towards the direction of sustainability, Sheffi claims that "sustainability doesn't mean much unless your suppliers and your suppliers' suppliers are sustainable." Dumoulin's attitude that "if a supplier isn't at the top of the sustainability generation, we go to them with the information and open up a dialogue" is necessary to enable the fashion industry to transition into sustainability. New technologies serve as media to convey shared information and knowledge to enable every company in the supply chain to join the sustainability journey.

These two aspects mutually improve each other. Without a new sustainable design philosophy and branding image, the whole supply chain can hardly be vertically integrated. Similarly, without the common efforts from each section of the supply chain, the sustainable design philosophy and branding image can hardly be built. For example, we can hardly say Apple has a sustainable design philosophy and brand image until Foxconn's (Apple's contract manufacturer) manufacturing and logistics facilities are sustainable. Similarly, without Apple's huge profits generated from its sustainable design and branding, Foxconn can hardly be convinced to join the sustainability conversion also (Lacefield, 2018). As a result, the entrepreneur's technological innovations should both materially support the new sustainable business models and physically integrate the whole supply chain to make the fashion industry's transition to sustainability possible.

LIMITATIONS AND FUTURE RESEARCH

Although there is some information on technology supporting supply chain sustainability in the fashion industry, there are still some questions to be answered. Future research could include what kind of technology, specifically, or a specific sub-industry in the fashion world. It can also be beneficial to learn more about sustainability in other industries.

REFERENCES

Amed, I., Berg, A., Brantberg, L., & Hedrich, S. (2016). *The state of fashion 2017.* Retrieved from https://www.mckinsey.com/industries/retail/our-insights/the-state-of-fashion

Aoaeh, B. L., & Morales-Hellebo, L. (2018). *Where will technological disruption in the fashion supply chain come from?* Retrieved from http://www.refashiond.com/blog/2018/10/25/where-will-technological-disruption-in-the-fashion-supply-chain-come-from

Barbosa-Póvoa, A. P., da Silva, C., & Carvalho, A. (2018). Opportunities and challenges in sustainable supply chain: An operations research perspective. *European Journal of Operational Research, 268*(2), 399–431. doi:10.1016/j.ejor.2017.10.036

Basak, A., Seddiqe, M. I. S., Islam, M. R., & Akanda, M. O. F. (2014). Supply chain management in garments industry. *Global Journal of Management and Business Research, 14*(11), 23–28.

Benton, D. (2018). *Exclusive interview: Bolloré logistics, sustainability development manager, mathilde dumoulin.* Retrieved from https://www.supplychaindigital.com/company/exclusive-interview-bollore-logistics-sustainability-development-manager-mathilde-dumoulin#

Brun, A., & Castelli, C., RayeCarol, C., & Doris, K. (2015). A luxury brand management framework built from historical review and case study analysis. *International Journal of Retail & Distribution Management, 43*(10/11), 1083–1100. doi:10.1108/ijrdm-07-2014-0103

CB Insights Research. (2019). *Fashion forward: How tech is targeting waste & pollution in the $2.4t fashion industry.* Retrieved from https://www.cbinsights.com/research/fashion-sustainable-technology/

Edge Fashion Intelligence. (2018). *Fashion industry waste statistics.* Retrieved from https://edgexpo.com/fashion-industry-waste-statistics/

Ganeshan, R., Jack, E., Magazine, M. J., & Stephens, P. (1999). A taxonomic review of supply chain management research. *International Series In Operations Research And Management Science, 17*, 839–879. doi:10.1007/978-1-4615-4949-9_27

Kaiser, S. B. (2012). *Fashion and cultural studies.* Berg Publishers.

Kazlacheva, Z., Stoykova, V., Georgieva, K., & Ilieva, J. (2018). Application of innovative technologies in fashion design education. *IOP Conference Series. Materials Science and Engineering, 459*(1), 012080. doi:10.1088/1757-899X/459/1/012080

Lacefield, S. K. (2018). *A pragmatist's take on sustainability: Interview with Yossi Sheffi.* Retrieved from https://www.dcvelocity.com/articles/20180607-a-pragmatists-take-on-sustainability-interview-with-yossi-sheffi/

Langert, B. (2016). *One year later: Mcdonald's supply chain, sustainability chief Francesca Debiase.* Retrieved from https://www.greenbiz.com/article/one-year-later-mcdonalds-supply-chain-sustainability-chief-francesca-debiase

Lu, C. (2014). *Zara supply chain analysis—The secret behind Zara's retail success.* Retrieved from https://www.tradegecko.com/blog/supply-chain-management/zara-supply-chain-its-secret-to-retail-success

Macchion, L., Da Giau, A., Caniato, F., Caridi, M., Danese, P., Rinaldi, R., & Vinelli, A. (2018). Strategic approaches to sustainability in fashion supply chain management. *Production Planning and Control*, *29*(1), 9–28. doi:10.1080/09537287.2017.1374485

McDean, C., Shillingford, K., & Frankel, S. (2018). *"People need reality" Alessandro Michele on his Gucci.* Retrieved from https://www.anothermag.com/fashion-beauty/10576/people-need-reality-alessandro-michele-on-his-gucci

Schumpeter, J. A. (1934). *The theory of economic development: An inquiry into profits, capital, credit, interest, and the business cycle*. Harvard University Press.

Steele, V., & Major, J. S. (2019). *Fashion industry.* Retrieved from https://www.britannica.com/art/fashion-industry

Thornquist, C. (2014). Basic research in art: Foundational problems in fashion design explored through the art itself. *Fashion Practice*, *6*(1), 37–57. doi:10.2752/175693814X13916967094795

Tu, M. (2018). *An exploratory study of internet of things (IoT) adoption intention in logistics and supply chain management.* Retrieved from https://nls.ldls.org.uk/welcome.html?ark:/81055/vdc_100057944694.0x00002c

United States Fashion Industry Association. (2019). *About the fashion industry.* Retrieved from https://www.usfashionindustry.com/about/about-the-fashion-industry

Wen, X., Choi, T., & Chung, S. (2019). Fashion retail supply chain management: A review of operational models. *International Journal of Production Economics*, *207*(C), 34–55. doi:10.1016/j.ijpe.2018.10.012

KEY TERMS AND DEFINITIONS

Entrepreneur: Innovators who bring any new problem-solving idea into use.

Fashion: A prevailing style of aesthetic expression during a particular time and context.

Fashion Industry: An industrial sector that meets the demand for apparel.

Supply Chain: A network between a firm and its suppliers to produce and distribute goods and services.

Sustainability: Meeting the needs of the present without compromising the ability of the future.

Sustainable Business Strategy: A business strategy that positively affects both the environment and the society.

Technology: The application of scientific knowledge for practical purposes in the industry.

APPENDIX: TRANSCRIPT OF INTERVIEW RESEARCH

1. Alessandro Michele: Interview Questions Focused on Fashion
    a. What are some challenges you may have to go through in the fashion industry?
        i. A hardship he had to endure was when he copied a design by Dapper Dan. It was seen as a counterfeit on a luxury level. He replaced the Louis Vuitton logo with the G for Gucci and changed the sleeves and presented the item at the Gucci Resort collection show in Florence.
    b. Are you open minded in using technology to influence fashion design? What would this mean for the brand?
        i. "We are not in the 80s when there were just magazines and books. Now it's like another world. You can't keep using the same language, that would be like singing where everyone else is dancing. I think the thing that is helping us and our company is that mine and Marco's [Bizzarri, Gucci President and CEO] way of working is really open to something different. When Gucci started, it was another age. If you bought a Gucci bag, you belonged to the jet set. The jet set doesn't exist anymore. I'm trying to speak to the world, to everyone. It's beautiful that people go into the store, but I don't want them to feel they have to. It's more that you can be exactly what you want to be. More than anything, fashion is an expression of a way of life, a point of view. It's like a universal language. And if you work with empathy towards people, it's very powerful."
    c. What kinds of resources do you apply to be in the fashion industry?
        i. "My Gucci universe is inclusive. It fragments to recreate in a contemporary way. It tries to achieve chemical effects through the use of different agents. It is a possible universe that sometimes uses an impossible language." With this, he tried to blur the lines between genders, genres and ages, making culturally diverse clothes and making them as inclusive as possible for everybody.
    d. How do you think the fashion industry could be improved?
        i. He mentions that by maintaining his freedom which he learned from his father, he is able to help himself and the company. It is about the way of working; the company must keep an open mind about it and always go the different route.
2. Francesca DeBiase: Interview Questions Focused on Supply Chain
    a. How much involvement does supply chain sustainability have in your workplace or area of study?

    i. "First, I want to say I'm really honored that I have this role, and I do have a seat at the table. Just being in all the meetings — it's really expected of me when whatever topic comes up, I'm going to be talking about sustainability. So, I certainly use this opportunity to talk about it in every occasion in those meetings. I think the big thing we're working on right now that's got me really excited is we, as a company, are working on a brand purpose."

  b. How has supply chain sustainability been improved in the last few years from your perspective?
    i. "What I get to do in my role is really figure out how we can fully integrate our sustainability vision and framework into our new brand purpose work. This means that in the future, there won't be any difference between what we talk about when we say what we stand for as a brand, and what we talk about when we say our sustainability framework. It'll be one and the same. I think that truly means we'll have mainstreamed sustainability into our company in the highest level possible. So, to me, that's super exciting."

  c. Do you think the supply chain sustainability could be improved for the better with the help of technology, or what will it take for companies to improve sustainability?
    i. "If you just look at some of the things we accomplished in 2015, it will attest to the fact that the team has been doing a great job. We are continuing to make progress to achieve our vision of sourcing all of our food and packaging sustainably. So, we're on track to meet our 2020 goals for all five of our priority products in sourcing. That's beef, fish, coffee, palm oil and fiber. And in Planet, which to me was a newer area, obviously, so I hadn't had direct responsibility for it in the past, we are on track to meet our waste and recycling goals there. With the work we've done just on those two pillars, I think that helped us be able to communicate bolder actions on climate change overall."

3. Mathilde Dumoulin: Interview Questions Focused on Supply Chain
  a. How much involvement does supply chain sustainability have in your workplace or area of study?
    i. Mathilde Dumoulin is a Sustainability Development Manager in Bolloré, which is "one of the world's leading transport and logistics operators providing services across 106 countries in five continents. Bolloré Logistics is all too aware of its responsibility to ensure that those operations are sustainable."

b. What can you say about recognizing technology playing a part in supply chain sustainability? What is your experience with it?
   i. "Bolloré Logistics also introduced its first hybrid shuttle in March 2015. Powered by highly efficient diesel and electric motors, the truck serves iconic retail stores from the Green Hub. The hybrid technology reduces fuel consumption and harmful atmospheric emissions such as CO2 and suspended particles by up to 30%. Those two key milestones reinforced Bolloré Logistics' position as a key actor for sustainable logistics in Singapore, combining economic growth with environmental protection. With such a major logistical network, Bolloré Logistics invests a great deal into monitoring, improving and ultimately reducing its carbon footprint. This commitment was first structured at a global level in 2000 with the creation of the Group Code of Ethics."
c. How has supply chain sustainability been improved in the last few years from your perspective?
   i. "For more than 18 years, Bolloré Logistics has had a sustainability and corporate social responsibility (CSR) agenda that has been implemented throughout every aspect of the business. In 2011, the company launched the "Save Program" – an eco-solutions program dedicated to its customers. "Traditionally, CSR and sustainability have been viewed perhaps as a 'nice to have' activity," says Dumoulin. "Bolloré Logistics has recognized it as a 'must-have,' fully integrated into the entire operation. It has to be a core pillar of everything we are trying to achieve."
d. Do you think supply chain sustainability could be improved for the better with the help of technology, or how can it improve?
   i. "Sustainability is no doubt a global issue, where more and more countries are looking at improving their own processes; and there are of course some countries that are more mature than others. Thus, in the process of seeking out suppliers who can align to its sustainability agenda, Bolloré Logistics drives a second approach. "If a supplier isn't at the top of the sustainability generation, in addition to our mandatory CSR criteria, we go to them with the information and open up a dialogue," says Dumoulin. "As a large group we have a responsibility to push and drive them to act and enable innovation. That's one of the keys to innovate. We share information and knowledge so that we can develop their sustainability capabilities and get them to come along with us on our journey."

4. Yossi Sheffi: Interview Questions Focused on Supply Chain

a. How much involvement does supply chain sustainability have in your workplace or area of study?
   i. Yossi Sheffi has written many books on supply chain. He tends to write about sustainability a lot, but he wouldn't call himself a "tree hugger." He takes an unbiased opinion when it comes to environmental sustainability in supply chain. Instead, he "takes a pragmatic approach to sustainability, balancing corporations' responsibility to protect the environment against everything else a business has to accomplish—including making a profit, providing jobs, giving back to the community, and providing goods and services that people want at a price they are willing to pay."
b. What can you say about recognizing technology playing a part in supply chain sustainability? What is your experience with it?
   i. "The classic one is recognizing that sustainability is a supply chain issue. Many companies are dedicated to sustainability within their own company. So, for example, all of Apple's own facilities are carbon-neutral. But that's nothing because Apple doesn't make anything. It's the factories that are the big energy consumers. So, the question really is, 'How do we make [Apple's contract manufacturer] Foxconn's facilities more sustainable?' And Apple is aware of this. In many cases, sustainability doesn't mean much unless your suppliers and your suppliers' suppliers are sustainable. Companies have to realize that people are going to judge them not just on their own internal sustainability efforts but on their entire supply chain's sustainability. You really need to conduct a lifecycle analysis of your product's entire supply chain, and that has to include how the end customer uses the product."
c. How has supply chain sustainability been improved in the last few years from your perspective, or what will it take for companies to improve sustainability?
   i. "At the end of the day, nothing will change until we have a willing consumer. And right now, people like you and me like to order things from Amazon, where products are being shipped out as onesies or twosies with all the packaging that that involves. That's not sustainable. But who is going to give up buying online? That's a question I always ask my students: 'Who's willing to pay more for sustainability?' Everybody raises their hands. Then I ask, 'Who's willing to stop ordering online because it's not sustainable?' No one raises their hand. Until consumers are willing to give up some convenience, it's not going to happen, at least not in any scalable way."

Chapter 6
Entrepreneurship in the Fashion Industry:
The Case of Carolina Herrera

Jose Manuel Saiz-Alvarez
https://orcid.org/0000-0001-6435-9600
Universidad Católica de Santiago de Guayaquil, Ecuador & Universidad Autónoma de Manizales, Colombia & CEIEF-Universidad de Santiago de Chile, Chile

ABSTRACT

The fashion industry employs more than 300 million workers in the world with a turnover of more than a trillion dollars, which is equivalent to being the seventh economic power on the planet. The presence of Latin America and the Caribbean in this industry is growing, where Carolina Herrera is of fundamental importance. The objective of this chapter is to analyze the critical success factors of this company to recognize it internationally as an icon-brand and to study the entrepreneurial spirit of the company to be an example for new generations (and even to competitors). A SWOT analysis will be made complemented by a PESTEL analysis to achieve these goals. The chapter ends with conclusions and perspectives after COVID-19.

INTRODUCTION

Fashion is a cross-sector concept that encompasses several industries, such as apparel, footwear, leather, jewelry, perfumes, and cosmetics (Brun et al., 2008). The fashion industry, as "a singular social object," is at the crossroads of arts, as part of the creative industry, and business, with the production of goods (Godart, 2010). This

DOI: 10.4018/978-1-7998-3568-4.ch006

duality explains why the core of this industry is to produce symbols – the "label" of top designers converting passive objects into symbolic ones (Leclair, 2017), and to maximize EBITDA (earnings before interests, taxes, depreciation, and amortization).

The case of CH Carolina Herrera, founded by the Venezuelan businesswoman and billionaire María Carolina Josefina Pacanins Niño, is different and unique compared to other fashion firms. One of the main differences is her social origin, so she did not need to work for a living, since she works for pleasure, passion, and to help others, especially women. A Spanish noble title created by King Felipe V in 1722, Marquis of Torre Casa, was awarded to Carolina Herrera after her second marriage to the aristocrat Reinaldo Herrera Guevara. She had always belonged to the upper social class, as she was the daughter of Commander Guillermo Pacanins Acevedo, governor of Caracas, between 1950 and 1958. Due to this fact, she met at thirteen years of age the Spanish designer Cristóbal Balenciaga Eizaguirre (1895-1972), one of the top couture designers in Spain.

CH Carolina Herrera entered the world of haute couture almost by chance, after having traveled to New York in 1980 with fabrics designed by her. He showed them to Diana Vreeland, fashion editor for Harper's Bazaar and director of Vogue, and she suggested to design dresses and see the market response. After having returned to Caracas, she ordered to be performed twelve dresses designed by her to build a small collection of 24 dresses. Back in New York, she sold them off in a friend's New York apartment. It was September 1980.

In April 1981, she presented her first full collection of couture-quality creations for women, featuring exaggerated shoulder and sleeve treatment, that was enthusiastically received by 400 members of the press and the Beautiful People at New York's exclusive Metropolitan Club. Three months later, in July, she attended with her husband the wedding of Prince Charles and Lady Diana Spencer, staying at Kensington Palace with Princess Margaret. Shortly after, she distributed her creations in the leading stores: Saks, Bergdorf, and Mark, and it was a best seller.

CH Carolina Herrera followed the typical step-by-step process carried out in startups. Her first sale was a pilot test for CH Carolina Herrera, who did not even need to rely on focus groups, as she had the contacts to join the market. She had not yet created a firm or similar, but this sudden success gave her the idea of setting up a formal company. She had everything ready to do it, publicity included, that was conceived and carried out by the Venezuelan publisher Armando de Armas.

The objective of this chapter is to analyze the success of CH Carolina Herrera as an entrepreneur. To achieve this goal, the author will apply a SWOT analysis (Strengths, Opportunities, Weaknesses, and Threats) to observe which factors affect the firm, and will analyze which key success factors have driven the firm towards the international recognition of CH Carolina Herrera as an icon brand. The study of the main traits of the entrepreneurial spirit of the company will serve as an example for the new generations that are struggling for business success in Latin America and the Caribbean.

BACKGROUND

A Brief Overview of the Fashion Industry

The fashion industry employs more than 300 million workers in the world, with a turnover of more than 1.3 trillion dollars (Gazzola et al., 2020; BOF & McKinsey, 2020). This achievement is equivalent to being the seventh economic power of the planet (The Sustainable Fashion Blueprint, 2018), as it is more than 2% of the world's Gross Domestic Product (GDP)(Shirvanimoghaddam et al., 2020). The economic importance of the fashion industry varies between countries, being Italy and France the most influential ones. Italy boasts some of the top names in fashion, including Guccio Gucci, Gianni Versace, Valentino Garavani, Roberto Cavalli, and Giorgio Armani, and France is home of legendary designers, including Coco Chanel, Yves Saint Laurent, Christian Dior, and Hubert de Givenchy. Latin America is far away from the Top-10 (Table 1), but the fashion industry is growing on the continent. However, its GDP participation (less than 1%) is still meager in relative terms.

Table 1. The World's Most Fashionable Countries

	Country		*Country*
1	Italy	6	India
2	France	7	Spain
3	UK	8	China-Hong Kong
4	Japan	9	United Arab Emirates
5	United States	10	Brazil

Source: CEOWorld Magazine Research

There are well-known fashion brands in Latin America and the Caribbean, highlighting Brazil, Mexico, Colombia, and, to a lesser extent, Chile. Brazil is the fourth world power in fashion with more than 30,000 fashion companies and recognized brands, such as Martha Medeiros, Carlos Miele, Bárbara Casasola, Giuliana Romanno and Lilly, and Renata Sarti. In Mexico, Pineda Covalín stands out, created by Cristina Pineda and Ricardo Covalín, in collaboration with the

National Institute of Anthropology and History, to exalt the mythology of the peoples and indigenous roots of Mexico, and Vittorio Forti, a company focused on men's fashion. Other growing Mexican brands are Doce Cero Tres, Domi, Gloom, Tamakura, Trista, Yakampot, Zelcus, and Ziutika.

Regarding Colombia, it is becoming a benchmark of the Latin American Fashion after the celebration of the Bogotá Fashion Week, where Colombian fashion brands such as Lina Hernández, Metalero, Álvaro Ávila, La P-pa Design (Stella Reyes), Fernanda Arias, Tatiana Apráez and Edén Jewelry stand out and are endowed with a growing international expansion. Finally, in Chile, although its importance in this industry is relatively minor, it can be mentioned Cravatta (only for ties, as seen in the trade name) and Ja Tori Jan (only shoes). That is why CH Carolina Herrera's history is unique, given her high capacity for conceiving new creations combined, at the same time, with a "glocal" (think global, act local) vision.

The key to this whole process of change is given by entrepreneurship located in the countries of Latin America and the Caribbean. Both necessity and opportunity entrepreneurship generate value and wealth for the company and society. This wealth creation accelerates with public-private collaboration and, also, when HEIs collaborate in the training of entrepreneurs. For this reason, the fashion design schools are essential, although, in the Carolina Herrera's case, she had not attended any of them, as she has a natural talent for design.

Entrepreneurship in the Fashion Industry

When talent, luck, innovation, and knowledge come together, the result is business success. Innovation increases firm performance and contributes to generating competitive advantages (Ünay and Zehir, 2012). To stay competitive and avoid being smashed by large companies, small-and-medium-sized enterprises (SMEs) need to establish and manage dynamic and non-hierarchical networks to respond to market opportunities. As a result, they ensure a quick response, unique products with competitive prices, and high product quality (Shamsuzzoha et al., 2013).

Innovation is the development of new products (product innovation), production processes (process innovation), business practices, or forms of organization (business model innovations) (Jin and Cedrola, 2018) to create first-order competitive advantages in firms. In the fashion industry, reduced lead time, lower operational costs, and increased flexibility reflect innovations in the production process. Three orientations—market orientation, learning orientation, and entrepreneurial orientation—were found to increase a firm's level of innovation, which in turn enhances its performance (Jin and Cedrola, 2018; Hult, Hurley, and Knight, 2004).

In a framework dominated by a global increase in life age, the fashion industry today has the opportunity to serve both young and old generations at the same time. Consumer satisfaction translates the firms into the need to diversify both business strategies and marketing approaches to satisfy the needs of retired consumers and millennials (Gazzola et al., 2020). Fulfilling these two antagonistic market niches is a challenge for CH Carolina Herrera. A challenge that has overcome it with the diversification of the product, and the high level of innovativeness and entrepreneurship required in fashion firms and employers to generate top-performing firms (Ünay and Zehir, 2012).

In 2009, the Copenhagen Fashion Summit, as the world's leading event on sustainability in Fashion (Eder-Hansen et al., 2017), launched the first sustainability program for fashion companies and defined Seven Priority Actions useful to have higher sustainability inside the industry: supply chain traceability, saving water, energy, and chemicals, workers' security and respect, sustainable material mix, circular fashion system, better wage systems, and the digital revolution. It is necessary to carry out constant improvements in entrepreneurship policies, with the creation of new manufacturing and design methods that reduce the use of productive resources, to carry out this sustainability multi-objective. This challenge is of particular importance for the future of the firm, as the chief custodians of this green conception of Fashion are Millennials and Generation Z (PwC, 2018).

Besides, market information is crucial in the fashion industry, especially for startups, and is guided by two approaches: retrospective and forward-looking. In the retrospective approach, the generation process is based on expressed customer needs and existing market relations; the dissemination is based on formal mechanisms; the use process is more instrumental. In the forward-looking approach, the generation process is based on latent customer needs and the evolutionary patterns of the future market relations; the dissemination process is more informal; the use of information is more conceptual. Applied to the fashion industry, the two approaches are complementary for firm performance. Still, they have opposite effects on product innovativeness because a forward-looking approach is positively related to product innovation, a retrospective approach seems to be negatively related (Cillo, De Luca, and Troilo, 2010).

The global business of fashion requires sophisticated management techniques, creativity, and innovation, given the rapid development of business strategies that relate to fashion management (Ünay and Zehir, 2012). It is essential to have intra-entrepreneurs within the company who innovate and know how to work as a team. Teamwork is one of the success factors within CH Carolina Herrera. Success factors that we will see in the next section.

Carolina Herrera's Key Success Factors

Although Carolina Herrera is not listed in the Top 10 luxury goods companies by sales (in US$m)(Table 2), it is one of the world's best-known fashion companies. According to Silva, Duarte, and Sundetova, fashion brands have only slight differences concerning the number of channels and features available to clients despite the price segment they belong to. As a result, fashion brands have functional channel integration, order tracking, online communication, and social media.

Table 2. Top 10 luxury goods companies by sales

	Name of the company	Country	Luxury goods	
			Sales	**Sales growth**
1	LVMH Moët Hennessy-Louis Vuitton SE	France	27,995	17.2%
2	The Estée Lauder Companies Inc	USA	13,683	15.7%
3	Compagnie Financière Richemont SA	Switzerland	12,819	3.1%
4	Kering SA	France	12,168	27.5%
5	Luxottica Group SpA	Italy	10,322	0.8%
6	Chanel Limited	UK	9,623	11.5%
7	L'Oréal Luxe	France	9,549	10.6%
8	The Swatch Group Ltd	Switzerland	7,819	5.4%
9	Chow Tai Fook Jewellery Group Ltd. 周大福珠宝集团有限公司	Hong Kong	7,575	15.4%
10	PVH Corp.	USA	7,355	10.7%

Source: Deloitte (2019)

What have been the keys to CH Carolina Herrera's success? A SWOT analysis will be used to synthesize these keys to success.

SWOT ANALYSIS

Strengths

The most critical CH Carolina Herrera' strength is the ability and empathy of the founder, such as happiness, talent, passion, self-confidence, luckiness, self-discipline, persistence, family support, the capacity to face challenges, improvement, optimism, teamwork, social entrepreneurship, leadership, and the ability to delegate in complex situations or when there is excessive work. These advantages make possible the organization to achieve sustained growth.

One of the characteristics of successful companies is given because they attract other companies to do business since companies pursue win-win strategies. As a result of this desire, the growth of successful companies tends to accelerate over time, which tends to generate strategic alliances.

In the case of CH Carolina Herrera, this progress accelerated after the signature of a strategic alliance with the Spanish company Puig. The Puig company is a family business founded in Spain in 1914. By combining brand purchase operations, mergers and acquisitions, and business expansion have led Puig to market 18 cosmetic and perfume-related brands (Nina Ricci, Carolina Herrera, Paco Rabanne, Jean Paul Gaultier, Dries Van Noten, Prada, Valentino, Penhaligon's, L'Artisan Parfumeur, Comme des Garçons, Christian Louboutin, Antonio Banderas, Shakira, Mango, Adolfo Dominguez, Agatha Ruiz de la Prada, Massimo Dutti, Victorio & Lucchino). For this reason, the strategic alliance with CH Carolina Herrera has strengthened both parties by complementing the products sold in the market by both companies. Also, this strategic alliance has a profound impact on international markets, which positively affects its greater corporate visibility and reputation, to reach new market niches with less purchasing power, so less affluent customers can buy haute couture dresses.

According to Rosener (2011), cited by Bello (2019), women have a creative ability to persist and pursue their desires; they are patient nurturers of children, a tenacity usually transferred into business; are good innovators, and possess managerial skills as every woman is a manager. Women are innately skilled managers because of their peculiar nature as home-makers; and are reliable and responsible regarding financial record-keeping.

Carolina Herrera's clients are often loyal to the brand once acquired. Brand loyalty has been linked to variables such as brand personality, perceived value, and brand engagement (Ahmad et al., 2020). This loyalty is related to the value perceived by the customer of the product purchased, as this is a distinctive and unique symbol of elegance. Each haute couture company targets very select types of clients who empathize with the company through the company. That is why it is difficult to break this fidelity, at least in the short and medium-term.

Throughout this loyalty process, timing in the production and distribution of the product is of fundamental importance. At this sense, Cerruti et al. (2016) identify four main characteristics of agile supply partnerships (ASPs): they are part of a portfolio of relationships to balance the rigidities of long-term strategic alliances; they have project-like features; are developed from a network of pre-qualified suppliers, and they are recurring and intermittent rather than continuous or isolated one-off short-term partnerships.

Product Diversification

One of CH Carolina Herrera's advantages is that she knows how to listen to her team, and most importantly, to her clients to co-create and satisfy their needs. In this sense, Acharya et al. (2018) suggest that knowledge-based interactions between the customers and the salesforce in those organizations form the core of knowledge co-creation. The co-creation process is essential in the haute couture industry, as it is one of the keys to placing itself in leadership positions in the sector. The absence of this co-creator process leads to the obsolescence of the product, which is crucial to avoid in the fashion industry if the company wants to keep up over time. A co-creation process directly linked to product diversification

A second key to achieve product diversification is to attain a fruitful development of trust between partners, endowed with clear, aligned, and shared objectives and roles between participating companies. Also, firms must develop strategies based on change management programs to reduce opposition to changes of personnel at different levels of each organization and of the network. One of the secrets for CH's success has been her willingness to share knowledge, competencies, and experiences with partner companies, and to dispose of human resources with the necessary technical skills and collaboration experience to impulse product diversification (Table 3).

Table 3. Product diversification at CH

Women	Men	Children
Accessories, bags, eyewear, fragrances, jewelry, makeup, shoes, small leather goods, women's wear	Accessories, bags, eyewear, fragrances, men's wear, shoes, small leather goods	Children's wear, shoes

Source: elaborated from CH's official webpage (chcarolinaherrera.com)

Fast Fashion

The fast-fashion business model integrates a short production and distribution lead times, matching supply with uncertain demand as closely as possible, and a highly fashionable also called trendy, items' design (Lee, 2016). To ensure the compliance with the fashion collection timing, the entire Product Development process has to be optimized through the analysis of both the flows of material and information (D'Avolio, Mandinelli, and Rinaldi, 2016).

An effective Product Development process is crucial for fast fashion. In the fashion industry, creativity has to be constant over time if the company wants to stay in business. But, in some industries, creativity is far away from increased automation.

For many industries, increased automation is a natural next step, albeit a disruptive and capital-intensive one for most manufacturers. As has happened in many other industries, robots can take on tasks that are repetitive or physically demanding or hazardous. They also offer workers the opportunity to re-skill. Workers can move into machine monitoring jobs, or into calibrating and maintaining automation equipment, and effectively participate in the enhanced productivity through wage increases in the short- to mid-term. There is a social catch: automation could lead to value migrating toward more technologically advanced countries. It may become economically viable for companies to move manufacturing from developing countries and thus closer to the consumer with shorter distances traveled and therefore reduced CO2 emissions. Manufacturers will no longer have to go to where labor is cheapest; they will become smaller, local, and highly configurable (Eder-Hansen et al., 2017).

The reason fast fashion businesses can afford to discount so heavily is that somewhere along the supply chain, someone has paid the price–be it environmentally or through sweatshop labor (Newbold, 2018). In the case of CH Carolina Herrera, environmental preservation is of increasing importance. In addition to the creation of professional work teams guided by respect for the workforce, the payment of fair wages, and the introduction of emotional wages (Table 4).

As things are today, the sector's minimum wages in most Asian countries are less than half of what can be considered a living wage. A real living wage (quantity of money earned to support a 4-members family) is frequently twice as high as minimum wages in the garment sector in developing nations, as brought forward, for example, by the Clean Clothes Campaign. As a result, in emerging countries, it would cost only about €1.35 to double the wages of those producing t-shirts that retail for €25 each (Eder-Hansen et al., 2017).

Table 4. Average per Item Prices in Fashion Brands (in euros)

Year	Items per capita	Spend per capita	Average price per item
2030	20.9	235.1	11.2
2025	19.0	222.0	11.7
2020	17.4	210.6	12.1

Source: Eder-Hansen et al. (2017)

Internationalization

CH Carolina Herrera signed in 2000 a commercial licensing contract with the Spanish firm Sociedad Textil Lonia, S.A., to start up the CH Carolina Herrera's expansion worldwide. As a result, Carolina Herrera inaugurated some stores in Europe, the United States, South America, and Asia. The firm aimed primarily at the market segment with high purchasing power, offering excellent quality and exclusive design products (Calvo-Porral and Calvo-Dopico, 2011).

If the company wants to increase sales volume by selling its products to customers with less purchasing power, the solution is to create new brands so as not to damage the corporate image and lose customers. Other fashion multinationals have followed this strategy. However, I consider that doing so can be very dangerous because clients do not want to lose their exclusivity when they buy clothes and accessories to these firms at prices focused on maximizing value for money.

When companies want to be global, internationalization is mandatory, as is the case of CH Carolina Herrera. But maintaining leading positions in such globalization is a complicated task, especially when firms move from the first to the second generation in family businesses, as is the case of CH Carolina Herrera. The company needs to know how the succession process will take place to avoid family tensions, as happened, for example, a few years ago at L'Oreal.

Weaknesses

Fashion companies focus significantly on supplier compliance with their code of conduct, employing further monitoring and auditing activities to prevent production problems in developing countries, improve overall supply chain performance, and set sustainability criteria for their suppliers (Turker and Altuntas, 2014). This strong dependence on the designers of the suppliers carries a reputational risk if suppliers do not comply with international standards in matters of safety, working conditions, and handling of toxic products. Therefore, it is essential that haute couture companies, as is the case of CH Carolina Herrera, carry out a constant process of supervision of their stakeholders to capture if they are separating from the collaboration agreement signed in the past. Failure to do so may damage the corporate image of the company, especially if the suppliers do not comply with international laws on employment and security. Claxton and Kent (2020) demonstrate the relatively low influence of designers on sustainable fashion strategy and their engagement at a tactical organizational level, so they develop a model for the integration of designers into the management of sustainable fashion business.

A second weakness deals with the push & pull factor. Push factors are those that encourage the company to search for international opportunities given a limited (and almost exhausted) domestic demand and pull factors are those that involve attractive conditions in foreign markets (Calvo-Porral and Calvo-Dopico, 2011). The reality is that it is challenging to choose one of the two strategies (push or pull) because market conditions change very quickly, and exogenous shocks can occur, as with the

COVID-19 pandemic today. Global companies must not lose the national markets from which they started so that the market can relate them to a specific country. Customers need to classify companies, even by nationality, as observed in sentimental consumption, because if they are organized, the pride of belonging is generated. The fashion world is no exception. This perception of customers makes the fashion world converge towards the most influential fashion countries (Italy, France, and Spain), which makes it very difficult to stand out, for example, a company from a developing country.

Opportunities

Digital platforms and digital marketing strategies are becoming prevalent in the fashion market, and many new brands have emerged with the development of e-commerce, which allows companies to engage consumers through virtual reality (Gazzola et al., 2020). This increase in digitization will be observed very intensely in the post-COVID economy, where many companies will carry out teleworking, and there has been a robust increase in electronic commerce of products and services of all kinds worldwide. As business opportunities, the following are cited: online shopping, extended producer responsibility, sustainability, and circular economy, and vertical integration.

Online Shopping

Both digitization and the advent of Industry 4.0 are leading to a transformation in the way of doing business (Table 5). Digital natives, classified in turn into millennials, centennials, and alpha generation, have accelerated the process of digitizing the economy, including the fashion industry. Based on ZMOT (Zero Moment of Truth) and FMOT (First Moment of Truth), the goal of any company is to ensure that its customers are loyal to the products and services produced and marketed by the organization so that they continue to buy them.

Within this loyalty process, big data plays a fundamental role. Big data is instrumental in enabling experimentation to discover new needs and aspirations of customers and plays a dominant role in knowledge co-creation (Acharya et al., 2018). Knowledge co-creation impacts re-organizing knowledge management and the usage cycle in knowledge-driven organizations. These knowledge-driven organizations gain competitive advantages through better knowledge of the market and the talent of their teams, which allows the company to achieve leadership positions within the sector. Leadership that enables it to reach new market niches, both domestic and foreign, in the medium term.

Table 5. Pros and Cons of Online Shopping

Advantages	Disadvantages
No environmental impact	Risk of Fraud
Lower prices	Usually no sales assistance
Easy price, product or service comparison	Shipping delay
Saving time and effort	Lack of touch and feel of the merchandise
Convenience	Lack of interactivity
A wider range of products/services	

Source: the author

Only shopping accelerates the transformation process of firms focused on attracting prospective clients because they display the most up–to–date collections and sell them online directly to their customers (Hines and Bruce, 2007). For this reason, fashion companies, defined as having to be always in tune with the changing tastes of the market, have to use ICTs (Information and Communication Technologies) intensively if they want to survive. Simply, a company that does not appear on the Internet does not exist for the most digitized consumers, especially for digital natives (millennials, centennials, and alpha-Gen). This process of constant digitization, therefore, is complemented by EPR (Extended Producer Responsibility) that will be analyzed in the next section.

Extended Producer Responsibility

Extended Producer Responsibility (EPR) is a policy approach where producers are given responsibility–be it financial and/or physical–for the treatment or disposal of products they put on the market. Such liability provides incentives to prevent waste at source, promotes eco-design, and supports the achievement of public recycling and materials management goals. In the case of clothing, a levy on clothing sales as part of an EPR could be used to support the fashion collection, sorting and processing of clothing, R&D into new recycling processes (House of Commons Environmental Audit Committee, 2019).

The most prominent areas in the field are sustainable retailing in disposable Fashion, fast Fashion, slow Fashion, green branding, and eco-labeling; retailing of second-hand fashion; reverse logistics in fashion retailing; and emerging retailing opportunities in e-commerce (Yang, Song, and Tong, 2017). Combining e-commerce and nature protection has led to the emergence of the circular economy as a mechanism for nature preservation.

Sustainability and Circular Economy

Fashion companies, as CH Carolina Herrera, are paying increasing attention to preserving the environment by combining sustainability and circular economy. This fact makes organizations capable of regenerating themselves by using organic or renewable materials designed to be reused and re-entered at the end of their life cycle in the biosphere, as opposed to the classical linear model of the industrial economy. As a result, the circular economy eliminates both waste and the consequent negative externalities on the external environment caused by the production.

Colucci, Tuan, and Visentin (2020) show that SMEs engage less in CSR talk (communicate about CSR) and walk (implement CSR) than large companies, as SMEs have fewer financial resources, in general than large firms. Companies targeting lower market segments or the luxury segment engage more in CSR talk. Shoe and leather companies engage most in CSR walk. The main reason for this different behavior deals with the purchasing power of consumers, as the price in the luxury segment is secondary, being more important than the social impact made with the purchase.

Also, Stringer, Mortimer, and Payne (2020) argue that self-transcendence values, ethic-related issues, and openness to change values have a positive impact on consumers, in aspects such as consumers' likeliness to purchase ethically marketed fast-fashion on animal welfare, nature, and worker welfare. As a result, the fur trade has declined (and in some countries disappeared) due to the increased animal protection awareness of buyers. A process accelerated with the introduction of synthetic skin-replacement materials into fashion.

Vertical Integration

Another aspect of having in mind is how the integration process, if any, has been produced. When firms have a significant degree of verticalization, meaning that the value chain (design, patterning, distribution, and store management) is integrated, they obtain competitive advantages, and take advantage of the entire value chain, thus maximizing their operating income. Also, its flexible structure, as well as its customer orientation and the advanced information technologies used, allow a flexible and swift response to the customers' demand and excellent market orientation (Calvo-Porral and Calvo-Dopico, 2011). As a result, the adoption of business strategies based on vertical integration is one of the best ways to strengthen the firm in the short term.

This strengthening of the organization tends to improve the company's relationship with stakeholders, and especially with shareholders, who observe how the value of their investment increases over time. An investment process must be continuous over time if you do not want to achieve obsolescence of the products and services offered to the market. However, for the vertical integration process to be successful, it is essential to ensure that information flows quickly within the organization to guarantee fluid decision-making, avoiding bottlenecks and X-inefficiencies.

Threats

Sharing Economy

From clothing libraries to baby clothes subscription services, upcycling and repair cafes, and peer-to-peer vintage sales on sites like Depop and peer-to-peer clothes sharing on apps like MyWardrobe HQ, there are many new circular business models linked to sharing economy. The relationship between physical products and individual ownership has been undergoing a profound evolution, as sections of society do not want the material items, but instead want the needs or experiences they fulfill.

Millennials and centennials are the primary adopters of the sharing economy, being the "social projection value" as the most significant predictor of intention to consume luxury fashion on a sharing basis (Jain and Mishra, 2020). The sharing economy helps to nature protection and helps to optimize the use of economic resources.

The sharing economy can adopt various forms of organization: (a) peer-to-peer product sharing (Benjaafar et al., 2019); (b) Large-scale service marketplaces (Allon, Bassamboo, and Çil, 2019); (c) Crowdsourcing (Hu, Shi, and Wu, 2019), and (d) Agent pricing (Li, Moreno, and Zhang, 2019). Applied to the fashion industry, this type of economy has barely developed so far, as they commercialize personalized and unique products. This exclusivity explains the high price paid for the final product, which makes it possible for a very select minority of customers to purchase this product.

Second-Hand Markets

Retailers could look to implement these, boosting the second-hand market and helping increase the opportunities for extending the useful life of clothing. The action could include: (a) Hiring or renting dress to customers so multiple clients can use them; (b) Recovering and reselling items customers no longer want, and (c) Developing 'subscription' models, which enable customers to swap clothes but also incentivize retailers to use garments many times before disposing of them (WRAP, 2018). One of the main reasons for developing second-hand markets is nature preservation. In the last two decades, not only the textile industry has doubled the production but also an average global annual consumption of textiles has increased from 7 to 13 kg per person and reached the threshold of 100 million metric tons of textiles consumption. More than two-thirds of the textile go to landfills at the end of their use, and just around 15% is recycled (Shirvanimoghaddam et al., 2020).

To achieve green transformation in the industry, companies need to develop useful dynamic capabilities, which entails changing their current organizational design by realigning their activities, partnerships, and routines with a changing external environment. As a result, internal assets are modified to influence clients and stakeholders (De Giau et al., 2020).

In short, Jin and Shin (2020) show there are three disruptors in the industry: born-digital brands, AI-enabled demand forecasting, and product design, and collaborative consumption. They find that disruptive business-model innovations keenly answer fundamental needs unmet by current business models, such as offering quality products at a competitive price, curated services, and sustainable consumption. At the same time, all three disruptors suggest effective operation models for handling demand uncertainty, inventory management, and timely responses to the market, all of which are inherent issues for current push supply chains and forecast-based, inventory-driven systems.

CONCLUSION

According to the International Labor Organization (ILO), more than half of all salaried workers (especially in emerging countries, where labor force in the industry is concentrated), will be displaced by automation techniques and advanced technologies. This change will also affect the fashion industry defined by the intensive use of labor, and the application of outsourcing in the production and distribution processes.

Hopefully, Carolina Herrera's success will serve as an example for other entrepreneurs in Latin America and the Caribbean with talent, training, enthusiasm, and the desire to work hard towards achieving a common goal. Therefore, to publicize this case of constant innovation and entrepreneurship to encourage other entrepreneurs to follow or imitate the trail of success is the final objective of the chapter.

The past is only for inspiration; what matters is the future. The African fashion industry has the potential to become one of the main drivers of the economy at no distant future date through the combination of local industry development creating jobs and training for local craftsmen and artisans and reducing unemployment in their communities, and women's empowerment by including them in the companies' manufacturing teams (Bello, 2019)

Also, fierce international competition, the advent of innovative technologies, and a sharp reduction of time-to-market are crucial challenges that the fashion industry faces today. These challenges require new ways of operating and require changes in the production and supply network configurations in the fashion industry (Macchion et al., 2015). Fashion is an art in motion, so the designers who best adapt to the needs of a competitive and profoundly changing market will be the ones that will survive in time. For this reason, CH Carolina Herrera needs to have a succession plan well prepared to achieve continuity for his company. In this way, CH Carolina Herrera's designs will continue to dress thousands of clients around the world for decades.

REFERENCES

Acharya, A., Singh, S. K., Pereira, V., & Singh, P. (2018). Big data, knowledge co-creation, and decision making in the fashion industry. *International Journal of Information Management*, *42*, 90–101. doi:10.1016/j.ijinfomgt.2018.06.008

Ahmad, Z., Menon, A. S., Mason, C., Shamsudin, M. F., & Sentosa, I. (2020). Does social media engagement moderate brand engagement and brand loyalty? Evidence from young consumers of Malaysian modest fashion industry. *International Journal of Psychosocial Rehabilitation*, *24*(2), 2500–2508. doi:10.37200/IJPR/V24I2/PR200546

Allon, G., Bassamboo, A., & Çil, E. B. (2019). Large-Scale Service Marketplaces: The Role of the Moderating Firm. In M. Hu (Ed.), *Sharing Economy. Making Supply Meet Demand* (pp. 165–192). Springer Nature Switzerland. doi:10.1007/978-3-030-01863-4_9

Bailey, S., & Baker, J. (2014). *Moda y visual merchandising*. Gustavo Gili.

Barkova, N. (2018). Mass customization in the fashion industry. *Vestnik Universiteta*, *5*(5), 85–90. doi:10.26425/1816-4277-2018-5-85-90

Bello, H. S. (2019). Female Entrepreneurship in the African Fashion Industry: A Review of Its Determinants and Characteristics. In C. Moreno-Gavara & A. I. Jiménez-Zarco (Eds.), *Sustainable Fashion*. Palgrave Studies of Entrepreneurship in Africa., doi:10.1007/978-3-319-91265-3_5

Benjaafar, S., Kong, G., Li, X. X., & Courcoubetis, C. (2019). Peer-to-Peer Product Sharing (pp. 11-36). In Sharing Economy. Making Supply Meet Demand. Springer Nature Switzerland.

BOF & McKinsey. (2020). *The State of Fashion Report 2019*. Available online: https://www.businessoffashion.com/articles/intelligence/the-state-of-fashion-2019

Brun, A., Caniato, F., Caridi, M., Castelli, C., Miragliotta, G., Ronchi, S., Sianesi, A., & Spina, G. (2008). Logistics and supply chain management in the luxury fashion retail: Empirical investigation of Italian firms. *International Journal of Production Economics, 114*(2), 554–570. doi:10.1016/j.ijpe.2008.02.003

Calvo-Porral, C., & Calvo-Dopico, D. (2011). "Carolina Herrera" Internationalization Strategy: Democratic Luxury or Maximum Exclusiveness? *European Research Studies, 14*(2), 3–25.

Cerruti, C., Mena, C., Skipworth, H., & Tavoletti, E. (2016). Characterizing agile supply partnerships in the fashion industry. *International Journal of Operations & Production Management, 36*(8), 923–947. doi:10.1108/IJOPM-03-2015-0181

Cillo, P., De Luca, L. M., & Troilo, G. (2010). Market information approaches, product innovativeness, and firm performance: An empirical study in the fashion industry. *Research Policy, 39*(9), 1242–1252. doi:10.1016/j.respol.2010.06.004

Claxton, S., & Kent, A. (2020). The management of sustainable fashion design strategies: An analysis of the designer's role. *Journal of Cleaner Production, 268*, 122112. doi:10.1016/j.jclepro.2020.122112

Colucci, M., Tuan, A., & Visentin, M. (2020). An empirical investigation of the drivers of CSR talk and walk in the fashion industry. *Journal of Cleaner Production, 248*, 119200. doi:10.1016/j.jclepro.2019.119200

D'Avolio, E., Bandinelli, R., & Rinaldi, R. (2016). How Product Development Can Be Improved in Fast Fashion Industry: An Italian Case. *IFIP International Conference on Product Lifecycle Management (PLM) 2015: Product Lifecycle Management in the Era of Internet of Things*, 718-728. 10.1007/978-3-319-33111-9_65

Da Giau, A., Foss, N. J., Furlan, A., & Vinelli, A. (2020). Sustainable development and dynamic capabilities in the fashion industry: A multi-case study. *Corporate Social Responsibility and Environmental Management, 27*(3), 1509–1520. doi:10.1002/csr.1891

Deloitte. (2019). *Global Powers of Luxury Goods 2019. Bridging the gap between the old and the new*. Author.

Díaz, P. (2014). *Comunicación y gestión de marcas de moda*. Gustavo Gili.

Eder-Hansen, J., Chalmer, C., Tärneberg, S., & Jäger, K. (2017). *Pulse of the Fashion Industry*. Global Fashion Agenda and The Boston Consulting.

Gazzola, P., Pavione, E., Pezzetti, R., & Grechi, D. (2020). Trends in the Fashion Industry. The Perception of Sustainability and Circular Economy: A Gender/Generation Quantitative Approach. *Sustainability, 12*(7), 2809. doi:10.3390u12072809

Godart, F. (2010). *Sociologie de la Mode*. Editions La Découverte.

Herrera, R., Araujo, D., Guerrero, G., & Tapia, F. (2020). Time optimization using augmented reality for the fashion industry [Optimización de tiempos utilizando realidad aumentada para la industria de la moda]. *RISTI-Revista Ibérica de Sistemas e Tecnologías de Informacao, 2020*(E28), 806–815.

Hines, T., & Bruce, M. (2007). *Fashion marketing: Contemporary issues* (2nd ed.). Butterworth–Heinemann. doi:10.4324/9780080468174

House of Commons Environmental Audit Committee. (2019). *Fixing fashion: clothing consumption and sustainability*.

Hu, M., Shi, M., & Wu, J. (2019). Online Group Buying and Crowdfunding: Two Cases of All-or-Nothing Mechanisms. In M. Hu (Ed.), *Sharing Economy. Making Supply Meet Demand* (pp. 319–346). Springer Nature Switzerland. doi:10.1007/978-3-030-01863-4_14

Hult, G. T. M., Hurley, R. F., & Knight, G. A. (2004). Innovativeness: Its antecedents and impact on business performance. *Industrial Marketing Management, 33*(5), 429–438. doi:10.1016/j.indmarman.2003.08.015

Jain, S., & Mishra, S. (2020). Luxury fashion consumption in sharing economy: A study of Indian millennials. *Journal of Global Fashion Marketing, 11*(2), 171–189. doi:10.1080/20932685.2019.1709097

Jin, B. E., & Cedrola, E. (Eds.). Product Innovation in the Global Fashion Industry. Palgrave Studies in Practice: Global Fashion Brand Management. doi:10.1057/978-1-137-52349-5

Jin, B. E., & Shin, D. C. (2020). Changing the game to compete: Innovations in the fashion retail industry from the disruptive business model. *Business Horizons, 63*(3), 301–311. doi:10.1016/j.bushor.2020.01.004

Kotur, A. (2004). *Carolina Herrera: Portrait of a Fashion Icon*. Assouline.

Koumbis, D. (2015). *Moda y retail: de la gestión al merchandising*. Gustavo Gili.

Leclair, M. (2017). "Dior and I": Understanding the combination of creativity and economy in the fashion industry. *Society and Business Review, 12*(3), 274–284. doi:10.1108/SBR-11-2016-0066

Lee, J. (2016). The Model of Fast Fashion Industry: A Case Survey of "Inditex," *Aktual' ni Problemy Ekonomiky = Actual. Problems of Economics, 185*, 430–436.

Li, J., Moreno, A., & Zhang, D. J. (2019). Agent Pricing in the Sharing Economy: Evidence from Airbnb. In M. Hu (Ed.), *Sharing Economy. Making Supply Meet Demand* (pp. 485–503). Springer Nature Switzerland. doi:10.1007/978-3-030-01863-4_20

Macchion, L., Moretto, A., Caniato, F., Caridi, M., Danese, P., & Vinelli, A. (2015). Production and supply network strategies within the fashion industry. *International Journal of Production Economics, 163*, 173–188. doi:10.1016/j.ijpe.2014.09.006

Mbonu, E. (2014). *Diseño de moda: creatividad e investigación*. Promopress.

Newbold, M. (2018). *Ethical footwear brand Po-Zu calls for consumers to 'Champion an Alternative Black Friday*. Fantha Tracks.

Olarte, C., Sierra, Y., & Mosquera, A. (2016). *Venta de moda femenina: una guía muy práctica*. ESIC.

Pavón Vieyra, M. A. (2017). *Administración de la moda MX: básicos para la gestión de pequeñas empresas de nueva creación*. NEILSA.

Posner, H. (2016). *Marketing de moda*. Gustavo Gili.

PwC. (2018). *Report Millennials vs. Generation Z.* Available online: https://www.pwc.com/it/it/press-room/assets/docs/cs_pwc_food.pdf

Rosener, J. B. (2011). Ways women lead. In *Leadership, Gender, and Organization* (pp. 19–29). Springer. doi:10.1007/978-90-481-9014-0_3

Sedeke, K., & Arora, P. (2013). Top ranking fashion blogs and their role in the current fashion industry. *First Monday, 18*(8). doi:10.5210/fm.v18i8.4314

Shamsuzzoha, A., Kankaanpaa, T., Carneiro, L. M., Almeida, R., Chiodi, A., & Fornasiero, R. (2013). Dynamic and collaborative business networks in the fashion industry. *International Journal of Computer Integrated Manufacturing, 26*(1-2), 125–139. doi:10.1080/0951192X.2012.681916

Shirvanimoghaddam, K., Motamed, B., Ramakrishna, S., & Naebe, M. (2020). Death by waste: Fashion and textile circular economy case. *The Science of the Total Environment, 718*, 137317. doi:10.1016/j.scitotenv.2020.137317 PMID:32088483

Silva, S. C., Duarte, P., & Sundetova, A. (2020). Multichannel versus omnichannel: A price-segmented comparison from the fashion industry. *International Journal of Retail & Distribution Management, 48*(4), 417–430. doi:10.1108/IJRDM-07-2019-0232

Stringer, T., Mortimer, G., & Payne, A. R. (2020). Do ethical concerns and personal values influence the purchase intention of fast-fashion clothing? *Journal of Fashion Marketing and Management*, *24*(1), 99–120. doi:10.1108/JFMM-01-2019-0011

Thompson, E. (2014). *The Wedding Dress: The 50 Designs that Changed the Course of Bridal Fashion*. Prestel.

Turker, D., & Altuntas, C. (2014). Sustainable supply chain management in the fast fashion industry: An analysis of corporate reports. *European Management Journal*, *32*(5), 837–849. doi:10.1016/j.emj.2014.02.001

Ünay, F. G., & Zehir, C. (2012). Innovation intelligence and entrepreneurship in the fashion industry. *Procedia: Social and Behavioral Sciences*, *41*, 315–321. doi:10.1016/j.sbspro.2012.04.036

WRAP. (2018). *Sustainable Clothing Action Plan 2020 Commitment: progress against footprint reduction targets 2012–2017*. WRAP.

Yang, S., Song, Y., & Tong, S. (2017). Sustainable Retailing in the Fashion Industry: A Systematic Literature Review. *Sustainability*, *9*(7), 1266. doi:10.3390u9071266

KEY TERMS AND DEFINITIONS

ASPs: Acronym of Agile Supply Partnership defined by the combination of a portfolio of relationships to balance the rigidities of long-term strategic alliances.

Circular Economy: A business strategy that consists of optimizing the use of productive resources to recycle waste generation and eliminate negative externalities on the environment.

Extended Producer Responsibility (EPR): It is a policy approach where producers are given responsibility–be it financial and/or physical–for the treatment or disposal of products they put on the market.

Fast Fashion: Designs that quickly come off the runway to capture current fashion trends.

Second-Hand Market: Economic agents (organizations and individuals) dealing with transactions of used goods.

Sharing Economy: Services and assets shared between private individuals, either free or for a fee, through the internet.

SWOT Analysis: Acronym of Strengths, Weaknesses, Opportunities, and Threats, it is a sort of analysis directed to have a complete view of a specific problem to be solved or analyzed.

Vertical Integration: It appears when a firm owns or controls the entire supply chain.

Section 2

Innovation and Entrepreneurship in Colombia

Chapter 7
Social Entrepreneurship:
Successful Factors of Organizations Developed by Adults in the Colombian Coffee Region

Jairo Alberto Vasquez Bernal
Uniagustiniana, Colombia

ABSTRACT

This chapter presents the fundamental elements related to the success factors of social organizations. The first step was bibliographic research on social entrepreneurship. This research established that social entrepreneurship improves the quality of life of vulnerable communities, which stands out for the social construction of products, services, and processes that allow social inclusion. Social entrepreneurship in Colombian companies has become a topic of analysis; however, it is still a developing area. The second step was to conduct a quantitative and descriptive investigation in the Colombian coffee region, specifically in the departments of Caldas, Risaralda, and Quindío. The sample distribution of the proportions determined the sample. The information was collected from non-profit companies. The results showed that the success factors are to offer quality services, to have committed human talent, and the adequate management of resources that the competitive advantage is the social need they satisfy, and the social benefit is the reduction of poverty.

DOI: 10.4018/978-1-7998-3568-4.ch007

INTRODUCTION

Social entrepreneurship is one of those concepts that has circulated for four decades, with different meanings, scopes, and purposes. However, as Dees (1998) expressed, this is not a new phenomenon, because there have always been social entrepreneurs since there have always been vulnerable communities with social needs.

Social entrepreneurship is understood as an alternative that improves the socio-economic situation of vulnerable populations. This type of entrepreneurship has the primary purpose of improving, promoting changes and innovations in the living conditions of a specific community. Social entrepreneurship is considered as an option to solve social problems related to infrastructure, coverage of essential public services like health, education, housing, food, transportation, public health, and environmental protection. This type of entrepreneurship generates economic resources, employment, and promotes social inclusion.

Social entrepreneurship allows the development of the communities through new alternatives of public or private innovation by enabling the creation of business models with positive social, cultural, economic, and environmental impact. By identifying the success factors and key elements in the social initiatives developed in the Colombian coffee region, it will allow us to understand the success that this approach has had in this region of Colombia.

CONTEXTUALIZATION

Social Entrepreneurship is an alternative for the economic and social development of underserved communities. According to Zahra et al. (2009) and Paul and Uribe (2017), social entrepreneurship is geared towards increasing social welfare based on social and environmental problems building proposals with social value. Social entrepreneurship is a relatively new term and is considered as an emerging discipline. The first publication using this term was in 1889, and it has been increasing its use, as is seen in Figure 1.

Based on this information, social entrepreneurship has been an area of knowledge for the past 40 years. The first academic publication using social entrepreneurship as a term was in a journal in 1989, stating that social entrepreneurship emerged from the practice done by the new types of organizations and interrelationships developed between the companies themselves (Ganne,1989). In the 21st century, it is showing an increase in the use of this term in different types of academic publications, as it is shown in Table 1. As the graph shows, in 2000, were found two publications only, but by 2019, it has been seen 299 publications so far.

Figure 1. Documents published by year
Source: Own Elaboration from Scopus Data, July 2019.

Table 1. Academic Publications

DOCUMENT TYPE	DOCUMENTS	PERCENTAGE
Article	1356	63.81
Book Chapter	318	14.96
Conference Paper	195	9.18
Review	96	4.52
Book	86	4.05
Editorial	20	0.94
Note	15	0.71
Erratum	8	0.38
Conference Review	4	0.19
Short Survey	3	0.14
Undefined	24	1.13
DOCUMENTS	2125	100

Source: Own Elaboration from Scopus Data, July 2019.

From these academic publications, 63.81% are articles in business, management, accounting, social sciences, economics-econometrics, and finance journals. 14.96% of the publications are in the books' chapters. In other lower percentages, there are publications in conference papers, reviews, and books; these publications were done in different countries around the world, as it is shown in Table 2.

Table 2. Countries that published academic content using the term of Social Entrepreneurship

COUNTRY/TERRITORY	TOTAL	PERCENTAGE
United States	647	30.45
United Kingdom	247	11.62
Spain	118	5.55
Australia	116	5.46
Canada	108	5.08
Germany	86	4.05
India	83	3.91
France	68	3.20
Netherlands	67	3.15
Italy	61	2.87
Sweden	60	2.82
Brazil	46	2.16
Malaysia	46	2.16
Denmark	45	2.12
China	44	2.07
South Africa	42	1.98
Portugal	38	1,79
Russian Federation	38	1.79
Switzerland	36	1.69
Belgium	34	1.60
New Zealand	34	1.60
Finland	29	1.36
Romania	27	1.27
Czech Republic	23	1.08
Mexico	22	1.04
Hong Kong	21	0.99
Colombia	20	0.94
Indonesia	20	0.94

Source: Own Elaboration from Scopus Data, July 2019.

As for 2019, the country with the highest production of documents using the term of social entrepreneurship was the United States with 30.45%, then the United Kingdom with 11.62%, and subsequently Spain with 5.55%. Colombia is ranked 27th with a share of 0.94%.

The importance of social entrepreneurship lies in two main aspects. One relates to the economic, social, cultural, and environmental benefits they generate, and the second relates to the actions that promote the improvement of social conditions. These conditions are defined with comprehensive actions aimed to benefit and support populations that are in socio-economic vulnerability by fostering the development of business capabilities based on the generation of entrepreneurial ideas.

To understand the background of social entrepreneurship, it is essential to recognize it as a tool that meets the needs of a specific population. Díaz-Foncea and Marcuello (2014) state that this type of entrepreneurial initiatives are developed in the context-specific characteristics, among which it is essential to mention:

- Companies engaged in the generation of social benefits with unique business proposals.
- Products or services that are oriented to meet needs with proposals of social value-
- Entrepreneurship projects design to focus on underserved populations.
- Projects are making fair use of renewable and non-renewable natural resources.
- Companies that distribute profits among the population of specific geographical areas allowing the "fair and equitable distribution of wealth."
- Entrepreneurship processes that allow the participation of the populations to solve specific problems.
- Economic benefits or profits are not the primary purposes of social entrepreneurship; they will only be a consequence.

According to Santos, Barroso, and Guzmán (2013), social entrepreneurship can generate economic, social, and environmental benefits within a region or community, including the following:

- The current socio-economic system concentrates wealth in a few owners of economic resources, technology, and knowledge. The majority do not enjoy those returns; in social entrepreneurship is sought to distribute wealth among the population.
- Environmental deterioration given using renewable and non-renewable natural resources is done indiscriminately in some cases until the end, deteriorating the ecosystems. Entrepreneurship, on the other handsets the sustainable use of the resources for present and future generations.
- The concentration of power in a few families allows the concentration of capital. Social entrepreneurship intends to the active participation of the society and the required distribution of the capital.

- Social entrepreneurship is important because it makes it possible to reduce poverty, allowing the population the satisfaction of basic needs, access to services, and training.

Continuing with the contextualization of social entrepreneurship, it is essential to mention and review the factors of success of this practice, since they are the reason why customers choose a company or a product creating a competitive advantage to the rest of the actors in the market segment. Some of these advantages may be the location, alliances between companies or associations, the type and features of their products or services, human resources involved, among others (Feijoó, 2012). As well, the implementation of a strategy that effectively included the factors mentioned above (Morales,2011).

Hernández, Yescas, and Dominguez (2007) identified some of the factors of success like technology, innovation, delivery times, price, brand, customer service, the company's resources, staff costs, age of the business, characteristics of entrepreneurs. Similar to the factors reported by Vasquez (2002), this author indicates that the success factors are: Technology, innovation, technical support, quality, delivery times, price, brand, customer service, sales organization, and productive capacity.

CONCEPTUAL APPROACH

Social entrepreneurship is a concept that has been under construction for forty years. From different perspectives, without a general agreement, it is crucial to indicate that social entrepreneurship has been present with the development of humanity. Still, as indicated by Pirson (2015), in the common language, social entrepreneurship can be new. Likewise, Harding (2004) suggests that the growth of social entrepreneurship in global terms in the last decade has been outstanding; however, the precise meaning of the term remains a matter of debate." (p.40).

A situation ratified by Mair and Marty (2006) that, in the 1990s, social entrepreneurship became popular on the global stage as a 'new phenomenon' that is transforming the way we think about the creation of social value. Regarding social entrepreneurship, there are several definitions of this concept depending on the environment they are utilized, purpose, the objectives sought by the entrepreneur, and the scope of the activity.

A group of definitions is elaborated highlighting the social situation, as with Murphy and Commbes (2009). They affirm that social entrepreneurship is an opportunity to detect a social problem. It focuses their efforts on satisfying basic needs for the survival of disadvantaged populations, ensures a fair distribution of scarce resources, develops sustainable and environmentally friendly activities, or adapts technologies to local needs and infrastructure.

With a similar idea, Palacios (2010) indicates that social entrepreneurship is defined as the ability to recognize opportunities to solve social problems and is ratified with the definitions presented in the following table

Table 3. Definitions of social entrepreneurship based on the social situation

Author	Year	Definition
Alvord, Brown, and Letts	2004	Social entrepreneurship is the creation of innovative solutions that solve immediate social problems and mobilize the ideas, capacities, resources and social agreements necessary to achieve a sustainable social transformation
Guzmán y Trujillo	2008	Social entrepreneurship is understood as a type of entrepreneurship, which seeks solutions for social problems through the construction, evaluation, and pursuit of opportunities that allow the generation of sustainable social value, reaching new and stable balances concerning social conditions, through direct action carried out by non-profit organizations, companies or governmental agencies
Torres	2010	Social entrepreneurship is the process of creating organizations that respond to collective needs where social ethics and the integration of social services always prevail.
Bargster	2013	It is a specific type of entrepreneurship that seeks solutions for social problems through the construction, evaluation, and pursuit of opportunities that allow the generation of sustainable social value.

Source: own elaboration

The second group of definitions corresponds to the development of products or services with social value, as referenced by Austin, Svenson, and Skilem (2006), indicating that social entrepreneurship includes the identification, evaluation, and exploitation of opportunities that generate social value. Similarly, Bargsted (2013) suggests that social entrepreneurship is understood as any business initiative, with or without profit, whose main objective is the generation of social value. A similar proposal is expressed by Portales and Perez (2016), indicating that it is a mechanism through which a social and/or environmental problem is addressed while generating a product or service that meets the needs of the market.

A third group corresponds to definitions where value creation stands out. As indicated by Mair and Martí (2006), social entrepreneurship is a process of value creation through new combinations of resources. These combinations of resources are primarily intended to explore and exploit opportunities to create social value, stimulate social change, or meet new social needs.

Fileon, Cisneros, and Mejía (2011) also ratify this idea by indicating that it is a process of creating value through new combinations of resources. These combinations of resources are primarily intended to explore opportunities to create social value, stimulate social change, or meet new social needs. Also expressed by Moreira and Urriolagoitia (2011). There is a broad consensus that social entrepreneurship implies the creation of social value through innovative means and that it also contains elements inspired by the business world.

A fourth group bases its definitions on offers of goods or services to meet needs, as indicated by Dacin, Dacin, and Matear (2010). They explain that social entrepreneurship is the creation of new products, services, and business behaviors that in addition to meet the needs that society demand, it also implies a sustainable social transformation. Also, Navarro, Climent, and Palacio (2011) express that social entrepreneurship is defined as commitment-commitment, in creating new activity models that develop products and services that meet the basic needs of groups neglected by conventional social and economic institutions.

Also, in this fourth group, one of the concepts that best fit this research is proposed by Torío, Peña, and Hernández (2014). These authors affirm that social entrepreneurship refers to entrepreneurs whose objective is to generate social change, as the commitment is to create new activity models that develop products and services to meet the basic needs of groups neglected by conventional social and economic institutions. Also, social entrepreneurship is an approximation from the values of the initiative, the commitment, and the autonomous performance of the business projects and social scope.

A fifth group defines this concept on issues related to the increase of social welfare of the community, as defined by Zahra, Rawhouser, Bhawe, Neubaum, and Hayton, (2009). They establish that "Social entrepreneurship covers the activities and processes carried out to discover, define and exploit opportunities to improve social welfare by creating new companies or managing existing organizations in an innovative way (p. 522). Also, De Pablo and Uribe (2017), in this regard, indicate that social entrepreneurship is a company that seeks as the first objective the welfare of society, in parallel, seeks the care of the environment and the generation of economic profits. They are inclusive businesses aimed at contributing to the development and welfare of society (p. 74).

The sixth group relates to the common interest. In this respect, Gámez (2017) indicates the creation of companies characterized by having a social purpose of common interest. As benefits are reversed to achieve that objective, its organizational model is based on principles such as responsibility, transparency, democracy, participation, and social orientation. Common benefit, in the same way for Low (2006), is any action, initiative, or movement within the socio-economic sphere of private origin and oriented in favor of interest, general or common good.

The seventh group of definitions establishes that it is a discipline, as with Bargsted (2013), that sets social entrepreneurship as a complex discipline since it refers to a specific type of business and social activity based on the structuring and execution of social projects. Therefore, it involves developing, executing, and sustaining initiatives aimed at overcoming a social difficulty, and achieving a common benefit to a human group, whether through business or social-community activities. Like another type of entrepreneurship, it has the central elements of innovation and risk in the solution to a need or problem.

Likewise, Zahra et al. (2009) and de Pablo and Uribe (2017) indicate that social entrepreneurship is an emerging discipline aimed at increasing social welfare based on social and environmental problems, generating proposals with social value.

Finally, the term is related to the benefit it generates, as expressed by Valenciano and Uribe (2017). Social entrepreneurship is a company that seeks, as a first objective, the welfare of society; in parallel, it aims to care for the environment and generation of economic profits. It seeks a triple result, uses the tools of business and market model management to obtain benefits from all parties involved.

With the above, it can be established that social entrepreneurship is a discipline. It contains a set of structured knowledge with a defined purpose that identifies social problems related to public services, infrastructure, roads, shops, and the environment. Likewise, it is established by generating proposals with a social value that corresponds to the ultimate goal, which is to solve problems, through business models in which a project is a structure that describes logically how the organization develops and how it gives value in economic, social, cultural, environmental and service terms. All this, to achieve the fair and equitable distribution of wealth and, with it, a substantial improvement of living conditions in a given place.

METHODOLOGY

The methodological support of this research is based on research proposals that, in the field of social entrepreneurship, guide the process for obtaining, recording, and analyzing information, which allows, based on the conditions of the axis environment Colombian coffee, the maximum use of business success factors in social organizations.

The research approach includes quantitative and qualitative support to structure the study of success factors of social entrepreneurship that allow the development of social enterprises in Colombia (Hernández, Fernández, and Baptista, 2010). The research development process is carried out in several phases.

The first phase corresponds to documentary research, which aims to determine the state of knowledge of social entrepreneurship and, in particular, to identify factors of success. Databases support this process to understand, describe, analyze, and interpret information on the organizations that develop social enterprises.

The second phase is the collection of information. This is mainly focused on quantitative data. Since the units under study are representations of the population, selections are based on the following criteria:

- Type of merchant: non-profit entities: foundations, corporations, cooperative entities, other organizations, civilians, corporations, foundations, national agricultural, and peasant associations.
- Common entities: environmental entities; science, technology, culture, and research entities. Agricultural and peasant associations, including charity and social welfare associations. Entities of the solidarity economy, cooperatives, mutual associations, environmental entities
- Size: small, medium and large
- Economic activity: all economic activities
- Years of renewal: 2018 and 2019.

Based on these criteria, several databases were acquired. This process was done through the Chambers of Commerce of each city of interest to the project. By normalizing the bases, performing debugging in Excel, 230 records were obtained, distributed as shown in the following table

Table 4. Population distribution in the Coffee Axis

Department	Main City	Total Population
Caldas	Manizales	130 companies
Risaralda	Pereira	15 companies
Quindío	Armenia	85 companies

Source: own elaboration

To determine the sample size, the formula related to the process established by the master distribution of the proportions was used as follows:

$$n = \frac{Z^2 * P * q * N}{E^2 (N-1) * Z^2 * P * q}$$

Where:

Z = Value Confidence level = 1.64

P = chance of success = 95%

q = Probability of failure = 5%
E = Margin of Error in the sample = 6%
N = population size = 230

Based on these data, the sample size was determined as follows:

$$n = \frac{1.64^2 * 0.95 * 0.05 * 230}{0.06^2 (230 - 1) * 1.64^2 * 0.95 * 0.05}$$

n = Sample size = 31

The number of surveys conducted on social organizations in the municipalities of the three departments is 31.

The selection of the units under study was performed by proportional stratified sampling in each department. Based on this, the social organizations of the study were selected, as shown in Table 5.

Table 5. Sampling process

Department	Total of social organizations	Sample size
Caldas	130	18
Risaralda	15	2
Quindío	85	11
Total	230	31

Source: own elaboration

To obtain the primary information, a survey is carried out to 31 non-profit companies, including small, medium, and large sizes entities, specifically corporations, foundations, and cooperatives registered in the Chambers of Commerce's databases, using a standardized method of 20 closed and direct questions.

The above is taken as the foundation of the process, allowing the variables and aspects that are relevant to social entrepreneurship to be visualized. The survey also works as a powerful tool to do research. The survey process allows us to prepare and allocate data in an organized way to study several indicators and variables involved in this study. As indicated by Alvira (2011), the survey is a structured information capture tool, useful to describe something and to test hypotheses or models.

The construction and validation of the instrument were carried out based on the Delphi technique with some modifications (Trujillo, Hernández, Falco, Naite, Porro, and Valdivieso, 2014; Velásquez and Armas, 2015) through a successive process of experts, specifical directors of entrepreneurship centers and social entrepreneurs. This instrument is part of the research and the development process.

RESULTS

Regarding research in the Coffee Axis, the results are presented in four sections that are identification, context, success, and social entrepreneurship data.

Results of Identification Data

The identification data corresponding to the basic information of the organization are,

- Name of the organization or business name
- Direction
- City
- Registration date
- Email
- Name of the legal representative
- Economic activity
- Respondent's name

Based on the name of the organization or business name, the type of social organization is determined, as shown in Table 6.

Table 6. Type of social organization

Type Social Organization	Caldas	Risaralda	Quindio	Total	Percentage
Foundations	18	9	28	55	23.81
Associations	13	0	11	24	10.39
Corporations	14	3	7	24	10.39
Cooperatives	47	3	28	78	33.77
Money	37	0	5	42	18.18
Others	2	0	6	8	3.46
TOTAL	131	15	85	231	100

Source: own elaboration based on data from the Chambers of Commerce

In the coffee sector, specifically in the departments of Caldas, Risaralda, and Quindío, 33.77% of social organizations correspond to cooperatives, 23.81% to foundations, and to a lesser extent, funds, associations, and foundations, the percentage of others They represent committees, centers, societies. Regarding the share by cities, the main municipalities of each department were selected showing the following results

Table 7. Cities where the surveys were conducted

Departments	Total	Cities	Total	Percentage
Caldas	131	Manizales	114	49.35
		Riosucio	5	2.16
		Salamina	2	0.87
		Aguadas	2	0.87
		Belalcazar	2	0.87
		Neira	1	0.43
		Anserma	2	0.87
		Aranzazu	3	1.30
Risaralda	15	Pereira	12	5.19
		Marella	1	0.43
		Santuario	1	0.43
		Quinchia	1	0.43
Quindio	85	Armenia	64	27.71
		Quimbaya	5	2.16
		Calarca	6	2.60
		Montenegro	4	1.73
		Salento	1	0.43
		Finlandia	1	0.43
		Latebaida	1	0.43
		Circasia	3	1.30
TOTAL	231		231	100

Source: own elaboration based on data from the Chambers of Commerce.

58% of the social organizations are in the department of Caldas, and especially the city of Manizales (49.35%). In the Quindío department, they are 35%, specifically in the city of Armenia (27.71%), and the Risaralda department represents 6% and the city of Pereira 5.19%. Surveys were conducted by following these proportions.

About the publication dates, the number of published articles is indicated by years, as shown in Table 8.

Table 8. Registration dates in the Chambers of Commerce

Year	Total	Percentage
1996	2	0,87
1997	118	51,08
1998	9	3,90
1999	3	1,30
2000	4	1,73
2001	8	3,46
2002	5	2,16
2003	8	3,46
2004	4	1,73
2005	9	3,90
2006	3	1,30
2007	2	0,87
2008	5	2,16
2009	3	1,30
2010	3	1,30
2011	4	1,73
2012	2	0,87
2013	6	2,60
2014	12	5,19
2015	6	2,60
2016	10	4,33
2017	3	1,30
2018	2	0,87
TOTAL	231	100

Source: own elaboration

Regarding the registration date in the Chambers of Commerce, social organizations defined as cooperatives, associations, foundations, and regulated corporations began to be registered in 1996, and 51% of these companies were recorded in 1997.

Table 9. Gender of company representatives

Gender	Caldas	Risaralda	Quindio	Total	Percentage
Male	70	8	58	136	58.87
Female	61	7	27	95	41.13
Total	131	15	85	231	100

Source: own elaboration based on data from the Chambers of Commerce

In the identification data concerning gender in the Departments, males (58.87%) predominate as representatives of social organizations. The highest percentage of women locates in the Quindío department (41.13%).

Regarding firms, they are associated with small commercial companies (more than ten employees and less than 500) with legal minimum wages in force. These conditions allow us to identify the success factors of non-profit firms. It is essential to indicate that the largest proportion of this type of business are cooperatives and are mainly located in Manizales, as the main center of commerce, communications, and education of the region. By regulation, 51 companies were registered in the Chambers of Commerce in 1997.

Results Context Data

The second section corresponds to the context data, which correspond to general issues related to theory and practice in the field of performance of organizations, whose results are as follows:

It begins with the question of the sustainability reasons of the companies; the results are shown in Figure 2.

The representatives of the non-profit companies ESAL consider that companies are sustainable when they create economic value (17,02%), are competitive (10.64%), and generate well-being (10.64%) mainly. However, other reasons stand out as the management of resources, generate progress, through the process of administration and marketing, among others.

There are many problems that social companies solve, and the answers are shown in Figure 3.

Social organizations solve many social situations, specifically poverty (12.77%), employment (12.77%), and protection of human rights (12.77%). Some of them focus on specific issues such as drug addiction, financing, education, housing, food, and coverage of public services.

The factors that strengthen social enterprises are varied; the alternatives are shown in table 10.

Figure 2. Reasons for the sustainability of companies
Source: own elaboration

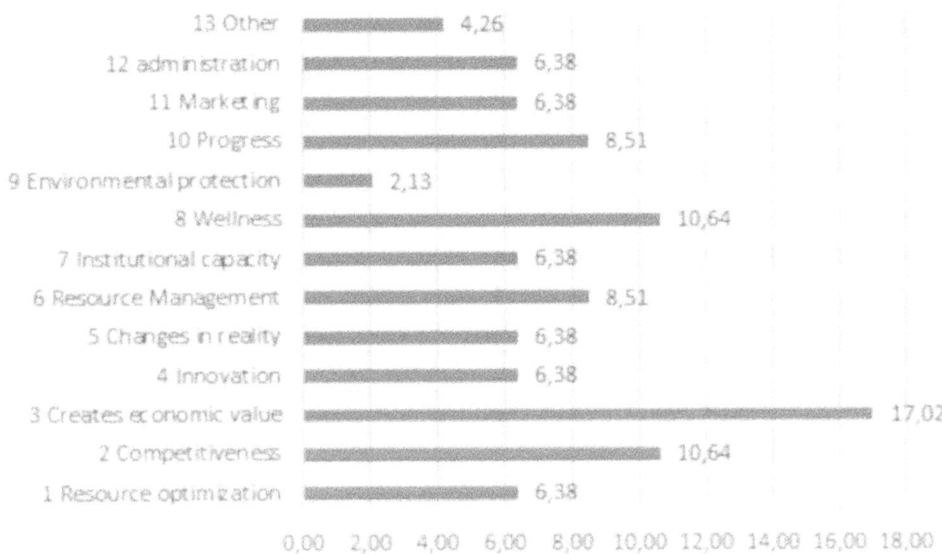

Figure 3. Problems solved by social enterprises
Source: own elaboration

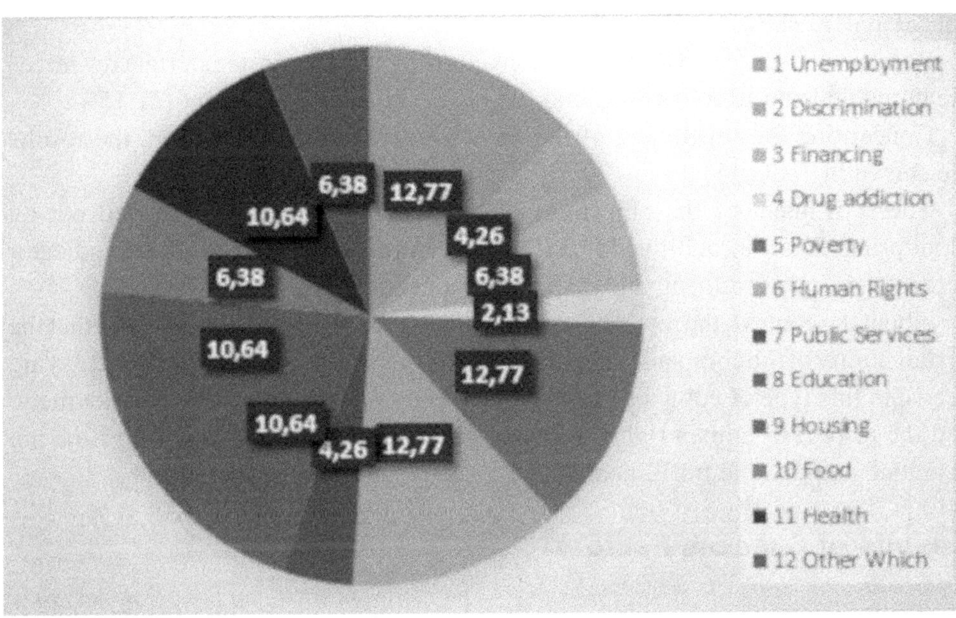

Table 10. Factors for the development of social enterprises

Factors	Total	Percentage
1 Business Units	1	1,92
2 Good organization	7	13,46
3 Adequate financing	4	7,69
4 Customer knowledge	4	7,69
5 Reinvest EBITDA	4	7,69
6 Long term vision	7	13,46
7 The good or service offered	10	19,23
8 Economic resources	1	1,92
9 Human Talent	12	23,08
10 Other Which	2	3,85
TOTAL	52	100

Source: own elaboration

The representatives of social firms consider that for the development of social enterprises, the most critical factors are human talent (23.08%), goods or services offered into the market, long-term vision (13.46%), and good organization (13.46%), among others.

Regarding the resources of social enterprises, the following alternatives are considered, as shown in Figure 4.

Representatives of social organizations consider that the most important resources are human talent (40.38%), financial (25.00%) and economic talent (21.15%)

Concerning the fulfillment of the objectives, precisely as verified, the results are shown in Table 11

The fulfillment of the objectives of the social enterprises is carried out by monitoring (32.56%), auditing (25.58%), and control (18.60%) and in lower indicator percentages, measurement, and review of budgets.

About the context, the representatives of the social organizations consider that the sustainability of the companies is in the creation of value proposals, that is, satisfying needs, in this type of companies solved problems such as poverty, unemployment, and the respect of human rights, for which human talent and long-term vision are essential, and that the fulfillment of the objectives is done by monitoring

Results of Success Factors

Regarding the success factors, they are considered to be those aspects of the company's performance to remain in the market, whose research results are as follows

Figure 4. Resources of social enterprises
Source: own elaboration

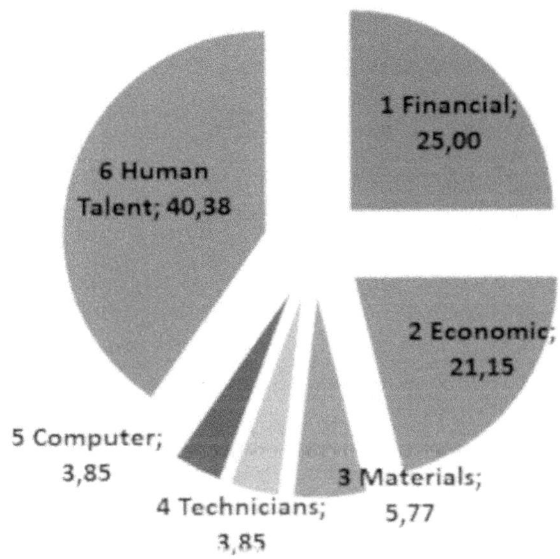

Table 11. Compliance with goals

Fulfillment	Total	Percentage
1 Audit	11	25,58
2 Control	8	18,6
3 Measurement	4	9,3
4 Tracking	14	32,56
5 Indicators	5	11,63
6 Budgets	1	2,33
7 Otra	0	0
Total	43	100

Source: own elaboration

It begins with the question about the success factors of social firms, and the answers are shown in Figure 5.

There are many reasons why social enterprises are thriving the most important are the following quality service (29.41%), human talent (21.75%), resources (9.80%) and service orientation (9.80%), and other aspects such as public relations, strategic planning, good service, administration, social work, and advertising

Figure 5. Success factors of social enterprises
Source: own elaboration

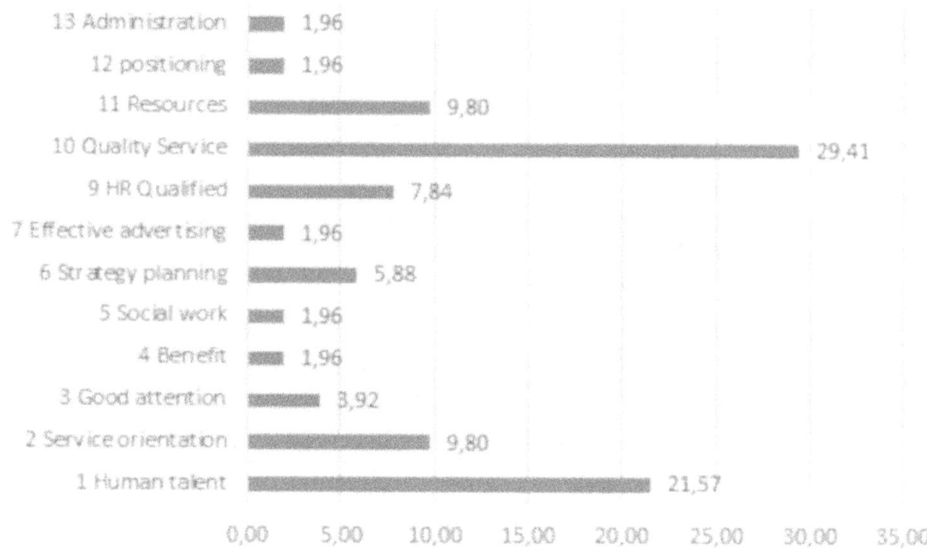

To determine what makes a social enterprise remain in the market, we ask about the competitive advantages. The results are shown in Figure 6.

Representatives of social companies consider that the competitive advantages of their organizations are the social need they satisfy (25.72%), exclusivity in their offer of products or services (20%), recognition obtained from their actions (17.14%), business approach on how goods and services are being offered (14.29%), and exclusivity (14.29%).

Strategies are fundamental for the positioning and recognition of social enterprises. In this regard, the results of the most used strategies are shown in Figure 7.

Social companies carry out many of the strategies of commercial and marketing companies (21.43%), to achieve recognition through promotion (12.50%), to encourage the use of the product or service through advertising (7.14%). They also use distribution strategies, such as positioning, product and service diversification, events, and alternative marketing, among others.

Human talent is essential in social organizations, so it is necessary to know what are the skills and/or competencies that are most valued. The results are shown in Figure 8.

The competences of human talent that mainly value social organizations are teamwork (36.07%), training (19.67%), communication (8.20%), proactivity (8.20%), creativity (6.56%).

Figure 6. Competitive advantages of the social enterprise
Source: own elaboration

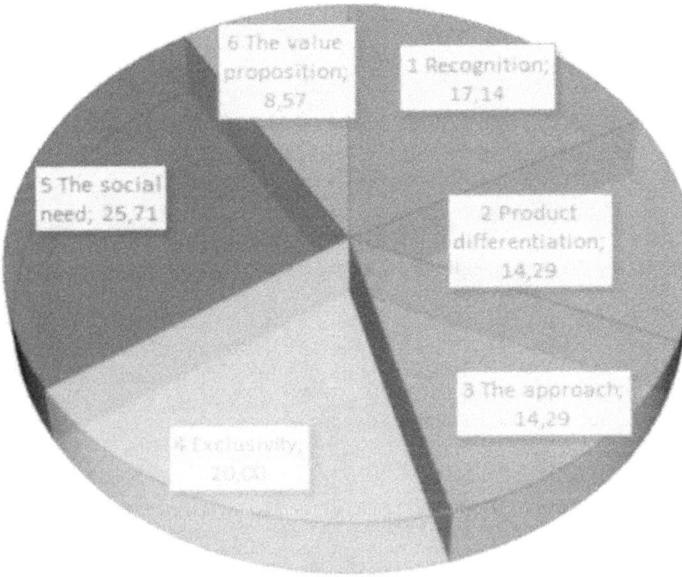

Figure 7. Strategies used by social enterprises
Source: own elaboration.

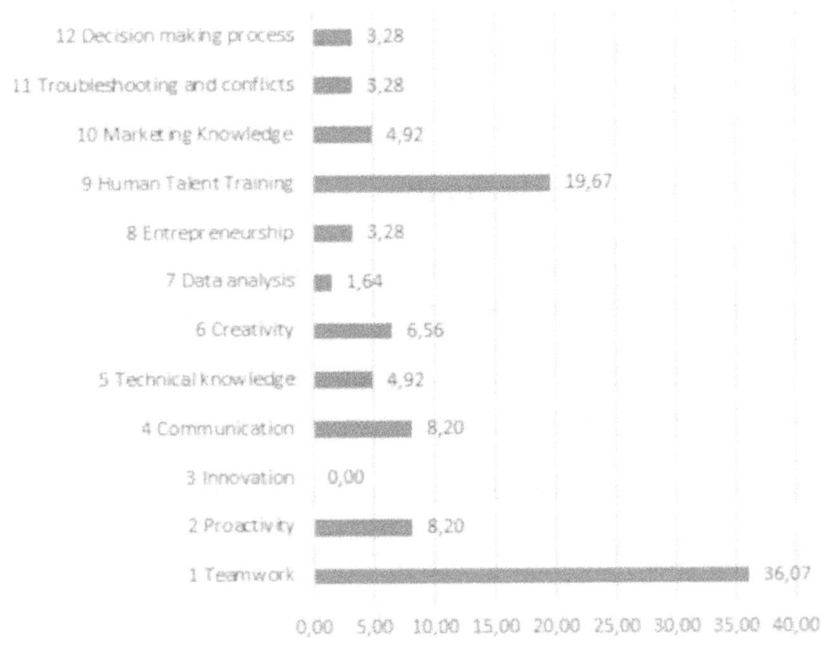

Figure 8. Human talent competencies
Source: own elaboration

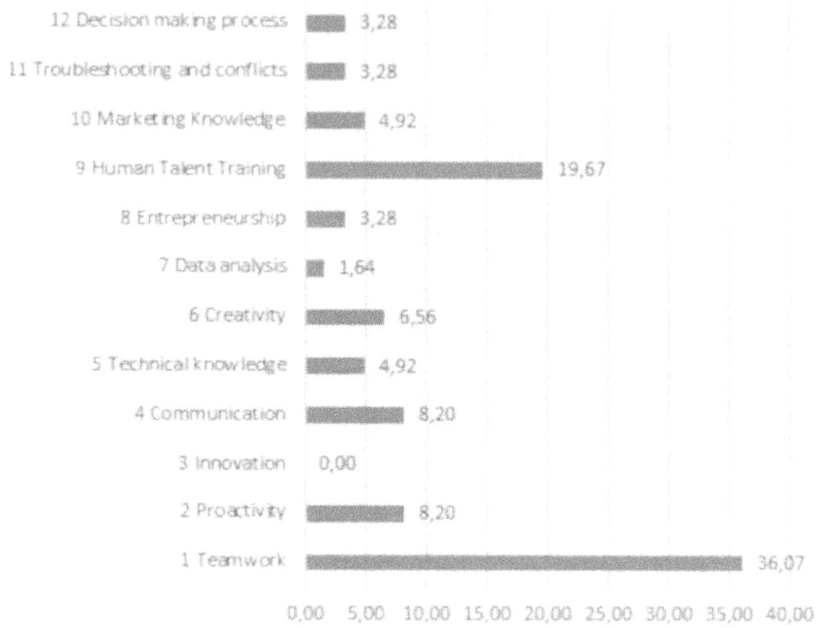

About the success factors of social organizations, it is established that the fundamental thing is to offer quality services, that is, that they fully satisfy the needs of the clients, and the commitment of human talent to the product and service. These companies also carry out marketing strategies to inform and persuade, and carry out promotional and advertising activities to stay in the market and valuing teamwork.

Results of Social Entrepreneurship

The effects of social entrepreneurship include the processes related to activities or actions for social benefit, the foundation of social organizations, presenting the following:

In this regard, it begins with knowing what aspect, function, or area they consider to be considered in social enterprises are assumed efficient. The answers are shown in Figure 9.

The aspect, function, or area that they consider efficient in social enterprises is to offer products with a quality process (32.14%) and the administrative area (19.64%). Since resources are scarce, and it is vital to manage it properly and the responsibility in the fulfillment of the established objectives (14.29%).

Figure 9. Appearance, area or efficient function
Source: own elaboration

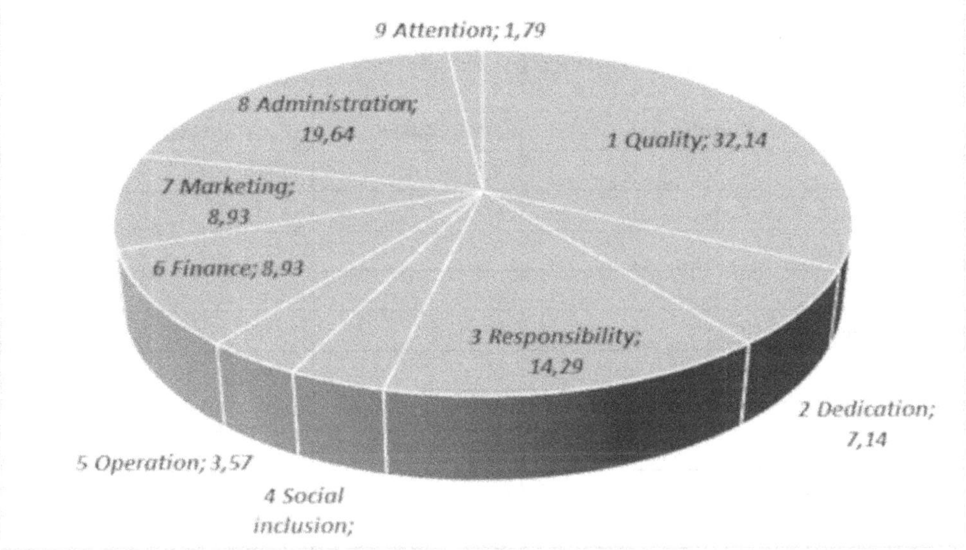

A functional aspect of companies is an innovation since the needs of the population are changing. In this regard, the representatives of social enterprises expressed the existence of this activity, as shown in Table 13.

Table 13. Innovation in social firms

Innovation	Total	Percentage
Yes	20	64,52
Not	11	35,48
Total	31	100

Source: own elaboration

The representatives report that in social enterprises, 64.52% carry out innovation processes in processes, products, technology, or services, 35.48% do not carry out innovation processes, since they concentrate on a single good or service in specific geographical areas, such as public services, for example, an aqueduct.

Regarding the corporate purpose of each of the companies associations, foundations, corporations, foundations, funds, societies, committees, offer various products or services, given by geographical area, social situation, needs, make these social are varied.

The companies within their work carry out activities of promotion by strengthening motivation. Social entrepreneurs highlight those facts, as shown in Table 14.

Table 14. Social activities performed by social firms

Social Activities	Total	Percentage
1 Health	10	12.35
2 Education	9	11.11
3 Public Services	2	2.47
4 Food	8	9.88
5 Social inclusion	11	13.58
6 Generation of resources	7	8.64
7 Job creation	2	2.47
8 Sports activities	3	3.7
9 Recreational activities	6	7.41
10 Cultural activities	7	8.64
11 Social awareness	5	6.17
12 Environmental protection	3	3.7
13 Religious activities	6	7.41
14 Other	2	2.47
TOTAL	81	100

Source: own elaboration

Social organizations carry out many activities. The ones that stand out the most are Social inclusion (13.58%), health days (12.35%), education process (11.11%), food delivery (9.88%), cultural activities (8.64%), resource generation (8:64%), and recreational activities (7.41%).

Social enterprises from their missionary principles generate social benefits, business people expressed them, and the answers are shown in Table 15.

The main benefit of social enterprises is the reduction of poverty (26.83%), but others stand out as family integration (24.39%), reduction of social problems (14.63%), or population with education (12.20%). These organizations direct to people who have resolved their economic situation, pensioners, or members of wealthy families who dedicate part of their income for social benefit, specifically to vulnerable communities, such as children, single women with children, disabled, and displaced population.

Social enterprises have many difficulties in their performance, as shown in Table 16.

Table 15. Social benefits

SOCIAL BENEFITS	TOTAL	PERCENTAGE
1 Poverty reduction	11	26.83
2 Increase in the coverage of public services	2	4.88
3 Population with education	5	12.2
4 Family integration	10	24.39
5 Reduction of social problems	6	14.63
6 Family integration	3	7.32
7 Financing	4	9.76
8 Other	0	0
TOTAL	41	100

Source: own elaboration

Table 16. Difficulties of social organizations

Difficulties	Total	Percentage
1 Difficulty to consolidate the team	1	2.7
2 Few economic resources	8	21.62
3 Insufficient infrastructure	5	13.51
4 Corruption	3	8.11
5 Many projects do not fit the real ones	4	10.81
6 Difficulty making contact networks.	1	2.7
7 Lack of ambition	5	13.51
8 Financing	1	2.7
9 Public Policies	9	24.32
10 Other	0	0
TOTAL	37	100

Source: own elaboration

Representatives consider that one of the current difficulties mostly affecting them are public policies (24.32%). Due to procedures and tax burdens, they have fewer resources (21.62%) to meet social needs and build infrastructures (13.51%) such as facilities, technological, and IT. The shortage of economic resources ends with a lack of ambition (13.51%) to offer other products, services, or to reach other markets (Table 17).

Table 17. Linking process for beneficiaries

Process	Total	Percentage
1 Conferences	11	20.37
2 Talks	13	2407
3 Workshops	7	12.96
4 POP material	1	1.85
5 Awareness programs	10	18.52
6 Advertising campaigns	4	7.41
7 Views	1	1.85
8 Voice to voice	3	5.56
9 Social networks	3	5.56
10 Other	1	1.85
TOTAL	54	100

Source: own elaboration.

Social companies are carrying out linking processes through talks (24.07%), conferences (20.37%), awareness programs (18,52%), and advertising material accompanied by information on social networks and voice to voice.

Regarding social entrepreneurship in social firms, quality is fundamental, accompanied by marketing strategies, and product and service innovation. Although some organizations concentrate their services on a specific group of the population, there is general business growth.

The most significant benefit that social firms offer to society is the reduction of poverty, as they carry out actions and activities to improve the social conditions of the population. But the most outstanding current difficulty is the public policies that limit the work of these organizations. As a result, talks, conferences, and awareness programs are forms of generalized communication between these groups of communities.

CONCLUSION

Social entrepreneurship began in the 1980s, so it is a relatively new discipline. From an organizational and legal perspective, it aims to solve social problems through business models that provide economic, social, cultural, environmental, and services value to achieve a fair and equitable distribution of wealth.

In the Coffee Axis, specifically in the departments of Caldas, Risaralda, and Quindío, and mainly in the cities of Manizales, Pereira, and Armenia, associations, corporations, foundations, cooperatives, and social organizations, generate a social benefit to vulnerable people, such as adults, elderly, children, single women, displaced population, with passing homes, community canteens, training institutions, activity centers, and marketers for common benefit.

The success factors of social firms are quality service, experienced human talent, the type of product or service, the planning strategy of the organization. It is also essential to take into account good care, social work, quality, and resources, among others, as their advantage is the social need they satisfy, and define by offering quality products. Firms that are efficient in the administrative area and dispose of adequate management of resources.

The social organizations carry out many activities; the ones that stand out the most are social inclusion, health days, education process, food delivery, cultural and recreational activities. As a result of the trajectory, exclusivity, and value proposition, the differentiation of product and social need satisfy these companies that achieve poverty reduction, family integration, and reduction of social problems by linking population through talks, awareness programs, conferences, voice to voice, and workshops.

REFERENCES

Alvira, M. F. (2011). La encuesta: una perspectiva general metodológica. Madrid, Spain: Centro de Investigaciones Sociologicas (CIS)

Austin, J., Svenson, H., & Skilem, J. (2006). Social and commercial entrepreneurship: Some, different, or both. *Entrepreneurship Theory and Practice*, *30*(1), 1–22. doi:10.1111/j.1540-6520.2006.00107.x

Bargsted, A. M. (2013). El emprendimiento social desde una mirada psicosocial. *Civilizar*, *13*(25), 121–132. doi:10.22518/16578953.133

Dacin, P. A., Dacin, M. T., & Matear, M. (2010). Social entrepreneurship: Why we don't need a new theory and how we move forward from here. *The Academy of Management Perspectives*, *24*(3), 37–57.

De Pablo, V., & Uribe, J. (Coords.). (2017). Experiencias de emprendimiento social en Iberoamérica. Almeria, Spain: Universidad de Almería.

Dees, J. G. (1998). Enterprising non-profits. *Harvard Business Review*, *76*, 54–69.

Díaz-Foncea, M., & Marcuello, C. (2014). Las empresas sociales en España: Concepto y características. *Gizarte Ekonomiaren Euskal Aldizkaria-Revista Vasca de Economía Social*, *8*, 23–36.

Feijoó, J.L. (2012). *El planeamiento estratégico en hotelería.* Buenos Aires, Argentina: Ugerman Editor.

Filion, L., Cisneros, L., & Mejía, M. J. (2011). *Administración de PYMES. Emprender, dirigir y desarrollar empresas*. Pearson Educación.

Gámez, J. (2017). Aproximación al emprendimiento social. *Revista Gestión y Finanzas*, *1*(1), 21–28.

Gámez, J., & Saiz-Álvarez, J. M. (2016). A Model of Social Entrepreneurship based on Distance Education y ICT. In A. Cotte, A. G. Muñoz, & G. Correa (Eds.), *Development, Growth, Environment and Social Equity* (pp. 1–25). Nova Science Publishers.

Ganne, B. (1989). Regional Dynamics of Innovation: A Look at the Rhône-Alpes región. *Entrepreneurship and Regional Development*, *1*(2), 147–154. doi:10.1080/08985628900000013

Harding, R. (2004). Social Enterprise: The New Economic Engine? *Business Strategy Review*, *15*(4), 539-43.

Hernández, G., Yescas, L., & Domínguez, H. (2007). Factores de éxito en los negocios de artesanía en México. *Estudios Gerenciales*, *23*(104), 77–99. doi:10.1016/S0123-5923(07)70018-9

Hernández Sampieri, R., Fernández Collado, C., & Baptista Lucio, P. (2010). *Metodología de la investigación*. McGraw-Hill.

Low, C. (2006). A Framework for the Governance of Social Enterprises. *International Journal of Social Economics*, *33*(5/6), 376–385. doi:10.1108/03068290610660652

Mair, J., & Marti, I. (2006). Social entrepreneurship research: A source of explanation, prediction, and delight. *Journal of World Business*, *41*(1), 36–44. doi:10.1016/j.jwb.2005.09.002

Morales, M.I. (2011). 50 Aniversarios del canje de la moneda. *Revista del Banco Central de Cuba*, 1-68.

Morales-Gutiérrez, A. C., Ariza-Montes, J., & Rodríguez, N. M. (2012). El emprendedor social y el E-empowerment de las redes virtuales. *CIRIEC – España. C.I.R.I.E.C. España*, *75*, 153–177.

Moreira, P., & Urriolagoitia, L. (2011). Emprendimiento social. *Revista española del tercer sector, 17*, 19-21.

Murphy, P. J., & Coombes, S. M. (2009). A model of social entrepreneurial: Discovery. *Journal of Business Ethics, 85*(3), 325–336. doi:10.100710551-008-9921-y

Navarro, A. M., Climent, V. C., & Palacio, J. R. S. (2011). Emprendimiento social y empresas de inserción en España. Aplicación del método delphi para la determinación del perfil del emprendedor y las empresas sociales creadas por emprendedores. *Revesco: Revista de Estudios Cooperativos, 106*, 150–172.

Pirson, M. (2015). *Social Entrepreneurship and all that Funk, Research Paper Series*. Fordham University Schools of Business Research; Humanistic Management Network.

Portales, L., & Pérez, O. (2016). Emprendimiento y Empresa Social como estrategia de desarrollo local. *Institut de Socio-Économie des Entreprises et des Organisations, 144*, 45–56.

Saiz-Álvarez, J. M. (Ed.). (2019). Handbook of Research on Digital Marketing Innovations in Social Entrepreneurship and Solidarity Economics. Hershey, PA: Information Science Reference (IGI Global). doi:10.4018/978-1-5225-8939-6

Trujillo Blanco, W. G., Hernández, J. J. R., Hernández, A. M. L., Falco, E. R., Naite, O. F. A., Porro, E. M., & Valdivieso Romero, J. F. (2014). Adaptación del cuestionario SF-36 para medir calidad de vida relacionada con la salud en trabajadores cubanos. *Revista Cubana de Salud y Trabajo, 15*(1), 62–70.

Valenciano, J., & Urube, J. (2017). *Experiencias de Emprendimiento Social en Iberoamérica*. Editorial Universidad de Almería.

Vásquez, C. O. (2002). La idónea implementación estratégica es condición necesaria para aspirar al éxito de la empresa. *Estudios Gerenciales, 18*(85), 41–66.

Velásquez, L. J., & Armas, M. (2015). Requerimientos estadísticos para la determinación de criterios e indicadores de desarrollo sostenible del Municipio Autónomo Caroní. *Universidad, Ciencia y Tecnología, 19*(75), 82–97.

Zahra, S., Rawhouser, H., Bhawe, N., Neubaum, D., & Hayton, J. (2008). Globalization of Social Entrepreneurship opportunities. *Strategic Entrepreneurship Journal, 2*(2), 117–131. doi:10.1002ej.43

KEY TERMS AND DEFINITIONS

Awareness Programs: Programs aimed at raising awareness among the most vulnerable population so that they change their ways of life to achieve a more economically sustainable life.

Colombian Coffee Axis: It is a geographical, cultural, economic, and ecological region of Colombia specialized in the production of coffee, and located in the departments of Caldas, Risaralda, Quindío, and Northwest Tolima, the southwest of Antioquia, the north and east of Valle del Cauca, and the capital cities of the first four departments mentioned.

Cooperatives: Type of organization characterized by collective property and equitable sharing of obligations and costs.

Non-Profit Entities: Mainly foundations, corporations, and cooperatives are defined as being focused on social improvements.

Social Entrepreneurship: It is an organization that uses business methods to address social problems through innovation and non-profit strategies.

Social Firms: Business for a social cause.

Social Value: It is the social importance in quantitative terms of social change.

Success Factors: They are the fundamental variables that determine business success.

Chapter 8
From Displacement to Entrepreneurship:
Case of the Wounaan-Nonam Community

Javier Andrés Reyes Ardila
Universidad EAN, Colombia

Omar Alonso Patiño Castro
https://orcid.org/0000-0002-4897-4897
Universidad EAN, Colombia

Catalina Lucía Ruiz Arias
Universidad EAN, Colombia

Paula Echeverry Pérez
Universidad EAN, Colombia

ABSTRACT

The violence that hits Colombia for more than 50 years forced many people, families, and communities to leave their original territories and seek refuge in the principal cities, especially in Bogotá, where displaced people from various regions of the country arrived. Victims of this situation, the Wounaan-Nonam community, were relocated in the periphery of Bogotá, under challenging conditions, some without the necessary infrastructure to live with a minimum quality of life standards, and in a completely different context and culture than the one they were used to live. This research seeks to help artisan women for developing production processes around Wérregue products. As a result, this community will improve their productivity, structure their organization, define marketing strategies, and promote their sustainability and growth while protecting and respect their cultural essence and heritage to generate higher and sustainable income for the artisans.

DOI: 10.4018/978-1-7998-3568-4.ch008

INTRODUCTION

The report *Indigenous Latin America in the Twenty-First Century. First Decade* (World Bank, 2015. p. 30) states that 49% of the indigenous population of Latin America lives in urban areas, far from their lands, for reasons, among others, associated with displacement, land dispossession, ecological depletion, conflicts, violence, and natural disasters. On the other hand, the International Labor Organization (OIT, 2015) shows that, in the processes of forced migration, the most affected population group are women, mainly due to the labor exploitation to which they are subjected, by outsiders or by members of the same community. Moreover, it obliges them to plunge into the informal economy as the only means of subsistence in urban areas.

Therefore, having signed the Sustainable Development Goals (SDGs), 170 countries around the world have acquired the commitment, among others, to eradicate all forms of poverty by 2030, eliminate existing inequality through the implementation of strategies for the empowerment of vulnerable populations, among which are indigenous people.

The situation as described is typical of the Colombian indigenous communities, which face the same problems, with the aggravating fact that a large part of the population has had to migrate to urban areas because of forced displacement, caused by the violence that has occurred and affected the country for more than 50 years.

In this sense, the contributions for the achievement of the SDGs can be to the attention of specific problems, which, from the perspective of social innovation, are solved accompanying processes to overcome them structurally, thereby generating benefits that can be sustained over time. As an example, processes with specific communities, such as the Wounaan-Nonam, can favor the method of insertion in urban areas of those who have very little chance of returning to their lands. Among other things, because their new generations are growing in different environments than those of its origin, and its customs and behaviors are much more city-dwellers.

This project has the goal of consolidating a community project based on the elaboration of handicrafts using ancestral techniques and inputs from Nature, especially in the region in which lived this community: mainly the South of the department of Chocó and the North of the department of Valle del Cauca, both in Western Colombia.

Per the above, the community intervention project began with the first phase to support the community in the design of products. Once consolidated, they move to the second phase of business accompaniment that gives them the necessary elements to ensure that their culture can be preserved through the craftwork of its members.

In the first part of our chapter, we present the bibliography that includes the most critical transformations taken place, in recent years, with the practice of design, and how this discipline has focused on social sustainability as an engine of structural change. This fact has become one of the fundamental axes of social innovation, changing the traditional concepts, leading it to focus on products and services with a much more commercial approach, thereby giving a very visible role to social innovation as the axis of change for societies.

The second part describes the field interventions and accompaniment done with Wounaan-Nonam women in 13 sessions, with which it was possible to strengthen the development of the community entrepreneurship project on handicrafts. To reduce the risk of vulnerability in which they find themselves, establish ways to avoid labor discrimination that affects them, thereby seeking to strengthen their culture and the possibility of oral transmission of ancestral knowledge that they carry out through artisanal work.

The third and last part of the chapter contains the most critical findings and future tasks that can be developed, so that this experience is not unique, but becomes the axis on which new works arise that contribute to the social and economic adaptation of the community.

INDIGENOUS PEOPLE AROUND THE WORLD - CURRENT SITUATION

According to the United Nations Organization (2010, pp. 1-3), the indigenous population is grouped into more than 5,000 different communities spread worldwide, with more than 370 million people, representing about 5% of the total population of the world. The indigenous population is the most significant source of cultural diversity, despite its minority population.

Language is the second element of diversity. Around 7,000 languages are being spoken in the world, of which 4% are spoken by 97% of the population. This situation evidences the significant problem that looms over indigenous communities, given that it is considered that more than 90% of these languages may disappear in a period not exceeding 100 years. Due to the problems mentioned above and the increased colonization processes, which not only tear their territory but also detach them from their culture, as history shows (U.N., 2010).

The aspect, as mentioned above, becomes more relevant if one considers that language is an essential component of culture and that it serves as a means to preserve ancestral knowledge through oral tradition. Besides, to providing collective and individual identity to community members, by which, with its disappearance, breaks the sense of belonging and community (U.N., 2010, p. 3).

Colonization and displacement bring other consequences, such as the alteration of the indigenous ways of life, which are closely linked to mysticism, spirituality, and attachment to Mother Nature. Their way of understanding the universe is given by understanding the sacred character of the territory, which they consider as the source of life, being part of their existence.

It can be affirmed that the particularities expressed above are lived by the Colombian indigenous people in the same or greater intensity. The unequal struggle that they have to face is usually lost because, on the other side, they always find compelling interests that make them the most prone group to vulnerability. Much more when their chances of development are diminished to the same extent that those interests captivate its inhabitants, who, at an early age, when they can decide freely, are seduced by the comforts and opportunities offered by urban civilizations.

The same report cited by the U.N. states that indigenous communities are more than 30% of the population living in rural areas and represent about 15% of the people living in poverty around the world. Likewise, the preservation of indigenous communities is not guaranteed, not even in developed countries in which there may be higher levels of social investment with which the conservation of these populations is intended. The indicators of quality of life and wellbeing are always below those in the majority of the non-indigenous population. Life expectancy is shorter, health services are precarious, in the majority of cases provided by the same community through the shamans, and the level of education is low.

After these processes of submission, abuse of power, non-legitimization, and violation of the individual rights of indigenous people, the possibility of extinction of indigenous communities has increased. As a result, there is a risk of cultural colonization, and a loss of territory and power, among other consequences of their current situation. Therefore, the conditions in which indigenous communities are submerged around the world suggest that they are becoming more acute over time, with a great possibility of extinction in a few years.

The situation mentioned above is different in China, where there are no high rates of inequality among indigenous communities. Poverty rates have declined significantly in China thanks to sustained economic growth since the 1990s, with the benefits despised for the indigenous communities (Table 1).

On the other hand, the International Labor Organization (2015) considers that the threat to the livelihoods of indigenous people has forced them to migrate, with the consequences that this brings for the population, especially for women who also of displacement are forced to work in conditions of high informality.

This implies that the processes of westernization are taking place in a forced way, compelling communities to live a method of coupling that is at the expense of their culture and customs, without which their insertion into new social and economic life forms is not possible. In this fact is the challenge, Western societies must strive to find opportunities to insert them into these new conditions but interpreting their way of seeing life and developing strategies to maintain their ancestral knowledge.

Table 1. World indigenous population and population in poverty

Country or region	Indigenous population (in millions)	Number of indigenous in poverty (in millions)
China	106	5
South Asia	95	42
Southeast Asia	30	15
Africa	22	17
Arabia	15	1
Central America and Mexico	12	9
South America	11	9
Rest of the world	9	2
Total	**300**	**100**

Source: World Bank (2015)

SITUATION OF THE WOUNAAN - NONAM INDIGENOUS COMMUNITY

The Wounaan-Nonam is a community with more than 500 years of existence that lives on the banks of the basin of Río San Juan, between the departments of Chocó and Valle del Cauca, in western Colombia. They are at high risk of vulnerability due to the high unemployment rates they have faced. Besides, associated with the same conditions that have arisen for indigenous people in other parts of the world: labor exploitation, social marginalization, and discrimination due to the state of being indigenous (Vía Plural, 2011).

The same characteristics of the territory have allowed the Wounaan-Nonam to be people of water and mountains. They are surrounded by natural jungle, in which, due to the existence of a good number of rivers, in addition to hunting, gathering fruits and growing products, have great opportunities for fishing. Its spiritual connection with its environment is made through the garments, which include the use of necklaces and body paint with inputs that come from the lush Nature of the region (Artesanías de Colombia, s.f.).

More than 500 Wounaan-Nonam people live now in Bogotá, the capital of Colombia, specifically in Ciudad Bolívar, since 2003, because of the armed conflict that has plagued Colombia for more than 50 years. That conflict forced them to leave their land on the Coast from Río San Juan, in western Colombia to the center of the country. These people have their cosmogony and elements of cultural identity that have not been replicated with intensity in their children born and raised outside their territory. These children have been educated in Western culture, despite efforts made by mothers to maintain some specific elements of its culture, such as language.

The limitations in the quality of life have caused the Wounaan-Nonam in Bogota, led mainly by women, to draw their hardened spirit. They are in an organizational process that allows them to generate independent sources of income, based on their ancestral knowledge around the weave made with palm fibers from the original region of the community.

One of the cultural elements that give Wounaan- Nonam the greatest identity is the use of Werregue palm fiber, with which they weave different products whose beauty and quality are recognized by society in general.

The acquisition of new resources is one of the aspects on which women want to leverage the support of their culture, thereby seeking to create decent and equitable work opportunities that favor their community and allow them to establish the preservation of their own customs programs.

EL WERREGUE – WOUNAAN - NONAM HANDCRAFTED WORK BASE

The Werregue is part of the mythology of the community. Its origin dates back to a dispute between its God, creator of life, Ewandam, and Satan, Dosat, who confronted each other because the first considered that the Wounaan-Nonam should not work because he gave them wellbeing and food, with "The Banana of Life." In an absence from Ewandam, Dosat handed them axes and other tools to cut trees and palms, learning to cut bananas for their livelihood. Upon his return, Ewandam saw his children working and began a dispute with Dosat for salting the sea. Seeking to prove who was more powerful, Ewandam created the palm of chontaduro and Dosat, the Werregue palm; that, although it does not produce any fruit; it was used by the Wounaan to create amphorae with anthropomorphic and zoomorphic figures that tell stories of the jungle, they see daily. Besides, Dosat created the platanilla, instead of the banana, and the cane, instead of the sugar cane, which gave rise to the Werregue and other inputs used by the community for the weaving of the different elements they make.

The Werregue is a spiny trunk palm that reaches up to 20 meters high, whose harvest can only be done on a new moon since if it is done at a different time, the leaf is damaged and doesn't serve to be used in crafts.

Although its more outstanding production, in large percentage spontaneously without the need for crops, occurs in Chocó, it is also produced in a part of Antioquia, where it is called Werregue or chuga, and in Nariño, where it is called guinul.

The fiber is initially harvested by cutting down the palms, work is done only by men, and women are responsible for tearing the buds from the tree, which they could only do with the permission of God Jai, spiritual owner from the Werregue.

With this palm, weave one of the most recognized handicrafts of Colombia, some of which, in the beginning, were kitchen and table accessories for the community. With the spiral technique, Wounaan-Nonam women make jugs, baskets, plates, cups, fruit trays, and accessories such as wallets or earrings.

The elaboration of the different artifacts is made from the use of a cord called soul or gut, around which it is woven, lining the gut, with the previously treated fiber coming from the Werregue, organized in very thin, dried threads to the sun.

What was initially only a work done with the natural color of the fiber then acquired color thanks to the intervention of the missionary nuns who influenced the application of natural dyes extracted from achiote, puchama, saffron, and other plants in the region. Also, in the design of larger pieces, they colored the fibers with naturally extracted dyes and shined it with a friction technique. Although there is complete freedom in the design, the figures of the baskets and other pieces commonly refer to situations of daily life, images of the past, elements of Nature and beliefs, or geometric figures.

With the pass of time, the community has developed better harvesting techniques, such as they no longer cut the palm. Still, they use special tools to cut the bud and, in the same way, improvements have been made in the finishing of their handicrafts (Artesanías de Colombia, s.f.)

THE IMPORTANCE OF DESIGN IN SOCIAL INNOVATION PROCESSES

Like any of the other arts, the design has evolved, becoming much more adjusted to new social realities. In this sense, Manzini (2015) states that the wide range of activities and its possibilities of application confuses its modern definition because the discipline has closed the gap between social and technical systems, which has placed the domain into a dynamic transformation to serve for social innovation projects, repeatedly.

The evolution of the concept of sustainability, the interpretation and adaptation of the designers to the demand of the contemporary world has generated the development of different design practices (Martínez et al., 2017). That is why current design practices are those that have come off the new interpretations of sustainability and innovation with a social approach and are those that involve more participatory methods during the process. Likewise, for McKenzie (2004, cited by Martínez et al., 2017), the vision of social sustainability as a concept that attempts to achieve a better quality of life for communities is identified in the current scenario.

New design trends indicate that the product-centered design is moving to one focused on people's purposes, in which the focus is broader. At the same time, the support of diverse actors and disciplines is needed to address broad research fields that result in the solution to the needs of the populations (Sanders and Stappers, 2008, p. 11).

Therefore, it is expected that today, we are talking about social design, in which different methodological and conceptual currents converge, such as participatory design, social sustainability, social innovation, and co-creation (Martínez et al., 2017). The purpose of this work approach is to approach small-scale community challenges, to serve the deployment of strategies that contribute to the local development of these communities, marking sustainable production processes with high differential value.

It is pertinent, then, to talk about participatory design with a social approach. For Ferruzca and Rodríguez (2011), it is conceived as a strategic factor, given that it not only contributes to improving the performance of initiatives and generating wellbeing for people but also contributes to competitive development at the local, regional, or country level. This is why the innovation processes carried out today and led by design are the product of the synergies of collaborative strategies between organizations and users.

In this sense, Espitia and Cedeño (2017) affirm that the potential of sustainable design within the so-called new waves of alternative economies (of the common good, of knowledge, of inequalities) will allow the living conditions to improve. As long as further research provides methodological elements and processes that will enable the design discipline to continue expanding its scope and in parallel contribute to reducing environmental impacts.

For Manzini (2015), social innovation has the potential to change the world, but, for this, a new culture and new practices that support it are necessary. Just as the industrial design did a century ago, generating and building a shared vision that expanded the meaning of this culture and practice throughout society, to the point of making it part of people's daily lives. Design is the combination of a new approach and culture focused on social innovation to generate global changes. Still, it must be a widespread activity in all socio-technical structures where we are involved daily. But this goal requires constant and continuous work of the entire design community. The design for social innovation is shown in Figure 1.

Faced with this new situation, social research must be directed towards social innovation. Under new developments related to market-oriented design and commercial innovation, it is seeking that there is a more significant investment in economic and intellectual capital. This fact leads to the formulation of public policies that legitimize and further support their contributions to the development of society in general (Ortiz, 2016; Cajaiba, 2014; Mulgan, 2006).

Figure 1. Design for social innovation
Source: Krois (2015).

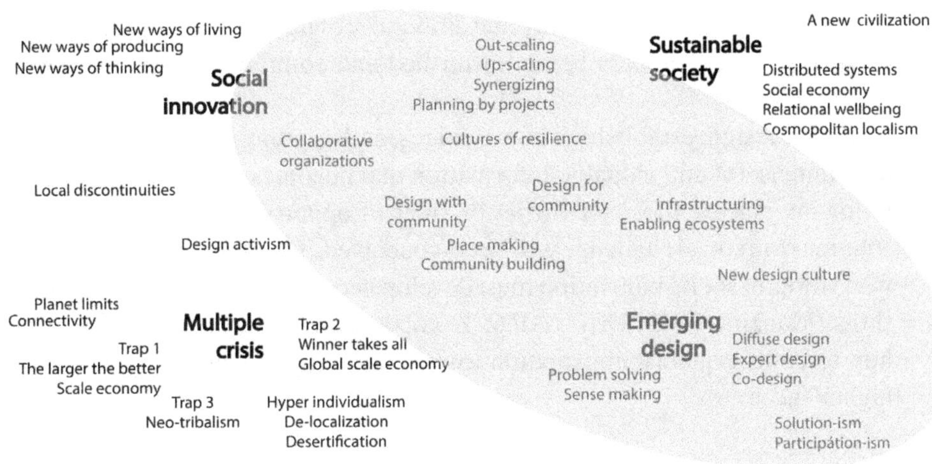

On the other hand, Tromp and Hekkert (2016), Ortiz (2016), Manzini (2015), Thackara (2013), Morelli (2007), Margolin and Margolin (2002), and Papanek (1985) suggest that social innovation requires some conditions that facilitate its development and generate long-term effects, such as those shown below:

1. Revert assistance solutions: leave aside the conceptual and material design of proposals that are aimed at generating passivity and conformity in the communities to which a solution is directed. It must instead be stimulated by the co-responsibility and dignity of the population.
2. Visualize users as active people: the population for which a social innovation project is initiated must be participants from the beginning to the end of the process. Since they are the beneficiaries and users of the final solution and, therefore, should be the primary source of inspiration in the co-design phases (Manzini, 2015) or in the democratization of solutions (Björgvinsson, Ehn, and Hillgren, 2010). This fact will prevent inappropriate solutions based on misunderstandings from designers.
3. Consider the impact of the context: it is also essential in the process of social innovation, consider the context, understood as a set of variables that are dynamic and complex (e.g., social, cultural, historical, economic, and institutional), which they will influence and affect the process of solving the social challenge.

4. Manage ambiguity and uncertainty: social innovation involves, in most cases, face open tasks; it doesn´t exist a unique solution and therefore, an assortment of scenarios marked by uncertainty and ambiguity of not knowing how to manage it can lead to the process being unfinished and community expectations are frustrated.
5. Research design: establishing how field research is going to be, is also essential to obtain useful and valuable information that becomes an input to find in the following phases, those territories or areas of opportunity on which possible solutions to a social challenge will be co-conceived. The reason why the designer who works in social innovation must develop necessary non-scientific research skills (Manzini, 2015; Ortíz, 2016; Tromp and Hekkert, 2016), which allows him to collect quality information to raise and implement the research with higher success.

SOCIAL INNOVATION - A NEW FORM OF APPROXIMATION TO SOCIAL REALITY

The new social conditions and its diverse manifestations have meant how the surrounded phenomena have changed. New methodologies arise to develop solutions to problems that overwhelm it.

Following the above, research methodologies must be adjusted according to the characteristics of the communities intervened and problems detected. Accordingly, for research in indigenous communities, we adapt the method used for the development of a social innovation project called the Double Hexagon Model. The method proposed by Jiménez (2017) and developed by Ruíz, Patiño, and Echeverry (2018).

According to the above, the double hexagon model is a methodological structure of facilitation for external agents - consultants and designers - that was developed and validated for the Colombian business context to guide innovation processes led by design within organizations, especially for MSMEs (micro, small and medium enterprises). This model is shown in figure 2.

Ruiz, Patiño, and Echeverry (2018) adapted the six phases of the methodological model to establish a model that would facilitate the accompaniment of entrepreneurship projects in vulnerable communities, working on the specific case of indigenous people. With this new proposal, the Rural Communities Intervention Model was established, consisting of seven phases shown in Table 2.

The adaptation of the methodology to the context conditions of the community took place under the following parameters:

- Inclusion of additional activities in the preparation phase to have more excellent knowledge and understanding of the socio-cultural conditions of the community.
- Establishment of an active role, facing the situations of the community with the responsibility and commitment necessary to develop creative and unique solutions to the identified problem.
- Absolute respect for people, understanding that they are the central axis of development of solutions within the framework of participatory design methodology.
- Clear definition of the role of facilitator, different from that of a consultant or advisor.
- Search for a deep and lasting social transformation of the community.
- Development of work phases in which the motivation towards creative and lateral thinking was sought.
- Discovery of knowledge transfer spaces and empowerment processes of community members.

Figure 2. Double hexagon model for social innovation
Source: Jimenez - Ibañez (2017).

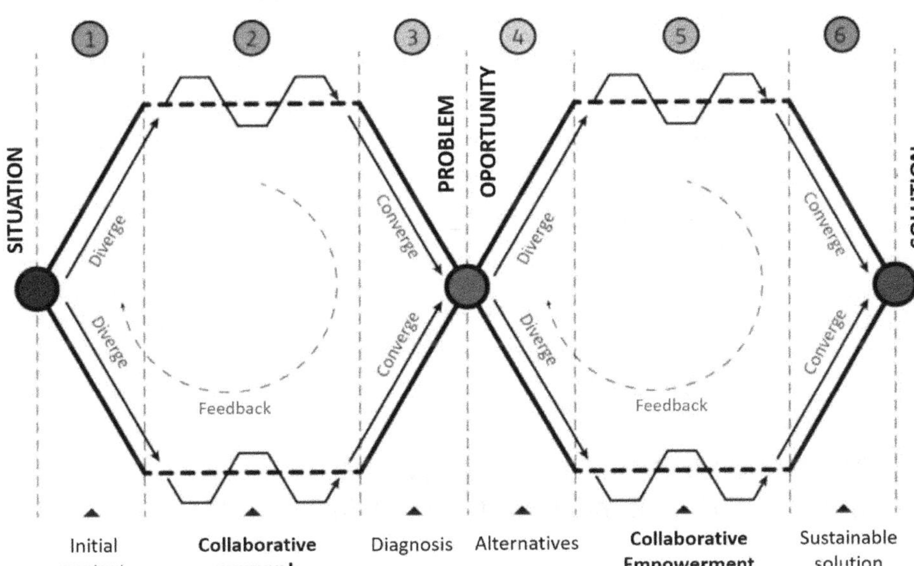

Table 2. Phases of the intervention model in rural communities

Phase	Objective	Activities
0. Preparation	Plan the activities to be carried out during the project and promote a first approach to the situation to define the fundamental aspects, scope, objectives, equipment, and work plan.	0.1 Identification and definition of the starting situation.
		0.2 Formulation of the project framework.
		0.3 Socialize the project with the community.
1. Initial context	Understand the elements of the context that will influence the activities on the field, to redefine them, if necessary.	1.1 Community characterization.
		1.2 Definition of the context where the community is immersed.
2. Collaborative approach	Design and define the methodological tools to use with the community and activities schedule.	2.1 Preparation of fieldwork.
		2.2 Field research with ethnographic and people-centered methods.
3. Diagnosis	Analyze all the information, make sense, and generate conclusions and findings to present to the community.	3.1 Interpretation of data.
		3.2 Socialization and validation of results.
4. Co-creation of alternatives	Design and propose possible models that are based on local potentials and vocations and personal motivations, jointly and collaboratively between facilitators and the community.	4.1 Definition of areas of opportunity.
		4.2 Design of business models.
		4.3 Deepening of business model alternatives.
		4.4 Selection of final models.
5. Collaborative Empowerment	Strengthen the proposed projects and establish commitments that allow the community to take ownership of the projects and can implement them without relying on external actors.	5.1 Validation and prototyping.
		5.2 Project specification and roadmap.
6. Sustainable implementation	Promote and ensure that the proposed business model is sustainable, scalable, and has a positive impact on the community.	6.1 Design of the sustainability strategy and impact measurement.

Source: Ruiz et al. (2018)

A PROCESS ADJUSTED TO THE PARTICULAR CONDITIONS OF THE WOUNAAN-NONAM COMMUNITY

As proposed, the process was developed in 13 work sessions, establishing the activities to be carried out in each of them according to the advances obtained in the previous ones; this made the planning undergo modifications throughout the intervention time. The development and progress of each session are below:

Session 1

In the place where artisan women work, the scope of work, their objectives, and roles that each of the actors had to assume were shared. It was an approach session to set the schedule, the times for each session, and the number of people to attend the meetings.

This session was the opportunity for artisans to show some of the pieces they make for a corporate client, who, besides, has participated in the design of some of these pieces and has taken with them an incipient process of training in design, finishes, and other technical aspects of production.

Session 2

At this stage, it was possible to establish a common language, in which all the participants understood the basic entrepreneurial and design concepts. The artisans also played the prominent role of this activity; they offered a clear explanation of each of the ideas handled by them in their production process.

Concerning the concepts of entrepreneurship and business, there were difficulties, as many artisans have been handling the Spanish language for a short time, and some essential words they wanted to use have not been heard until then. However, after their incorporation, they were similar to their own language with which the barrier presented was quickly overcome. This workshop also served to identify the lack of knowledge in money management, given that the little amount they receive daily.

This session advanced in the interest of artisans to learn on the management of a company to search for the economic independence of men. In the methodological, the understanding of the facilitator's role was reaffirmed, which must be careful in the handling of customs and beliefs and not try to impose since this can become a significant obstacle to the accompaniment process.

Session 3

It aimed at seeking that artisans refer to their past, to recognize their origin, territory, lifestyle, and their worldview from the foundational stories of the community. The Wounaan-Nonam are very proud of their birth, despite the remoteness in which they are from their territories, they recognize themselves as homeless people, committed to their family and their community, respectful of Mother Nature, and in the search for a total balance in their activities.

In this step, the business model started to made sense; by granting high value to its work from the meaning, understanding that processes of this type help them to safeguard their permanence over time. Although the approach focused on women,

men combined the weave of Werregue with wood without abandoning the essence of their art. The result was that they produced pieces different from those customarily elaborated by women.

The practice of using Werregue as the primary input to elaborate their handicrafts is disseminated over time through oral tradition, which is an activity as vital to them as their language. As a significant achievement of this session, we can highlight the confirmation of the essence of their art, which becomes the medium they use to publicize their culture. Each design is the product of a spiritual process at the time of weaving. This process connects with Nature, and with its territory, animals, and the tools used for hunting or fishing. As a result, their original works are unique and unrepeatable.

On the other hand, we identify the values that govern their lives and their weaving activities: trust, happiness, fidelity, spirituality, solidarity, loyalty, innocence, humility, and good listening towards his interlocutors.

Session 4

The objectives of this session were the identification of actors and groups that are part of the production process in a business mapping.

It was established that there are 20 women expert in weaving and a man who led the marketing and sales process. He is responsible for offering and selling their products to final customers who specifically demand them. Similarly, some women not belonging to the committee sell their products autonomously to their clients, in addition to women of the committee.

There are also the intermediaries, persons who buy the items from women and sell them to different third parties. The contact with the suppliers of raw material in their place of origin (Chocó). The institution Handicrafts of Colombia that, in addition to being one of the corporate clients, has provided training opportunities for artisans and finally, fairs or events that are used as a means to publicize the product to new markets, work that is mainly done by one man of the community.

As indirect actors, there are those women who are not part of the committee but want to join to contribute to the project of entrepreneurship and other related that do a job of placing potential clients without being considered commercial agents.

As for the business map, the supplier of the raw material in Chocó, some intermediaries of the raw material that offer it in Bogotá, a distributor that buys in bulk, Colombian Handicrafts, and customers, both national and international, participate in the process.

There is a need for women empowerment towards the process because, by tradition, it is men who the responsible for commercial and economic aspects.

From the methodological point of view, the graphic image of the system of their entrepreneurship, the actors, and the interactions that occur between them, generated concern to the same extent that it showed that they are not clear about the business concept. There is an excellent opportunity for improvement in this aspect.

Session 5

For the development of this part, the Business Model Canvas developed by Osterwalder and Pigneur (2011) was chosen to identify the areas of creation and delivery of value to customers and the economic benefit for the community.

Although the main objective of entrepreneurship is to provide further visibility to their culture, they fail to clearly define the value proposition offered to customers, considering that deliver a product in one of three categories: functional, accessories, and decorative.

Although their largest client is Artesanías de Colombia (Handicrafts of Colombia), they consider that high-income clients give the most outstanding value to them and foreigners with whom there is no personalized relationship except when they place orders directly to the artisan. Beyond the fairs, men of the community do not identify other marketing channels.

Their key activities are acquiring the raw material, the elaboration of the products, the technical training, and the promotion of their work; Its essential resources are the people, and its strategic partners are the suppliers of raw materials and handicrafts from Colombia. The cost structure is determined by the raw material, the most expensive aspect of the manufacturing process.

Expectations remained at the end of this phase are the need to understand which added value they can offer to customers, to give legal strength to the venture, and to create a management work scheme that allows the project to be conducted strategically.

Session 6

The methodology of social cartography sought to identify the capabilities and resources currently available to the Wounaan-Nonam group of artisan women.

In addition to their exceptional manual skills (fine motor skills) and creativity in design for good quality at work, artisans have developed the ability to communicate assertively with other members of the community, especially to their suppliers.

Just as the skills were determined, the expectations they have with the project were also defined, among which the desire to have their own land stands out, recalling their stay in the ancestral territory, which is conducive to the cultivation of palm, with which would significantly reduce the costs associated with manufacturing.

Although considered master craftswomen, they believe that they should remain in constant training so that they can perform in management areas related to their activity. In this case, in conclusion, a training project should continue and that it can be considerably improved to the extent that there is the specialization of the work that contributes to improving the productivity of this group of women artisans.

Session 7

The search for an immediate challenge faced by artisans to strengthen the business model is the goal of this phase of the methodology. In this sense, as it happened in an earlier stage, it was affirmed that understanding the needs of the client was of vital importance to be able to offer a product that generated value. Generating a certification of origin of the work can be an excellent alternative to add value for customers.

To get to know the client better, it is established that you must go out to the field, to have direct contact with him, to know about his expectations and desires to be able to elaborate handicrafts more in line with that client profile that wants to buy the product.

On the other hand, it emerges as a decision to work on a price list with which artisans can determine the sale price of each manufactured handicraft, leaving aside the subjectivism with which that value is set today.

For the project, the challenge of eliminating the signs of discomfort that are perceived among the workshop attendees is established since, although they were clear before starting, no immediate results are obtained.

Session 8

The session was developed to prepare the community for co-creating with the facilitator, the tools to be used in the fieldwork for the client's knowledge. Given that there are four relevant moments in the management of the service: desire, search, use, and purchase/sale, artisans women conducted an activity in which they could ask themselves what they would like to ask their clients about each one of those moments?

In the moment of desire or need, the artisans want mainly to know what makes the customer fall in love with a handmade product, why they make the decision to buy it, and what people value when they buy a handcrafted product to some ancestral ethnic group.

For the moment of the research, women want to know through which channels the client looks for this type of product, and in the future, how things would be easy when looking for them. They also wanted to know from their costumers what other handmade product categories they would be interested in. Finally, at the time of purchase: it was defined of great relevance to know where customers usually buy the handmade products they have. Transversally to each one of these moments, they want to know what gives their customers joy and disappointment regarding each of those four (4) moments.

In this phase, it becomes clear that the women's community has always focused on selling a product without thinking about the activities behind the sale of it. It must have associated a service that can generate more perceived customer value. The community admits clearly and sincerely, not having a more excellent knowledge of its customers because they have not recognized the importance of approaching them to know what they want to see as novel to buy.

As a fact to highlight, the community begins to understand that there are no limitations to start exploring new design concepts. Although there is a turnaround in product lines other than those that have traditionally characterized Wounaan-Nonam culture, this may come to have much more welcome by customers looking for different types of handmade products other than traditional handicrafts.

The progress in the methodology led artisans to do pre-meeting work that allowed the workshop to flow much faster and more efficiently. Group work was a factor that boosted creativity and aroused the mood of the group.

Session 9

This was a critical moment for the community; they could face to face with the client, and that brought them essential benefits for the future development of their project.

The craft exhibition was held at the facilities of EAN University, in Bogota (Colombia), with two fundamental purposes:

1. To foster a space in which women could establish - for the first time for the majority - a closer business relationship with their real potential clients.
2. To carry out a generative session in which users will play a fundamental role in contributing ideas and information that would be valuable to adjust a business model that adapts much more to the needs of people.

Despite the normal anxiety caused by these types of situations, women were empowered and led the presentation of their products, subtly guiding clients through the three moments of the session: the registration, the craft show, and buying handicrafts. Women were able to talk more closely with people and show them to live how a handicraft is woven and the previous spiritual processes that are carried out. Finally, the generative session, in which users participated, contributing with ideas and identify their needs, their thinking, feeling, and dreaming; information that would serve to guide later through design, new product concepts.

The public, made up of students, teachers, and guests, showed closeness, admiration, respect, and recognition not only to handicraft products but also to the hard work that these women must carry out when weaving to finalize a product.

The visual exhibition presented throughout the session highlighted the Wounaan-Nonam culture, the ancestral artisan work carried out by these women, and delivered, the attributes that shape the meaning of this ethnic group's handicraft products and that many people do not know.

At the end of the event, both artisans and the public generated mutual empathy, understanding the reality of the other party. Attendees showed much more interest in participating after having verified from the artisans what handicrafts represent in terms of culture, weaving, and figures that shape a kind of "mysticism" in their crafts.

As an advance in the methodology, the confidence developed by artisans about the quality of their product, they understood that there are times when they should assume a more obvious leadership and developed communication skills and analysis of their relationship with the environment and the customer in particular.

Session 10

After the client approach session, it was essential to understand the results obtained in it.

In the first instance, with the company of the facilitator, the artisans found four types of potential clients, of which they chose two to focus all their efforts on the design and commercialization of their products: those of exclusive taste ("Chic") and those of different taste ("Selective").

When defining strategies for these two types of customers, the artisans considered that they could also be impacting those of a third type: "The believers," who, due to their general characteristics, are more likely to value and buy handmade products regardless of the Design style; is traditional or modern. This fact indicates that what is designed for the two (2) chosen extreme users will be easily adapted to the tastes and preferences of this third type of customer.

The analysis begins to reveal that the primary needs of these customers are oriented towards:

1. Find products with modern styles that generate more value to them, unlike what is currently found in the market.
2. Find a proposal that also adds value in terms of the point of contact of the sales channels, given that users generally state that they do not usually quickly locate handmade product stores that are served by indigenous artisan communities.

This session concludes that it was important for artisans to understand that customers have different ways of perceiving and valuing handmade products, giving additional attributes to it. They believe that their current work is not meeting the needs of these customers, perhaps, because the value proposition is below what they aspire to find together so that entrepreneurship and brand -which is not yet defined - start generating recall and market positioning.

On the methodological side, the need to generate closeness with customers is proven, trying to have significant experiences in which the first-hand concept a customer has about a product when he knows details of its origin.

Session 11

This session helped to identify the general principles on which the community should develop the different designs and the entire craft production process. The artisans were contacted with a couple of entrepreneurs of the sector to generate an alliance that allows them both parties, benefit from a win-win relationship to create opportunities to expand in terms of new concepts towards the two product lines chosen.

Based on the work of the previous session, it was established that the design should focus on two lines: i) products that, in addition to decorative, are functional and ii) accessory products that are as new, differentiated, and original.

The three principles chosen for the work were:

1. Ancestral design adjusted to Western needs: Exclusive products that not only decorate a space but also incorporate a modern practical and functional design.
2. Products that evoke meanings: Products that tell their story and provide information about their authentic Nature.
3. Dynamic renewable design: a set of products released every certain period, under the concept of "collections." These products must share characteristics and design criteria, which will give the customer a promise of value in terms of dynamism and exclusivity of the product offer.

The two ventures were chosen to make this first rapprochement with the community align in values and philosophy to what the Wounaan-Nonam artisan community is and the vision they have towards respect for Mother Nature, sustainable design, and social justice.

This session allows us to conclude that strategic alliances can open the doors for new product lines to start generating more value in design and meaning to customers.

For the artisans, starting to explore the weaving in new product concepts will be a challenge. Still, the attitude and conviction with which they have assumed the results of the research drive them to adapt their technique to start a path of co-ideation and co-creation with other entrepreneurs of handmade products.

In the methodological, time management becomes an essential quality for new developments. It is recommended to take action leading the community to connect with actors that can provide some support to their project. Besides, give more responsibility to the community to begin articulate and ensure in a certain way, that they should strive once the design process is completed to continue implementing the recommended.

Session 12

Once customer needs and design principles were defined, efforts focused on the co-ideation of a brand identity, with a name and a logo that represented what the community is and its ancestral work. As a result of this work, five proposals were designed in which key elements such as hands, connection with nature, spirituality, dignity, strength, spiritual and religious uses associated with the materials of the products - the fiber of the Werregue palm and the Chocolatillo -, the woman as transmitter and carrier of ancestral knowledge.

The community has shown that there are many elements that they and their customers value regarding the process that is carried out for the production of handicrafts, which do not necessarily have to do only with the final finished product. Likewise, it recognizes the importance of creating a brand identity for the client that shows what their ancestral knowledge in weaving in Werregue represents for them so that their products recover the real economic value and cultural significance that they have been losing.

The methodology used allows us to conclude that participatory design with users is the central axis of this stage of co-creation. The clarity and precision that precedes the session help contextualize the participants and create a friendly environment that fosters creative mental states and avoids having to shorten or have to accelerate the pace of the workshop due to time wasted.

Session 13

The activities of this last workshop sought the compilation of the strategic aspects necessary to give future solidity to the entrepreneurship project, worked throughout the process. The brand identity was defined as a positioned strategy as a handicraft producer, as shown in Figure 3.

Figure 3. Wharki logo
Source. Wounaan-Noman community

Warkhi

Experiencia ancestral

The problem on which the workshop was developed was that people want to find handmade products that fit their needs: i) decorative and functional spaces (homes and offices), and ii) personal feeling authentic and original. To provide a fit solution, the value proposition focuses on offering:

1. Collections of 100% handmade pieces, which combine the magic and spirituality of the Wounaan-Nonam ancestral weave, with the best of avant-garde design to give: elegance, sophistication, and originality
2. Each piece tells a story and provides information on its authentic Nature
3. Support of a brand 100% operated by and for the benefit of the Wounaan-Nonam women indigenous community of Colombia. Survivors of the armed conflict.

The customer segment served will be men and women between 30 and 60 years old, who want to find high-end products, authentic and original, with personal assistance at the points of sale (Showrooms). These customers use social networks (Facebook and Instagram) and other support tools, such as Whatsapp, e-mail, and digital blogs.

The key activities are i) raw material supply from the Chocó, always under conditions of respect for Mother Nature, ii) co-design of products with strategic allies, iii) prototyping and validation with customers, iv) manual weaving process by artisan teachers, and v) product promotion (marketing).

The essential resources are i) physical: point of sale (showroom), ii) intellectual: brand (registration and protection), databases, iii) human: master artisans who guarantee the high quality of the products, iv) economic: fund consisting of a percentage (reserve) of total sales in the month, to reinvest in the venture.

The strategic partners are i) raw material suppliers in Chocó, co-working spaces to establish an exhibition and sales point - Showroom, ii) Vivamaria (entrepreneurship for co-design of the accessories line), iii) Manosabia (entrepreneurship for co-design of the functional line), and iv) universities, for training and entrepreneurship training.

Regarding the cost structure, this is composed of i) raw material: Werregue, quitasol, palma mona, among others, ii) logistics: transport of raw material and travel to fairs and points of sale, iii) marketing: packaging, visual and written communication and, iv) production: prototype design. The new business mapping is shown in Figure 4.

Figure 4. New business mapping
Source: Co-elaboration with the Wounaan-Nonam community

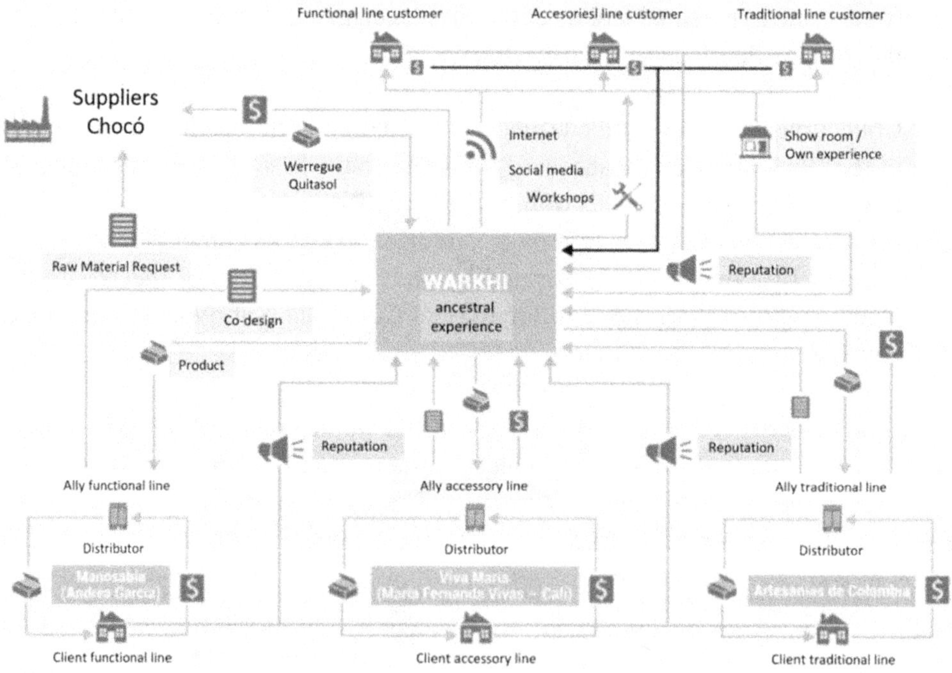

THE WOUNAAN-NONAM COMMUNITY AGAINST A DIFFERENT PERSPECTIVE FROM THE FUTURE

The Wounaan-Nonam community, after the fieldwork carried out during 13 sessions, has found its meaning to the artisan work in which they work. A new business model was developed within the framework of the social economy, benefiting the community in general, and each of the actors involved in the process of design, production, and marketing of handicrafts. They understood it as a possibility of creating new value for their work, which results in a better quality of life for all.

The conception of their handicrafts as the fundamental axis of creation and implementation of a venture with a social sense is aligned more clearly with the expectations of a market that seeks innovation and design in the products it purchases. The added value they give to their crafts has to be evaluated from two different points: the commercial, that places them with a product that offers new alternatives to the market with prices that are affordable to buyers, and the cultural, with which they manage to give permanence to an ancestral tradition and art whose chances of survival are limited to the few opportunities they have to make them visible.

From an utterly social perspective, with the initiative and start of entrepreneurship, decent and quality employment is provided to a population that, in its vulnerable situation, does not have formal workspaces and that amid informality, can create mechanisms to improve their quality of life. The purpose of interventions has a more significant impact when it is received by the group of women, the majority in the community, and responsible for the artisanal work of production.

With the process carried out, the Wounaan-Nonam have consolidated a broader portfolio of products and designs which, together with the creation of a brand identity around Warkhi, are intended to generate recall and market positioning. As a result, connections are much more solid with clients, seeking to offer them much more than an artifact: the representation of an ancestral culture. Although the community is immersed in adverse social conditions, with these new possibilities, they can maintain the cultural principles and some of the community's customs before migration. The commercialization of products of their culture is the best indicator of this.

Despite their cultural connotation, the pieces have evolved in such a way that they combine the designs of the tradition with modern design concepts by creating unique pieces that tell stories, which have a background beyond beauty shown outside. But this is only one of the important achievements of the process. At the end of the activities, community members have appropriated management tools that allow them to be more efficient in carrying out some of the work.

By determining a minimum viable business model, it has been achieved that indigenous people move from a scheme of exploitation of ideas that generated no value to another in which new concepts of products and different ways of relating to the environment prevail.

Beyond economic aspects, this experience has left other gains for the community. With the completion of the first phase of accompaniment, women have developed empowerment that they did not have before. This experience allowed them to have clarity regarding the scope of the project and its possibilities for the future, thus bringing a source of new income with more excellent stability that can help them in the maintenance of cultural patterns in future generations. Also, leaving a historical legacy as proof of the resilience that they had to arm themselves to survive after moving to the peripheral areas of Bogotá.

In this same sense, women have understood that the processes of social innovation have allowed them to close a little the gap of labor inclusion that affects not only their community but all those that must have migrated from their territories towards the big cities. Their empowerment and overcoming mental blocks of insertion in a culture that is initially inhospitable have been a critical factor to believe in themselves by appropriating new models to be closer to manage business ideas.

CONCLUSION

The conclusions of this work can be presented from two perspectives. From the first perspective, it is essential to note that project planning should be as flexible as possible to the same extent that the results obtained in some of the scheduled sessions were not achieved and should be reformulated, affecting the scope given to each moment of work. Despite this, with the methodology used, it was possible to find the minimum viable business model, the ultimate goal of the intervention.

As a discipline to support entrepreneurial processes or to search for better options for a community, our experience with the project demonstrates that design is a tool that offers the possibility of finding new ways of planning, structuring, and implementing strategies to promote local community development. This strategy works when it is adapted to each population, regardless of the complexity of the problem encountered.

Essential elements to keep in mind that were critical factors of the process were the facilitator with the role of accompaniment rather than the intention to advise. The creation of an environment in which people appropriate the process and the search for meaning to it by those who carry out the activities allow the release of prejudices and rigid mental models and are incentives for creativity. Also, the development of tasks in less formal spaces, with a language closer to people, gives way to the spontaneity with which fun is a catalyst for the fears that formality can generate and a proactive attitude. These facts make a profound difference compared to other models of approach and work with this type of community.

Despite the methodology and the environments, very close interaction with the community is achieved, which results in a high level of creativity that favors innovation and allows the collective construction of appropriate solutions for all and in which they feel involved and responsible for success.

Workshops must be preceded by a preamble to find the meaning of the activity and identify dreams to be achieved. As a result, with this vision, they can trace the way forward for their achievement.

Now, from the second perspective, the business, the result has been the finding of a solid business model that meets the needs of the community, with perfectly-identified and classified clients that were not previously served, with the criteria of design, production, and offer to exist.

Although the community did not have a clear sense of its value proposition, some aspects were identified and potentialized. So, at the end of the process, they found the pillars of their marketing strategy.

While in other contexts, it may sound like a business axiom, the participants recognized the importance of the client in the process and defined the co-design as one of the strategies, which added to the quality, authenticity, and artisanal production with ancestral techniques. It became a significant differential to develop in the search for the objective of attention to a market that knows their products but now are not considered potential customers.

It is not enough to have developed that new business conception in the community; there steals a lot of work to do. The next phases of the investigation will focus on training in more advanced business issues to help them for improving their production processes, optimizing the management of raw materials and self-organization, and defining the roles to increase efficiency.

REFERENCES

Artesanías de Colombia. (n.d.). *Canasto Werregue Mediano*. https://artesaniasdecolombia.com.co/PortalAC/Productos/canasto-Werregue-mediano_284

Björgvinsson, E., Ehn, P., & Hillgren, P. (2010). Participatory design and democratizing innovation. In *Proceedings of the 11th Biennial Participatory Design Conference* (pp. 41-50). Sydney: ACM. 10.1145/1900441.1900448

Cajaiba, G. (2014). Social innovation: Moving the field forward. A conceptual framework. *Technological Forecasting and Social Change*, *82*, 42–51. doi:10.1016/j.techfore.2013.05.008

Espitia, P. E., & Cedeño, M. (2017). Formulación de una línea de investigación en Diseño sostenible para la innovación y el emprendimiento en Colombia, a partir del análisis de las líneas y grupos de investigación registrados en el Sistema de Ciencia Tecnología e Innovación (CTI). *ArDin. Arte. Diseño e Ingeniería*, *6*, 24–45.

Ferruzca, M., & Rodríguez, J. (2011). Diseño sostenible: Herramienta estratégica de innovación. *Revista Legislativa de Estudios Sociales y de Opinión Pública*, *4*(8), 47–87.

Gámez, J., & Saiz-Álvarez, J. M. (2012). Microcredits for Women Entrepreneurship: Are They an Effective Tool to Avoid Family Impoverishment? In M. A. Galindo & D. Ribeiro (Eds.), *Women's Entrepreneurship and Economics. New Perspectives, Practices, and Policies* (pp. 167–177). Springer. doi:10.1007/978-1-4614-1293-9_11

Jiménez, J. E. (2017). *Análisis y desarrollo de un modelo de tutorización integral basado en el Design Thinking orientado a la innovación estratégica en empresas colombianas* (Tesis Doctoral). Valencia, España: Universidad Politécnica de Valencia.

Krois, K. (2015). *Watch & read Eco-Social Design according to Ezio Manzini*. https://designdisaster.unibz.it/watch-read-eco-social-design-according-to-eziomanzini/

Manzini, E. (2015). *Design, when everybody designs. An introduction to design for social innovation*. The MIT Press. doi:10.7551/mitpress/9873.001.0001

Margolin, V., & Margolin, S. (2002). A "social model" of design: Issues of practice and research. *Design Issues*, *18*(4), 24–30. doi:10.1162/074793602320827406

Martínez, P., Barana, M., Rocha, R., & Paschoarelli, L. (2017). Innovación, design y sostenibilidad social: nuevas tendencias para el desarrollo local en la contemporaneidad. *Revista de Arquitectura, 19*(2), 68-77.

Morelli, N. (2007). Social innovation and new industrial contexts: Can designers "industrialize" socially responsible solutions? *Design Issues*, *23*(4), 3–21. doi:10.1162/desi.2007.23.4.3

Mulgan, G. (2006). The process of social innovation. *Innovations*, *8*(2), 145–162. doi:10.1162/itgg.2006.1.2.145

OIT. (2015). *Derecho de los pueblos indígenas y tribales a un desarrollo incluyente sostenible*. ILO.

ONU. (2010). State of the world's indigenous people. New York: Department of Public Information & Center for Indigenous People's Autonomy and Development (CADPI).

Ortíz, J.C. (2016). Diseñando el cambio. La innovación social y sus retos. *Economía Creativa, 6*, 9-35.

Osterwalder, A., & Pigneur, Y. (2011). *Generación de modelos de negocio*. Editorial Deusto.

Papanek, V. (1985). *Design for the real world* (2nd ed.). Thames and Hudson.

Ruíz, C., Patiño, O., & Echeverry, P. (2018). *Emprendimiento social en comunidades indígenas*. Ponencia.

Saiz-Álvarez, J. M., & Coduras, A. (2020). Aspects of Work-life Balance of Women in Entrepreneurship. In M. T. Lepeley, K. Kuschel, E. Eijdenberg, & N. Pouw (Eds.), *Exploring Wellbeing of Women in Entrepreneurship. A Global Perspective* (pp. 123–142). Routledge.

Sanders, E., & Stappers, P. (2008). Co-creation and the new landscapes of design. *CoDesign, 4*(1), 5–18. doi:10.1080/15710880701875068

Thackara, J. (2013). *Diseñando para un mundo complejo. Acciones para lograr la sustentabilidad*. Designio.

Tromp, N., & Hekkert, P. (2016). Assessing methods for effect-driven design: Evaluation of a social design method. *Design Studies, 43*, 24–47. doi:10.1016/j.destud.2015.12.002

United Nations Department of Public Information & Center for Indigenous People's Autonomy and Development (CADPI). (2010). *State of the world's indigenous people*. Author.

Vía Plural. (2011). *Desplazamiento forzado comunidad Wounaan-Nonam en Bogotá*. https://es.scribd.com/document/54865446/Desplazamiento-Forzado-ComunidadWounaan-Nonam-en-Bogota

World Bank. (2015). *Indigenous people's policy brief. Still among the poorest of the poor*. Author.

KEY TERMS AND DEFINITIONS

Business Model Canvas (BMC): Developed by the swiss Alexander Osterwalder in his doctoral theses, it consists of strategic management and a lean startup template for creating business scenarios and applications.

Chocó: It is one of the thirty-two departments of Colombia, located in the northwest of the country, in the Colombian Pacific region. It includes the forests of the Darién and the basins of the Atrato and San Juan rivers. Its capital is the city of Quibdó.

Chocolatillo: Also called Guarumo, it is a type of tropical herb used to make handicrafts.

God Jai: According to the Wounaan-Noman cosmology, it is the spiritual owner of the Werregue.

Indigenous People: Formed by 5,000 different communities spread worldwide, which represents more than 370 million people (about 5% of the world population).

Sustainable Development Goals (SDGs): Commitment, among others, signed by 170 countries to eradicate all forms of poverty by 2030 and eliminate existing inequality through the implementation of strategies for the empowerment of vulnerable populations, among which are indigenous people.

Werregue: It is a spiny trunk palm harvested in Colombia only that reaches up to 20 meters high, whose harvest can only be done on a new moon since if it is done at a different time, the leaf is damaged and doesn't serve to be used in crafts.

Wounaan-Noman Indigenous Community: Living on the River San Juan, it is one of the indigenous people in Colombia that are at risk of extinction due to displacement and violence.

Chapter 9
Open Collaborative Innovation at Colombia's National Spectrum Agency

María del Pilar Ramirez-Salazar
https://orcid.org/0000-0002-9462-0897
Universidad EAN, Colombia

Carlos Salcedo-Perez
https://orcid.org/0000-0002-4433-5537
Universidad EAN, Colombia

Sara Esperanza Castañeda Valenzuela
Agencia Nacional del Espectro, Colombia

ABSTRACT

This chapter describes the implementation of the Open Collaborative Innovation Program in Colombia's National Spectrum Agency (from Spanish, ANE). Six universities participated in the program. The model implemented was based on previous models developed by Ramírez-Salazar; Chesbrough; VanGudy; and Davila, Epstein, and Shelton (2008). The objective of the implementation was to propose solutions to reduce the number of complaints related to the illegal use of the spectrum in Colombia. The innovation challenge for universities was to find answers to solve the problem previously mentioned. Three solving teams were formed. Movimiento Espectral was the winning team with its solution called "Clausula de la Cultura." The model was validated by ANE executives who deemed it adequate to conduct external projects that provide solutions to institutional challenges.

DOI: 10.4018/978-1-7998-3568-4.ch009

INTRODUCTION

Between 2010 and August 2017, the Colombian National Spectrum Agency (ANE) received over 1,075 complaints related to the illegal use of the spectrum. Complaints were related to Blockers and Broadcasting, Networks and/or services, television, TMC-PCS-Trunking, and others, which occur when the spectrum is used with expired or non-existing permission, and when signal amplifiers or blockers are used (Correa, 2015). These complaints increase the workload at the Surveillance and Control Unit because of the time it takes to go to locations to verify the information received. Also, it prevents the ANE from providing the right telecommunication services that use the radioelectric spectrum.

Decree 2573, issued in 2014 established the general guidelines of the Online Government Strategy, indicating that all those organizations which are part of the Public Administration, as shown by Article 39 of Law 489, issued in 1998, are subject to fulfill what is established thereof. The Manual of the Online Government Strategy, published by the ICT Ministry to accomplish such strategy, proposes the use of open innovation to find solutions to problems through collaboration with stakeholders.

The project presented in this chapter demonstrates that the use of the strategy of open, collaborative innovation between the ANE and universities allows for the creation of ideas to reduce the illegal use of the spectrum in Colombia; therefore, the ANE can optimize its surveillance and control processes.

This study starts with the diagnosis of the ANE to find out the current state of the implementation of open collaborative innovation. The chapter continues with designing a model of open collaborative innovation with the participation of the ANE and universities. Then, it comes to the implementation of the model by using a pilot test, and finally, the presentation of the final design of the strategy, along with the implementation plan, conclusions, and recommendations.

This chapter is a descriptive, cross-sectional study since data is collected at a single moment, and variables are described, analyzed, and correlated at a given single moment (Hernández-Sampieri et al. 2015). It is quantitative research since percentages are obtained, and data can be compared.

This article is divided in four parts: [1] Introduction, research problem and objectives; [2] referential and conceptual framework, including information related to the ICT industry, electric radio spectrum, the ANE, and concepts dealing with open innovation, the open collaborative innovation model, and some successful cases of application of this strategy in Colombia; [3] methodology; and [4] the design of open innovation proposed lessons learned, recommendations and conclusions.

RESEARCH PROBLEM

The Open Collaborative Innovation Strategy is a model that goes beyond the limits within an organization; thus, the cooperation of people from outside the organization is relevant to provide customers with innovative goods and services. By using this innovation method, enterprises can optimize resources and create world-class goods and services, saving time and money. Its importance lies in the combination of internal and external knowledge to find solutions to problems, needs and opportunities faced, to start new projects, mainly on Research and Development, and to make such projects last over time.

According to Law 1341, issued in 2009, one of the functions of the ANE is to surveil and control the Colombian radioelectric spectrum; the current situation is that there is a high number of complaints about the illegal use of such spectrum. Therefore, the open collaborative innovation strategy can be used as a mechanism by which the ANE can generate interaction with internal and external clients. The guiding question for the innovation challenge then is: How to reduce the number of complaints about the illegal use of the spectrum in Colombia?

OBJECTIVES

General

To design the Open Collaborative Innovation Model at the ANE, in collaboration with six universities from Bogota, to control the use of the spectrum, aimed at reducing the number of complaints about its illegal use.

Specific

- To elaborate on a diagnosis of the current situation of the illegal use of the spectrum in Colombia.
- To design an Open Collaborative Innovation Model between the ANE and six universities aimed at reducing the number of complaints about the illegal use of the electric radio spectrum.
- To implement the Open Collaborative Innovation Model through the application of a pilot test.
- To present the final design of the strategy of Open Collaborative Innovation to the ANE along with its implementation plan, conclusions, and recommendations.

CONCEPTUAL AND REFERENTIAL FRAMEWORK

ICT's first started with the transistor (it operated as an electric switch and codified binary), which became the boost of such digital technologies. The ICT massive use and its popularization were caused by the reduction of prices of this central device. This effect relates to the Moore's Law (the processor's speed and total processing power of computers duplicate every 12 months) and its quick expansion to the Metcalfe Law (the value of a communication network is proportional to the square number of connected users of the system).

At least three revolutions related to knowledge have been identified. *The First Industrial and Technological Revolutions*, by which machines replaced the workforce, occurred between the end of the XVIII Century and the beginning of the XIX Century. *The Second Industrial and Technological Revolutions* occurred after 1850. They were characterized by the invention of the engine of internal combustion, electricity, and the automobile and airplane designs. *The Third Industrial and Technological Revolutions* revolved around the use of ICT's during the 1960s and beginning of the 1970s in the United States; it was centered on microelectronics, computers, and telecommunications. Its roots can be traced to 1806 when Bell invented the telephone. Telecommunications facilitated the capacity of interconnection and data and information processing, which was achieved by the innovation and synergy of microelectronic devices as well as by the power of informatics, availability, and easiness of telecommunication (Quiroga-Parra, 2016).

The Colombian ICT Industry

Infrastructure, production and/or sale of ICT goods, production of telecommunication services (where Internet services become the starting point of a new industry), digital platforms, research activities, development, and innovation compose the ICT Value Chain in Colombia (MINTIC, 2015). Efforts from private enterprises have significantly broadened access to a variety of goods and services, both of telecommunications as well as of information technologies. The ICT industry's income has grown at an average annual rate of 9.9% in nominal terms from 2002 to 2012, equivalent to 5.4% of the nominal GDP (Fedesarrollo, 2013).

According to the World Economic Forum, in 2016, Colombia ranked 68 (with a score of 4.1) in the Networked Readiness Index (NRI), which measures the maturity of countries in regards to ICT. Colombia ranked behind Chile, Uruguay, Costa Rica, and Panama, and ahead of Brazil, Ecuador, and Peru. The best rank for Colombia was 58 in 2011, and the most critical problems identified dealt with regulatory and political environments, low impact of technology in businesses, and high tax rates (Medina, 2017).

In 2017, the First Big ICT Survey in Colombia stated that 72% of households in Colombia have at least one smartphone; 75% of people evaluate its home Internet service positively, and 77% do the same with its workplace Internet service. However, still, 36% of households do not have Internet access. Yet, only 8% of these households do not have so because there is no Internet coverage in the geographical areas where they are located (Ministerio de Tecnologías de la Información y las Comunicaciones, 2017).

ICT Industry International Trends

Considering development topics from political perspectives and international ICTs regulation, it is possible to determine three working lines: massive broadband use, migration to new generation networks, and the analysis of markets as well as the identification and regulation by relevant markets, which means that law and policies revolve around infrastructure and digital services and the promotion of those markets that compose it.

Although Colombia has improved its international position, especially in ICT use, there is still room to move forward in the development of infrastructure tailored to provide services. Adequate development of infrastructure is a must to increase the number of services that users can demand, improve quality, and reduce prices.

The global trend in telecommunications is oriented towards the integration or convergence of technologies, networks, services, markets, etc. In this environment, the traditional definition of telecommunication services fades due to the regulatory implications that arise as technological convergence allows the development of competition among networks, resulting in better use of services. Thus, technological convergence makes it possible that a single provider can supply multiple services through the same telecommunications network, enabling the entrance of new competitors, increasing competition. The opening of markets worldwide has overthrown barriers to competition in such sectors, increasing the number of providers as well as the services demanded by users (CRC, 2010).

The Radioelectric Spectrum

Electromagnetic Waves

A wave is created by distress that goes from one place to another without matter. A means is that substance or material that transports the wave. Every particle of the means is temporarily displaced, but it goes back to its original position. The highest point from the equilibrium position is the wave's crest. A trough is a point with the lowest point from the equilibrium position (GESP, 2010).

Electromagnetic Spectrum

The electromagnetic spectrum is how radio frequencies that make telecommunications possible are transmitted. The ANE states that the radioelectric spectrum is how electromagnetic waves that make telecommunications possible, are sent and they are administered and regulated by each country's governments; radio electric and electromagnetic spectrums are composed by waves, each of them with different frequencies (Palacio, 2015).

By Article 75, the Colombian Political Constitution established that the electromagnetic spectrum is subject to the administration and regulation of the State, which will intervene to prevent monopolistic practices. Therefore, the State must guarantee equal access opportunities to it.

The National Spectrum Agency (ANE) in Colombia

It was created based on Law 1341 issued in 2009, as a National Special Administrative Unit ascribed to the Ministry of Information and Communication Technologies. Later, Decree 4169, published in 2011, modified its legal nature. Also, it granted it legal personality with technical, administrative, and financing autonomy, as well as its equity, in charge of supporting technical assistance for administration, planning, surveillance, and control of the radioelectric spectrum, and working along with other entities with similar responsibilities.

Administration of the spectrum involves technical, economic, and legal aspects. Internationally, the administration of the spectrum is performed by the International Telecommunication Union, a United Nations agency in charge of affairs related to information and communication technologies. This includes international coordination for sharing the radioelectric spectrum (GESP, 2010).

Once the regulatory framework is established, it is implemented in the country. Management, planning, grating, surveillance, and control of the radioelectric spectrum are under the guidance of the ANE. The assignation is in charge of the Ministry of Information and Communication Technologies.

OPEN INNOVATION

Open innovation is a model used by firms to intensively use internal and external knowledge for boosting and accelerating their innovation processes to expand markets (Chesbrough, 2006). Open collaborative innovation refers to people or organizations that change or introduce new things into a business, then becoming referent for others (Ramirez-Salazar, 2016). External innovations are organized into collaborative units in which external and internal motivations are emphasized, relations are informal, and there is a technological exchange (Almirall, Lee, and Majchrzak, 2014).

Open innovation implies a constant interaction between enterprises and a wide range of external parties such as users, clients, suppliers, universities, research centers, competitors, and the community. Nowadays, enterprises have mechanisms such as alliances, joint ventures, investment or access to risk capital, licenses, open-source code platforms, development communities, crowdfunding, mass personalization, and the use of innovation intermediaries (Bernal-Torres, and Frost-González, 2015).

Key Factors for Success

A "key factor for success" in the context of open innovation is defined as an element of organizational management that needs to be used effectively, aimed at increasing the probability of success when applying open innovation in an organization. The decisive factors for open innovation are grouped as follows: leadership, management facilitators, and business processes.

Leadership relates to the characteristics and behaviors of managers and decision-makers. Management facilitators deal with the relation between group and individual factors (about administrative matters such as mission, organizational strategy, physical and financial resources, organizational structure, and corporate and communication systems). Business processes consolidate innovation variables such as communication and workflow, decision-making strategies, methods to create a plan, and progress (Bravo-Ibarra, León-Arenas, and Serrano-Cárdenas, 2014).

Advantages

By using open innovation, organizations can create competitive advantages that make them different from others; besides, such benefits cover all interested parties involved in the process. It brings advantages to research groups, allowing them to build capacities in emerging areas, to identify competencies and abilities required by their members, and to generate resources to motivate research.

Open innovation also benefits governments and NGOs by boosting entrepreneurship, technology transfer, and knowledge-based economies. It also brings advantages for clients and users of products and services created through it, since they obtain quality products (at lower costs in many cases).

The Open Innovation Collaborative Model

According to the model developed by Ramírez-Salazar (2016), seven aspects guide the path to follow a program of open, collaborative innovation, being them:

1. Innovation Challenge: it is the need, problem, or opportunity presented to the firm. So, the challenge is to reduce the number of complaints about the illegal use of the spectrum in Colombia.
2. Internal and External Knowledge: know-how coming from people outside the organization, along with knowledge from the organization's workers. In this case, the universities working to solve the challenge are going to provide their experience.
3. Paradigm Change: it is the different way of doing things in a process or procedure; it is one of the most relevant aspects of creativity and innovation, by which people discover other ways to obtain better results.
4. Leadership: it refers to the person in charge of a project, which stimulates the creativity of participants. Usually, the leader is the person who coordinates the open innovation project.
5. Interinstitutional and Transdisciplinary Teams: the operational teams are composed of people coming from different organizations and various fields of knowledge, who get together to work towards a common objective. In the case analyzed in this chapter, groups were composed of students from different universities from Bogota.
6. Communication: it refers to the body, oral, and written language that allows the practical narrative expression among people who participate in the project. It is their part of the process in which it is evident that ICTs are used as an effective communication channel.
7. Creative Solutions: it refers to the answer to an organizational problem or need, which is chosen by a group of experts. The process developed includes exploration, creativity, prototype, and pitch, in which the solution is presented to the organization's top management to analyze the feasibility of its implementation.

To work correctly, the open innovation model needs to be supported on six principles that help to consolidate and reinforce the relations among the parties; these are: [1] respect to the identity related to social and institutional characteristics that are part of a person or organization; [2] trust, which becomes the security felt by the people and the organization when they get involved in a project; [3] respect agreements, which guide the procedures during the project; there must be consensus among the parties involved whenever a decisions is taken; [4] flexibility, which is the easiness to participate and interact during the development of the process, and must be available to all participating members of a project; [5] commitment, which is one of the main aspects to highlight; people must assume responsibility that comes when tasks are assigned, and under no circumstances people can leave such tasks undone; it is better to quit if functions are not going to be performed with the quality and during the spam of times expected; [6] to recognize the job done is essential; the work of each individual and of the team as a whole must be valued and praised. There are many ways to recognize the work of people and groups; a fundamental way of publicly acknowledge the work of every person in a project is by press articles or publications in other media.

Successful Cases in Governmental Organizations

This part of the chapter shows cases of open innovation developed by governmental organizations working together in collaboration with universities. It is essential to The information presented in this part of the chapter was taken from the "*Biblioteca del Centro de Innovación Pública Digital del Gobierno en Línea*"[1] (Library of the Public Innovation Center of Online Government).

CGT Bogotá

For the "*Sistema Inteligente de Transporte para Bogotá*" (Intelligent Transportation System for Bogota), the integration of different systems that apply ICTs for monitoring and operating the transportation in the system was contemplated. Besides, it was considered to have online information in real-time to provide prompt responses to incidents and emergencies.

This application permits communication between citizens and the city government through the report of incidents. In this way, descriptions of incidents reach operators who manage resources of the city to provide timely and quick responses. An analysis was performed to communicate the project in the most suitable way, and a communication plan was created, which included videos and documents that can be disseminated by different media.

When the Intelligent Transportation System for Bogota was implemented, the response times to transportation incidents were reduced 15%; besides, the average speed increased from 18 km/h in 2015 to 21 km/h nowadays.

Bogotá Cambalachea, Banco de Tiempo de los Ciudadanos

Bogotá Cambalachea is a digital web platform with the dynamics of a time bank, whose main objective is to exchange skills, knowledge, and services between citizens. By using the platform, users can offer their services to other people who can acquire them in exchange for the time that takes to perform them (without the need to pay any money for it). This platform has been useful to social groups that can invite other people to participate in change initiatives.

This program is aimed at Bogota inhabitants who are open to new ways of exchanging and experience things and recognize ICTs as tools to stimulate community work and collaborative behavior in social environments; besides, they also have skills and knowledge that can provide to the community. Currently, the platform has 1862 users, 885 registered offers, and 60 exchanges of services and/or understanding have been done since March 2016. Communities have used *Bogota Cambalachea* within the city to call citizens to collaborate in social initiatives.

Public Bikes Management

ArcosSoft developed platforms for automatized lending, operation, and manufacturing of systems of public bikes that help to preserve the environment and contribute to social development through the optimization of urban public transportation. The platform consists of a software (Website and Mobile App for the interaction with the user) and hardware (electronic and wireless physical structure) for the parking of public bikes.

Most places rank very low, taking into consideration the traffic problems in medium-sized cities and analyzing the results of the first report on the environment quality of Colombian urban areas. Therefore, institutions, as well as communities, must develop projects to help to preserve the environment. Under such circumstances, cities are trying to create pedestrian and bikers-friendly public spaces, where they play the leading role in the context of promoting more sustainable transportation. It is essential to highlight the creation of social movements that encourage its use and to encourage people to think critically about this transportation way as part of a lifestyle that generates an impact on society. Colombian cities endure problems, such as narrow and inadequate streets unfit to support high vehicle traffic; huge demand for transportation, especially for short rides; absence of real traffic control dealing with inappropriate car parking; and the need to increase space for other transportation means. These factors have held back mobility and increase traffic chaos in cities. That is why Local Authorities, together with the Ministry of Transportation, are executing the "*Plan Piloto de Bicicletas Públicas*" (Pilot Plan of Public Bikes). Even though bikes are a valid mobility option for medium-sized cities, it is necessary to think about mobility as a transportation service; it is at this point that ICTs can support this transportation means under an automatized system of lending of shared public bikes.

Cátedra-Bancoldex

Its objective is to design an open, collaborative innovation model for *Bancoldex* (a Colombian development bank), aimed at finding solutions to Colombian entrepreneurial growth. PPT *Programa de Transformación Productiva* (Program of Productive Transformation) and *INNpulsa Colombia* (an entrepreneurial program) joined the project, providing academic institutions with challenges from a variety of industries.

The open, collaborative innovation model was a lecture at the national level, in which teams from different participant Colombian universities were given various challenges coming from enterprises or industries; at the end of the academic semester, the teams presented their solutions for them. All participants well accepted it, and the appropriation of the dimensions, components, and principles of the model was evident. It was proven that collaboration is essential in this model, as well as the networks formed between professors and leaders of the *Catedra Bancoldex* in each institution (Ramírez-Salazar, 2016).

METHODOLOGY

Based on Hernandez Sampieri, Fernández, and Baptista (2015), this a descriptive, transversal research since data are collected on a single moment, and variables are described, analyzed, and correlated on a given moment. The process used in this study is the Open Collaborative Innovation Model, which takes the following steps: [1] Population, [2] Challenge Contextualization, [3] Analysis of Ideas, [4] Ideation, [5] Prototype Creation.

Population: The population for the development of the innovation project in the ANE is composed of those representatives from participant universities; they were students who were taking their apprenticeship at the ANE during the first academic semester of 2018. Eight students joined their internship at ANE through the project through the "*Estado Joven*" Program.

The innovation team was composed of 50% by men and 50% by women. 50% of the participants were between 21 and 23 years old. The remaining 50% were older than 23 years. Students from six universities participated in the project: *Universidad del Bosque, Universidad EAN, Universidad Konrad Lorenz, Universidad INCCA, Universidad Cooperativa de Colombia,* and *Universidad Militar*. The majors studied by participant students were: electronic engineering, law, business, business administration, and international trade. Students were at the junior and senior years of their majors.

CHALLENGE PROPOSED

The ANE receives high numbers of complaints about the illegal use of the spectrum. Such objections can be grouped as: complaints about the unauthorized use of the spectrum, use of the spectrum with an expired or non-renewed license, and use of amplifiers or radio electrical signal blockers without the corresponding authorization. In such cases, fines ranged from 2,000 Colombian Minimum Current Legal Salaries when an offender is a person, up to 15,000 Minimum Current Legal Salaries when the offender is a legal entity. Depending on the case, penalties imposed are the suspension of the licenses, termination of services, and/or confiscation of equipment. See Table 1.

Table 1. Consequences of the Illegal Use of the Spectrum in Colombia

ADMINISTRATIVE	LEGAL
· Immediate cease of non-authorized operations · Preventive seizure of assets · Administrative Penalizing Process · Final seizure of assets · Penalties	· Felony: the illegal presentation, access, or use of telecommunication services. · Penal Code Article 257: Anyone who access renders, trades, or uses any telecommunication service without the corresponding authorization.

Source: the authors based on information taken from www.ane.gov.co

Considering that there are cases of illegal use of the spectrum in Colombia, the ANE has been implementing a policy to exercise preventive and corrective surveillance and control, favoring such a preventative approach over a penal system to achieve a flexible and efficient use of the spectrum in Colombia. Regardless of the efforts taken by ANE, there is no reduction in the number of complaints about the illegal use of the electrical radio spectrum.

Figure 1 shows how there are complaints about the illegal use of the spectrum all over the country. Cundinamarca is by far the administrative region with the highest number of complaints, even surpassing both Antioquia and Valle. Those three regions are also the most populated areas of the country. It is essential to clarify that many complaints are related to illegal use of the spectrum in rural areas, where there are additional transportation difficulties, which makes their verification difficult.

Context Analysis

To have more in-depth knowledge about the problem to be solved, participants started the process of Open innovation with the application of the brainstorming technique, obtaining the results showed in Table 2.

Figure 1. Number of complaints by the department in the Second Semester 2017
Source: the authors based on information obtained in the ANE's PQRSD Database

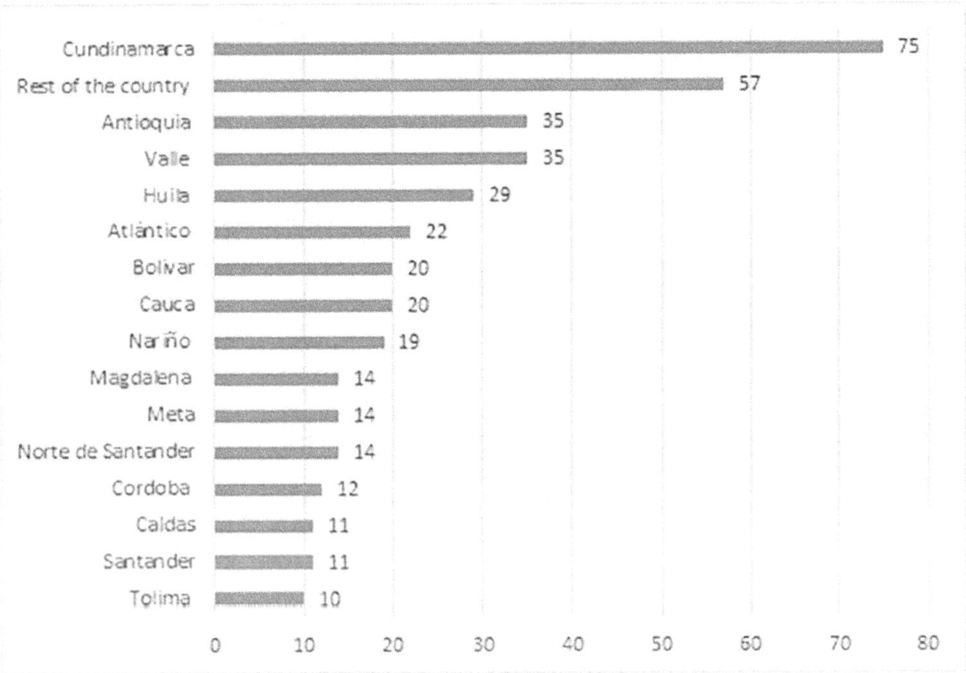

Table 2. Brainstorm Results

The Illegal Use of the Spectrum		
Causes	**Consequences**	**Actions to take**
· Lack of regulation · Inadequate use of social media · Brand not positioned · There are no tools to interact with users · Insufficient response time to complaints · No penalties · Lack of knowledge by control entities · Lack of knowledge about regulations · Lack of a unit in charge of dealing with complaints · Inadequate website · Not enough financial resources · Untimely communication of ICT topics · Not enough involvement from citizens	· High interference rates · Heavy workload due to the high volume of complaints received and research to inquire about interferences · Inadequate use of the spectrum due to lack of information about regulations · Enterprises legally authorized to use the spectrum have problems using it · Uninformed citizens	· To develop communication strategies about the ANE · To create a permanent communication channel · To implement penalties · To train workers · To develop and improve an app or website · To design mechanisms to offer timely and correct information · To position the brand · To interact more with clients by social media · To train in innovation, creativity, and Design Thinking · To speed up internal processes · To increase the number of information channels

Source: the authors, based on the results obtained by participants after the brainstorm

Next, participant teams developed a SWOT Analysis, aimed at having more detailed information on the case. The resulting SWOT Matrix served as a tool to analyze and assess the situation to be worked. The results are presented in Table 3.

Table 3. SWOT Matrix: How to reduce the number of complaints about the illegal use of the spectrum

Strengths	Weaknesses
Preventive training aimed at having a correct use of the spectrum	Inappropriate use of communication tools such as social media
Budget cuts that place limits to some ANE activities	Lack of coverage all over the country, which makes surveillance and control difficult
Telecommunications technological innovations	The heavy workload of employees at the Surveillance and Control Unit due to high numbers of complaints
Participation of universities in the process to solve the problem	Inadequate level of knowledge and expertise by employees
Education of citizens as well as communication through society segmentation	Difficulties in reducing response time to complaints
	Administrative and financial wear out due to repetitive complaints
	Unsatisfactory response time to complaints
	Lack of resources for mass communication
OPPORTUNITIES	THREATS
Increasing the use of ICTs in administrative and operational processes	Clandestine use of non-authorized networks
Deployment of infrastructure via the *Vive Digital* Plan	Possible lack of investment by the Government in activities related to spectrum management
The positioning of the function of electromagnetic spectrum control	A new regulation that limits investment and/or use of telecommunications infrastructure
Use of ICTs to strengthen the communication process	Lack of knowledge about ANE activities
Interest by the ANE to find mechanisms for optimal use of the spectrum	Lack of identification with the ANE
The direct relation between the ICTs Ministry and the ANE	Lack of permanent assistance during the process
	Culture of illegality

Source: the authors based on results from the SWOT Matrix creation process

To finish with the contextualization stage, an ANE expert was interviewed about the current situation of the agency regarding the challenge proposed. The results of the interview are shown next in Table 4.

Table 4. ANE Experts' Perceptions about the Challenge Proposed

TYPES OF COMPLAINTS FOR THE ILLEGAL USE OF THE SPECTRUM · Use without having the proper license · Use without considering the authorized technical specifications
REASONS FOR THE COMPLAINTS · Use of the spectrum for an economic benefit · Lack of knowledge about legal requirements · Illegal culture
SERVICE WITH THE HIGHEST NUMBER OF COMPLAINTS · Sound broadcasting
ACTIONS TAKEN TO REDUCE THE NUMBER OF COMPLAINTS ABOUT THE ILLEGAL USE OF THE SPECTRUM · Information campaigns focused on authorities and students (training) · "ANE in the Regions" Campaign (conducted outside Bogota; massive concentrations not allowed)
IMPACT ON THE SURVEILLANCE AND CONTROL UNIT · Heavy workload during visits and technical analysis · Difficulties in seizing equipment · Reprocessing due to repetitive complains
AVERAGE TIME TO DEAL WITH A COMPLAINT · Approximately four months (without including the penalizing process that might take up to a year)

Source: the authors

Proposing and Selecting Ideas

Once the analysis of the problem was completed, the creation of ideas started with brainstorming leading to the results shown in Table 5.

To analyze the ideas presented, every member of each team assumed a role: mediator, defender of the concept, and opponent to the idea. Once the exercise was over, each team proposed three ideas so it could keep going with the evaluation. The results of such experience are presented in the next part of the chapter.

Evaluation of Ideas

For this innovation project, the evaluator team was formed by a multidisciplinary group composed by the General Director of the ANE, the Vice President of the Surveillance and Control Unit, the Advisor assigned to the Surveillance and Control Unit by the General Direction, the Coordinator of the Spectrum Technical Team, and the Coordinator of the Spectrum Research Team. Such a committee was in charge of selecting the winning idea. They had to score on a scale from 1 to 5 each of the impact factors already established. The results of such evaluation are presented in Table 6.

Table 5. Results after Brainstorming

How to Reduce the Number of Complaints about the Illegal Use of the Spectrum?	
Idea 1	To educate and communicate
Idea 2	To train workers
Idea 3	To develop specialized software to manage complaints
Idea 4	To design an advertisement strategy
Idea 5	To develop projects of spectrum management in collaboration with universities
Idea 6	To increase penalties
Idea 7	To impose penalties aimed at promoting knowledge about the spectrum
Idea 8	To associate license granting to the promotion of information about the spectrum
Idea 9	To implement interactive tools to be in permanent communication with users
Idea 10	To develop strategies for the positioning of the ANE
Idea 11	To analyze offenders
Idea 12	To implement training tailored to offenders
Idea 13	To create a mobile app for the ANE
Idea 14	To include a clause of spectrum broadcasting

Source: the authors based on the brainstorming process

Table 6. Consolidated Results of the Evaluation of Idea

	Group ANE A NEW WAY OF THINKING									
	IDEA, ANE en el mundo					IDEA, Aprende y Capacitate				
Issue to evaluate/Evaluator	1	2	3	4	5	1	2	3	4	5
It fulfills the needs of the organization	4	3	4	5	4	4	3	5	5	4
It fulfills the needs of the users	5	2	4	4	4	4	2	5	5	4
It is technically feasible	4	4	4,5	5	4	4	4	5	4	4
It is financially feasible	3	2	4,5	5	4	4	4	4	4	3
Degree of innovation of the idea	4	2	4,5	4	3	2	3	5	4	1
It is aligned with organizational processes	4	3	5	4	4	4	4	5	4	4
Level of impact on the problem	3	2	4	4	4	3	2	5	4	4
Score per evaluator	27	18	31	31	27	25	22	32	30	24
Final score	26,6					26,5				

	Group SPANE									
	IDEA Identificación del					IDEA Amonestación				
Issue to evaluate/Evaluator	1	2	3	4	5	1	2	3	4	5
It fulfills the needs of the organization	4	4	3	5	4	4	4	4	3,5	4
It fulfills the needs of the users	4	3	3	4	4	5	3	4	3,5	4
It is technically feasible	3	4	4	4	4	3	3	3	3	3
It is financially feasible	3	4	4	3	4	2	4	3	3	4
Degree of innovation of the idea	3	5	3	3	1	3	4	3	3	2
It is aligned with organizational processes	4	5	3	4	3	4	5	4	3,5	4
Level of impact on the problem	2	2	3	3	2	2	2	3,5	3,5	1
Score per evaluator	23	27	23	26	22	23	25	25	23	22
Final score	24,2					23,5				

	Group MOVIMIENTO ESPECTRAL									
	IDEA Digiespectro					IDEA Clausula de la Cultura				
Issue to evaluate/Evaluator	1	2	3	4	5	1	2	3	4	5
It fulfills the needs of the organization	4	4	4	4	4	4	4	4	4	4
It fulfills the needs of the users	5	4	3,5	3,5	4	5	4	4	4	4
It is technically feasible	4	4	4	3,5	4	4	3	4	3	4
It is financially feasible	4	2	4	3,5	4	4	4	3	3	3
Degree of innovation of the idea	4	4	4,5	4	3	4	5	5	4	5
It is aligned with organizational processes	4	3	4,5	4	4	4	4	5	4	4
Level of impact on the problem	3	2	4	3,5	3	3	5	4	3,5	3
Score per evaluator	28	23	29	26	26	28	29	28	26	27
Final score	26,3					27,4				

Source: the authors based on results obtained in the evaluation of ideas

Considering that five evaluators were evaluating seven issues, the maximum possible score was 35 points per evaluator. An arithmetical average of the scores provided by each evaluator was calculated to obtain the final score.

SELECTED IDEA

Group: Movimiento Spectral Movement
Idea: Spectral Culture Clause

The idea was to include, in the contracts that grant the use of the spectrum, a clause by which the licensee is obliged to communicate, by use of mass communication media, information about the ANE and regulation applicable to spectrum management. This fact will benefit the ANE since it will be able to reach all users without needing to spend additional resources in an advertisement. This clause will be implemented in radio broadcasting licenses (radio spots), TV (TV ads), mobile phones (text messages and ringtones), and traditional phone service (phone call advertisement). See Table 7.

Table 7. Clause of the Spectral Culture Strategy

Why It Solves the Problem?
Because it dramatically reduces problems that cause illegal use of the spectrum such as: · Lack of knowledge about the ANE · Lack of knowledge about the electromagnetic spectrum · Lack of knowledge about regulatory aspects to using the spectrum · Lack of knowledge about how to obtain licenses to use the spectrum · Legal and administrative consequences of the illegal use of the spectrum
Resources required
ANE Public officers who will be in charge of working with the ICT Ministry to approve contract modifications
Results expected
A reduction in the number of complaints about the illegal use of the spectrum
Indicators to measure the clause' effectiveness
Percentage of decrease in the number of complaints about the illegal use of the spectrum Results of a survey tailored at measuring the knowledge users have about the spectrum

Source: the authors

Awarding

Awarding occurred after ideas were evaluated. The team called *Movimiento Espectral* won the challenge with its idea *Clausula de la Cultura* (Culture clause), obtaining a final score of 27.4 points. Each member of the team was rewarded with three days of paid leave and a gift. The second and third places each got two days of paid vacation and a gift.

A Proposal of Open Innovation Strategy for the ANE

Considering the project between the ANE and the universities and based on open innovation models proposed by Ramirez-Salazar (2016); Chesbrough (2009); Van Gundy (2007); and Davila, Epstein, and Shelton (2008), an open innovation model for the ANE was suggested. Such model follows the following steps:

1. Problem identification: ANE workers can do this.
2. Challenge definition: every challenge must deal with problems that affect the organization, and solutions to them must create new knowledge for the ANE (new technologies, procedures, services, goods, etc.).
3. Choose participants: the person in charge of the innovation process in the organization must decide, according to organizational needs and the type of problem, who will participate.
4. Protocols and agreements to establish criteria that will guide the open innovation project. At this point, the responsible for the project must fill its corresponding planning form.
5. Call to communicate the invitation to join the innovation challenge. The ANE Communications Team can support the effort at this time. The organization can use databases, social networks, research groups, and any other useful tool.
6. Ideation, to create ideas according to the rules of the process.
7. Evaluation of solutions proposed to be developed by an internal and multidisciplinary team composed of employees with the knowledge and expertise required to choose the best choice.
8. Awarding, once choosing the best options for the organization, awards will be conferred upon the winners.
9. Implementation of the solution, after the innovation project is finished, the ANE can decide to implement the solutions proposed. To implement them, the organization must consider its strategic alignment, budget, human resources, and any other factor that might have to affect the implementation.

Figure 2 shows a graphic description of the steps explained previously.

Lessons Learned

The following are lessons learned during the open innovation collaborative process developed at the ANE:

a) The commitment from Top Management generates confidence and security to participants, incentivizing them to work on the proposed challenges effectively.

b) The leader must have explicit knowledge of the topic to obtain the best results, increasing his/her capacity to guide, support, and answer questions from the team throughout the process.
c) The leader must have leadership and teamwork capabilities.
d) A multidisciplinary team can contribute to having different points of view about the problem, therefore, improving the process.
e) It is essential never to restrict or discourage ideas.
f) The leader of the process must never try to redirect the ideas of the innovation team.
g) Spaces for creativity must be generated, and resources for innovators to be creative must be provided.
h) Keeping the team motivated is a crucial factor for success.
i) Awards granted to winners must not be tied to future contracts, since this generates uncertainty to both parties involved.

Figure 2. ANE Open Collaborative Innovation Model
Source: the authors

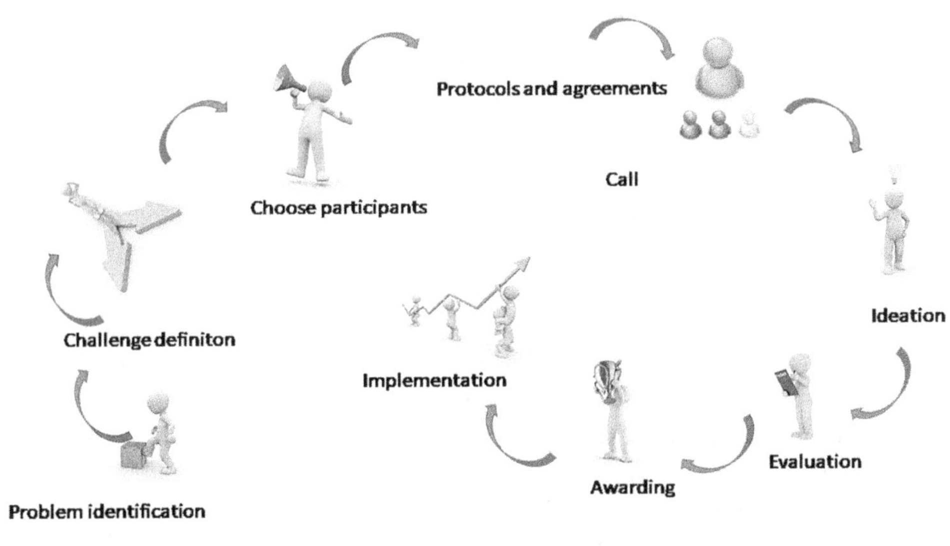

RECOMMENDATIONS

The following are recommendations for the ANE based on the open, innovative, collaborative process developed in such organization:

To keep developing joint programs with different clients and users, since this is an opportunity to optimize its processes at low costs and gaining the best from people outside the organization who could provide ideas to solve problems.

To promote a culture of innovation as a process of permanent change that will allow the development of new organizations' skills and abilities. This implementation will require continuous support from Top Management to reach the proposed objectives.

To adopt the strategy of open innovation will contribute to generating an environment in which behaviors to innovate in a sustainable and prosperous manner will be supported and encouraged.

To apply the strategy of open innovation in its daily activities so it will become a mechanism to create competitive advantages.

CONCLUSION

- It was a pertinent project; besides, it was the first time the ANE joint universities for an innovation process. The ANE obtained valuable ideas that can be applied to optimize the use of the spectrum in Colombia. Statements proposed in the project will be evaluated in coordination with the ICT Ministry, the ANE Surveillance and Control Unit, and the ANE Communications Team to implement initiatives to reduce the number of complaints about the illegal use of the spectrum.
- The evaluating team was highly satisfied with the results, given the participants' potential to propose innovative ideas to solve the problem suggested. Once ideas were analyzed, evaluators concluded that ideas' implementation leads to a significant reduction in the number of complaints about the illegal use of the spectrum; besides, they can contribute to the positioning of the organization as well as the widespread knowledge of spectrum-related topics.
- There has been significant progress in coverage, access, and spread of ICT's, answering the needs of dynamic private industries eager to invest and to a public government that established rules that boost ICT's development.
- Enterprises make more use of the Open Innovation Model because it allows them to make intensive use of internal and external knowledge, intending to accelerate internal innovation and to expand to new markets for the external use of innovation.
- Open innovation strengthens organizational innovation capabilities and allows enterprises to use a set of methods, techniques, and strategies to create and develop innovations more efficiently.
- For effectiveness and to obtain the results expected, open innovation must be aligned with the organizational strategic direction.

- Human resources play an essential role in the innovation process because own, acquired, and interiorized experience and knowledge contribute to the development of new abilities, ideas, ways of doing things and manage businesses, and use of resources.
- The Open Innovation Model is complemented with Knowledge Management since it allows the analysis of the validity of some of the organizational strategies and processes.
- Open innovation has become an essential tool for government enterprises to manage and strengthen them, therefore increasing public value and services to citizens.
- The University-Government relation gains importance when knowledge embodied in university students is used to strengthen public enterprises' management.
- The ANE must interiorize open innovation into its organizational culture. By doing so, it will create competitive advantages that benefit all population and contribute to the strengthening of its management as a government agency.
- The first innovation project between the ANE and universities allowed the generation of ideas that might help to reduce the number of complaints about the illegal use of the electromagnetic spectrum.
- To have a Top Management commitment to implement innovative processes (as it was the open innovation project) plays on ANE's favor because the agency can keep going on implementing the proposed open innovation strategy.
- The proposed open innovation strategy adapts to the ANE needs and will contribute to developing similar projects to provide solutions to problems.

REFERENCES

Agencia Nacional del Espectro. (2010). *Cartilla #1*. Conceptos del Espectro Radioeléctrico.

Agencia Nacional del Espectro. (2010). *Cartilla #2*. Gestión del Espectro.

Agencia Nacional del Espectro. (2010). Cartilla #3. Uso eficiente del Espectro Radioeléctrico. Author.

Agencia Nacional del Espectro. (2016). *Cuadro Nacional de Atribución de Bandas de Frecuencia*. Author.

Agencia Nacional del Espectro. (2017). *Manual de Calidad*. Author.

Álvarez-Aros, E., & Bernal-Torres, C. (2017). Modelo de Innovación Abierta: Énfasis en el Potencial Humano. *Información Tecnológica, 28*(1), 65–76. doi:10.4067/S0718-07642017000100007

Benegas, L. A. (2002). *Telecomunicaciones para comunicarse eficientemente - Libertas 19.* Eseade.

Bernal-Torres, C. A., & Frost-González, S. (2015). Innovación abierta en empresas colombianas: Reto a superar. *Revista Venezolana de Gerencia, 13*(70), 262–267. doi:10.31876/revista.v20i70.19996

Bravo-Ibarra, E. R., León-Arenas, A. P., & Serrano-Cárdenas, L. F. (2014). Explorando las principales ventajas y factores de éxito de la innovación abierta en las organizaciones. *Revista Entramado, 25*, 44–59. doi:10.18041/entramado.2014v10n2.20220

Cadena, E. (2013). *Gestión del Espectro Radioeléctrico en Colombia.* Universidad Distrital Francisco José de Caldas.

Chesbrough, H. (2006). *Open Innovation. The new imperative for creating and profiting from technology.* Harvard Business School Press.

Davila, T., Epstein, M., & Shelton, R. (2008). *Making Innovation Work, How to Manage It, Measure It, and Profit from It.* Seventh Printing & Pearson Education.

Fedesarrollo. (2013). *El sector TIC: la nueva locomotora de la economía colombiana. Informe trimestral TIC.* Author.

Fernández, N. J. (2007). *El universo de las radiaciones.* Eudeba.

GESP. (2010). *Introducción a la gestión del espectro radioeléctrico. Grupo del Espectro.* Colegio Oficial Ingenieros de Telecomunicación.

González, R. Y., & García, F. E. (2011). Innovación abierta: Un modelo preliminar desde la gestión del conocimiento. *Intangible Capital, 7*(1), 82–115.

Hernandez Sampieri, R., Fernandez Collazo, C., & Baptista Lucio, P. (2006). *Metodología de la Investigación* (4th ed.). Mc Graw Hill.

López, J., & García, A. (2010). *Innovación abierta: Desafíos organizacionales de este modelo de gestión de innovación para las empresas, Red de redes científicas de América Latina y el Caribe, España y Portugal.* Universidad de A Coruña.

Medina, D. (2017). ¿Qué le espera al sector. *El Espectador.*

Ministerio de Tecnologías de la Información y las Comunicaciones. (2015). *Comportamiento macroeconómico del sector TIC en Colombia.* Panorama TIC.

Ministerio de Tecnologías de la Información y las Comunicaciones. (2017). *Primera Gran Encuesta TIC 2017: Estudio de Acceso*. Usos y Retos de las TIC en Colombia.

Ministerio de Tecnologías de la Información y las Comunicaciones y Agencia Nacional del Espectro. (2012). Monitoreo del Espectro Radioeléctrico. Manual de Gestión Nacional del Espectro Radioeléctrico - Título V. Author.

OpenDemocracy. (2017). *Innovación abierta en el sector público*. Author.

Ramírez, A. (2011). *Gobierno abierto y modernización de la gestión pública: tendencias actuales y el inevitable camino que viene*. Instituto Universitario de Investigación Ortega y Gasset.

Ramírez-Salazar, M. P. (2015). *Modelo de innovación abierta colaborativa para la banca de fomento: Caso Bancoldex* (PhD Thesis). Universidad Nebrija.

UNESCO. (2004). Las tecnologías de la información y la comunicación en la formación docente. Guía de Planificación. Organización de las Naciones Unidas para la Educación, la Ciencia y la Cultura. UNESCO.

Vangundy, A. (2007). *Getting to Innovation: How Asking the Right Questions Generates Great Ideas Your Company Needs*. Amacom.

KEY TERMS AND DEFINITIONS

Bogotá Cambalachea: It is a digital web platform with the dynamics of a time bank, whose main objective is to exchange skills, knowledge, and services between citizens.

Cátedra-Bancoldex: Established in Bogota (Colombia) at EAN University, its objective is to design an open, collaborative innovation model for Bancoldex (a Colombian development bank), aimed at finding solutions to Colombian entrepreneurial growth.

INNpulsa Colombia: It is the entrepreneurship and innovation agency of the National Government, which accompanies the acceleration of high-potential ventures and the innovative and financing processes that allow companies in the country to scale to generate more economic development, equity, and opportunities for all Colombians.

Intelligent Transportation System: A system used in Bogota (Colombia) and defined by the integration of different transportation methods that apply ICTs for monitoring and operating the transportation system in the city.

National Spectrum Agency: It is a Colombian entity that assists the Ministry of Information Technologies and Communications in the planning, allocation, surveillance, and control of the radioelectric spectrum in Colombia.

Open Innovation: It is a model used by firms to intensively use internal and external knowledge for boosting and accelerating their innovation processes to expand markets.

PQRSD Database: The database used at ANE to integrate data related to ICTs and the use of it in Colombia.

Transistor: A small semiconductor device defined by operating as an electric switch and codified binary, which became the boost of such digital technologies.

ENDNOTE

1 http://centrodeinnovacion.gobiernoenlinea.gov.co/es/biblioteca-conocimiento

Chapter 10
Values and Administrative Practices for Generations Associated With Organizational Innovation

Gustavo Adolfo Gil Angel
Fundación Universitaria del Área Andina, Colombia

Jorge Gámez-Gutierrez
Universidad de la Costa, Colombia

Robinson Ernesto Calvo
Escuela Colombiana de Carreras Industriales, Colombia

ABSTRACT

Generational analysis and studies are a recent research trend that analyzes social, cultural, political, and economic changes within the framework of the digital revolution. In this work, an approach is made to the generational phenomena in the SMEs. The objective is to identify the correlations between entrepreneurship and management operations from the logic of individual values and the practices of SMEs managers and owners in Bogotá, from the Blackman model, according to their correspondence with the generational classification taking into account your date of birth. The sample is 383 entrepreneurs from Bogotá, and it was found that there are significant differences associated with generations in skills and abilities, risk management, honesty, responsibility, and work in the provision of services and facilities.

DOI: 10.4018/978-1-7998-3568-4.ch010

INTRODUCTION

Startups and firms in Colombia are developing environments to guarantee their functioning and durability. The vast majority of companies are created by entrepreneurs aged between 25 and 34 years old, 75.6% by opportunity, and 24.4% by necessity. Also, men over 55 years are creating companies (54.7% by opportunity and 44.2% by necessity). Startup creation links to high family income, as many entrepreneurs (13.1% men and 5.2% women) earn more than seven monthly minimum wages (Escadón-Barbosa et al., 2015).

Differences between generations refer to the different speeds at which they receive information, the capacity and taste of parallel work and multitasking, the preference of some for text and others for images, networking, immediate satisfaction for the job and the frequency of rewards and the differences between games and "serious work" (Gértrudix et al., 2010). Also, seniors and young people have different ways of working: managing interruptions, using mobile phones, the frequency of e-mail consultation on their computers, and the use of PDAs (Ferrer, 2010). Regarding work in the company, after 11 years of age, there seems to be no difference in the behavior of young people. Concerning young adults they have a poor understanding of their information needs and find it challenging to develop effective strategies of information search. Children and young people carry out few attempts to verify the veracity of the information obtained (Cabra-Torres and Marciales-Vivas, 2009).

In the European Union, it is common to see SMEs in networks, as part of supply chains formed by large national and foreign companies. In this case, specific products and services do not compete with mass manufacturing products made by massive companies and adapted according to customer requirements for niche markets linked to customer service. In Latin America, most MSMEs do not have these qualifications (Rabellotti, 1997; UN-Cepal, 2004; Dini and Stumpo, 2019). Besides, business performance is inertial due to its small capital, managers without sufficient knowledge in business management, restricted access to credit and local markets, and little innovation (Confecámaras, 2018). In Colombia, SMEs have the same problems: The promotion of long-term strategies is still incipient; there is a lack of a strategic vision about the role of MSMEs in productive transformation; The effectiveness of public entities and the fragmentation of small-scale support actions limits their ability to produce visible impacts (Dini and Stumpo, 2019; Consejo Privado de Competitividad, 2018).

Zapata (2004) considers that the non-professional management of entrepreneurs - managers of SMEs, the influence of the environment, the deficiencies in internal control, and the inability to associate to face national and transnational competition compromise their sustainability. In turn, Pérez (2004) found that underutilization of installed capacity, lack of advanced technology in processes, lack of leadership, and little autonomy of bosses to achieve the objectives, and low participation of employees in the planning of the activities of the company, compromise the performance of SMEs. Finally, Confecámaras (2016) considers that internal and environmental variables in the firm affect their ability to continue in the market and grow, as well as affect moderately the qualified personnel in the multiple tasks to be performed within the organization. As a result, SMEs do not become medium and large companies. In this paper, managers' performance working in 383 companies belonging to the industrial sector of Bogotá will be analyzed, according to the generations described and their characteristics.

THEORETICAL FRAMEWORK

Below is the theoretical support of companies, family businesses, generations, work, and family balance, management strategies, and practices.

Business

Micro, small and medium enterprises participate with 25% of the regional gross domestic product (GDP) in contrast to the countries of the European Union, where this figure reaches, on average, 56% (Dini and Stumpo, 2019). In Colombia, the business sector borders the 900,000 companies that are strengthened with more than 75,000 new companies each year; in the capital, there are more than 350,000 companies (OCM, 2007), and around 50,000 are being born. During 2017, entrepreneurs created 70,022 companies and 253,243 businesses of individuals, which represents a growth of 7.3% over the same period in 2016. These new companies are in the commercial sector (38%) and the manufacturing industry (9.7%) (Confecámaras, 2018).

Family Businesses

According to the Superintendence of Societies (1971), family firms have at least two partners with the same consanguinity up to the second degree, or partners being married. These family members exercise economic control, Financial or administrative about the company. In essence, in a family business, more than one individual from the same family has the company as a way of life. It is a company run and controlled by one or more members of a family (Becker, 1978). The motivation of those who create and manage a family business is that they remain and endure over time (Gersick et al., 1997).

Values in family businesses are a crucial factor in the performance of these organizations and manage to become a competitive advantage that can be preserved over time. (De la Garza et al., 2011). These companies maintain values such as commitment, respect, hard work, responsibility, credibility, and justice (García, 2009; Ittner and Larcker, 2003).

Family businesses are concerned not only with financial returns but also with non-economic objectives (Astrachan and Jaskiewicz, 2008; Kleiny Kellermanns, 2008; Chrisman et al., 2003; Sharma, Chrisman and Chua, 1997). Due to non-economic advantages and socio-emotional wealth, family businesses emotionally link to the affective dimension of the family, that is, families desire to control the firm to preserve the family's ties and values to perpetuate the family dynasty and its lifestyle, prestige, and image (Berrone, Cruz and Gómez, 2012; Dyer, 2003; Gómez, Cruz, Berrone and de Castro, 2011; Zellweger, Nason, Nordqvist and Brush, 2013; Cabrera, Déniz and Martín, 2014). According to Astrachan and Jaskiewicz (2008), the total value of a company is not only composed of the generated financial value, as it is generally assumed in traditional monetary theory. Emotional components also have an impact on their assessment, given that strategic decision making in family businesses is strongly influenced by the family (Chrisman, Chua, and Steir, 2005; Dyer, 2003; Rutherford et al., 2008; Sharma et al., 1997).

Family businesses are thought for the long term (Christman and Sharma 1999). In Latin America, they have an average age of 57 years - large companies - which on average, are in their second generation. The oldest is in Chile and Mexico -77 years- and at the other extreme, the youngest in Honduras -42 years-. In an intermediate group, there are two groups: one with an average age between 69 and 55 years (companies in Argentina, Spain, and Brazil), and the other between 48 and 43 (companies in Peru, Colombia, and Costa Rica).

Table 1. Comparison of generations

Generations	Traditionals	Baby boomers	X-Gen	Y-Gen	Z-Gen
Birth years	1930 - 1945	1946 - 1964	1965 - 1976	1977 - 1995	1995 - 2012
Work ethic	Dedicated and loyal	Question everything	Self-reliant	Sense of entitlement	Master of multitasking
Work-life balance	Duty before fun	Big imbalance	Clear balance	Flexibility	Flexibility
Work characteristics	Rule followers	Value ambition and youthfulness	Flexibility	Achievement and goal-oriented	Leverage technology for any task

Source: Own elaboration based on the Institute of Child Nutrition (2018).

As seen in Table 1, generations are, according to Gértrudix, Durán, Gamonal, Galvez de la Cuesta, and García (2010): Baby boom (born between 1946 to 1964), Baby burst (1965 to 1976), Eco baby boom (1977 to 1997). Tapscott (1998) considers that there are Digital Immigrants (Baby boomers), Digital adaptive (X-Gen) born between 1965 to 1979, Digital natives (Y-Gen or Millennials) from 1980 to 2000, and Digital avatars born in the 21st century. Finally, Boschma (2008) considers that they can be explained as Baby boom (1945-1955), X-Gen (1960-1985), and the Einstein Generation (1988 - present). See Table 2.

Table 2. Years and generations

Year	Theory	Author
1983	Globalization	Theodore Levitt
1998-2008	Demographic evolution	Don Tapscott (1998), Gerri Sinclair, and Bruno Cerboni (2008)
1982	Teoría de las edades de las audiencias	Philip Palmgreen and Daniel Raybum
2008	Theory of gratifications and motivations in the use of the Internet	Jay Blumler
2008	Maslow's Inverted Pyramid Theory	Jeroen Boschman
2008	Digital citizens vs. digital natives	Genius Roca
2008	Form and degree of interaction with the information	John Palfrey and Urs Gasser

Source: Own elaboration based on the Institute of Child Nutrition (2018) and Finra (2018)

Conventional wisdom paints a vivid picture of millennials and their attitudes on investing. Some of the common assumptions about millennials include: Millennials have lofty goals, income challenges and debt are critical barriers to investing; Millennials, being overconfident in general, are also overconfident in their financial lives; Millennials are wary of the financial services industry and, by extension skeptical of financial professionals; Millennials likely overestimate the investable assets needed to work with a financial professional; Being digital natives, millennials naturally gravitate toward robot-advisors; and Millennials as a group are homogenous and so likely have similar investing attitudes and behaviors across demographic subgroups (Finra, 2018).

Regarding communication skills, promotions, and repetitive work Institute of Child Nutrition (2018), believes that generations behave like this (See Table 3).

Table 3. Increasing Generational Performance

Generations and performance	Traditionals	Baby boomers	X-Geners	Millennials
Communications Skills	Give fast feedback	Be sure they know why work tasks matter	Use face-to-face interaction instead of e-mail	Treat them in a professional manner
Promotions	Help set project-based of time off	Give recognition for jobs well done	Allow them to earn recognition	Don´t let them get bored
Repetitive job assignments	Do not allow them to take on the bulk of these assignments	Assign tasks that push their limits	Give them credit for results	Assign tasks that push their limit

Source: Own elaboration based on the Institute of Child Nutrition (2018).

Green and McClelland (2019) consider that age does not determine gender role attitudes, nor is period accompanied by traditionalism (Lynott and McCandless, 2000). Instead, these differences between people are more associated with life experiences—the ages of Boomers in 2018 range from 54 to 72 (Hughes and O'Rand, 2004). Living in post-war anxiety, the Boomers participated in anti-war movements, multiple revolutionary social activities, and, of course: "sex, drugs, and rock 'n roll" (Green and McClelland, 2019). As Baby Boomer men entered the workforce, they struggled economically. Boomers experienced the stress of shifting expectations from blue-collar work toward high-end white-collar work, requiring postsecondary credentials (Hughes and O'Rand, 2004). At the time, Boomer men lacked economic security, which harmed their ability to support a family and put further strain on their relationships. This fact is reflected in the Boomers reporting the most family-work conflicts of any other generation, including ranking highest in family centrality (Bennett, Beehr, and Ivanistkaya, 2017).

Millennials are a cohort that consists of many children of Baby Boomers. Millennials are not clearly defined in their birth years. However, many of them were born anywhere between the early 1980s to the early 2000s (Hegelson, 2017 and Kohut et al., 2010). Millennials have experienced a wide array of social movements, as a free sexual expression has become more widely accepted and encouraged than in any other generation before, and this is especially true for males. When it comes to the workforce, men are less likely to feel financial pressure to support themselves and their families (Kohut et al., 2010). Because of this, men are increasingly choosing professions that are more suited towards their own individual needs, having a more "loving what I do" attitude towards their career (Schawbel, 2012). Many Millennials see the Baby Boomer cohort as being the one that incurred the financial debt, leading to depression that lasted from 2007-2012, and from which society is still recovering (Gregoire, 2017; Schawbel, 2012; Stein, 2013).

Reference Framework

Confecámaras (2016) indicates that between 2011 and 2015, the number of formal companies increased by 15.7%. In 2011 the stock of companies in the country was 1,197,573 productive units, 280,620 societies, and 916,953 natural persons. Five years later, this stock amounted to 1,379,284, with a total of 370,318 companies and 1,008,996 natural persons. In this same period, a total of 1,033,211 signatures entered the market, and 991,911 were canceled, which is equivalent to an average gross entry or birth rate of 23.1% one and an exit rate of 19.5%. Thus, the average net entry rate is 3.6%. These figures indicate that in the country, for every 100 formal companies, 23 new companies enter the market, and around 19 come out.

The National Competitiveness Report (INC) for 2018-2019 shows some progress in infrastructure investment, health and education coverage, investment attraction, macroeconomic strength, royalty reform for non-renewable resource extraction, and reduction of unemployment and informality. Labor, poverty reduction and inequality, the end of the conflict against the FARC, and the entry into the OECD are just some of the country's recent achievements (Consejo Privado de Competitividad, 2018). In the Global Competitiveness Index elaborated by the World Economic Forum, Colombia moved from 61st place (among 140 countries) in 2015 to the 66th place (between 137) in 2017. With the new methodology, it moved from the 57th place (between 135) to the 60th position (between 140). In the Competitiveness Yearbook elaborated by the World Institute for Management Development (which compares Colombia with the 61 highest-level economies), the country dropped from 51st in 2015 to 58th in 2018. Finally, in the World Bank's Doing Business ranking, Colombia ranked from the 51st position to the 59th one in the same period.

Regarding university and business relations, which can enhance ideas, resources, research contracts, and joint publications or patents, it was found that between 2015 and 2017, 11 technology licenses from universities have been achieved through the OTRI. Other facilitating entities are technological development centers, innovation centers in companies, among others. Companies and the Government link the least number of researchers, although that is where there would be a more effective transfer of knowledge and technology. Regarding patents, patent applications had a significant increase in Colombia, as from 2,049 in 2007 to 18,552 in 2016. During this period, 3,110 patent applications were filed nationally. The number of patents filed nationally increased 163% in the period, from 235 in 2007 to 620 in 2016 (Consejo Privado de Competitividad, 2018, p. 354).

Regarding innovation, own resources constitute the primary source of financing for business ACTIs, with 73.4% in the services sector and 80.9% in industry. Private banking provides about 15% of funding for manufacturing companies and 11.3% for service companies. Public resources play a minimal role in manufacturing companies (0.6% of financing) and 4.6% for service companies (Figure 11). Between 2012 and 2016, investment in ACTI (technology and innovation) in the services sector and manufacturing industry was concentrated on machinery and equipment purchases and R&D activities (35.1% and 28.8% of the total, respectively). According to the DANE's Technological Development and Innovation Survey, the main obstacle that companies identify to innovate is the shortage of own resources (24% of companies). Secondly, there is the ease of imitation by third parties (19%) and uncertainty regarding the demand for innovative goods or services (17%). For those companies that intended to innovate, the main obstacles related to resources: both shortage of own resources and access to external financing to the company and information on public support instruments (Consejo Privado de Competitividad, 2018, p. 362).

Colombia Enterprises and Performance

Amid the implementation of the peace process agreements in Colombia signed in 2016, the priority of governments is focused on correcting low economic growth. Other indicators have had a stable behavior such as inflation - between 3% and 4% -, moderate interest, low volatility of the exchange rate, average economic growth - between 2% and 3% - the one-digit unemployment rate, and perception of investment-grade risk rating agencies (ANDI, 2018; Fedesarrollo, 2019; World Bank, 2019).

The country's competitiveness has made progress, measured in the World Bank's Doing Business ranking, from 76th place in 2006 to 34th in 2015, the year since stagnation is seen. As seen before, in the WEF's IGC, Colombia moved from 61st place (among 140 countries) in 2015 to 66th place (among 137) in 2017 and, with the recent methodological change, from 57th place (between 135) to 60th (between 140). In the Institute for World Competitiveness Yearbook Management Development (IMD), the country fell from 51st position in 2015 to 58th in 2018. These classifications show that the country has not progressed in the relative position in Latin America, either because Colombia moves back and other countries' progress, as is the case of Uruguay and Peru (Private Competitiveness Council, 2018; DNP, 2017; National Trade Council, 2018). The low productivity can be explained in part by the high transport costs concerning Latin America, a shortage of qualified technical talent according to the needs of the productive sector, precarious institutions, and low state capacities to solve problems such as corruption and to guarantee the presence of the State and the provision of public goods in rural areas. Second, the Colombian economy is still closed due to non-tariff barriers and cumbersome foreign trade procedures, and an inefficient tax system. Third, Colombia is weak in business innovation (Private Competitiveness Council, 2018; DNP, 2017; EAFIT, 2015; DNP, 2013). The source of future growth is in productivity, so Colombia must bet on development based on increased productivity (DNP, 2017; OECD, 2017). The State intends to encourage innovation with poor results: Between 2015 and 2017, 11 technology licenses were obtained from universities, PhDs are concentrated in academia rather than in companies (88.9 of researchers), the State and few researchers link, and the evolution of patent applications shows 2,049 applications in 2007 compared to 18,552 in 2016 (Private Competitiveness Council, 2018, p. 354; DNP, 2013).

During 2018, the manufacturing industry performed favorably; Between January and October 2018, production increased 3.2% and total sales 3.5% compared to 2017. Entrepreneurs consider that production was close to 3.1%, total sales of 3.3%, and Domestic sales 2.8% in the Joint Industrial Opinion Survey. Besides, the utilization of installed capacity was 79.8% for 2018, while in 2017, it reached 76.2%. Regarding the reported production, 87.6% rated their orders as high or usual in 2018, better than in 2017 (79.6%). Inventories of manufacturing production were high for 17.5% in 2018, according to business people, while in 2017, stocks rose to 21.4%. In general, the main obstacles for entrepreneurs during 2018 were the lack of demand, the cost of raw materials, aggressive marketing strategies, the exchange rate, smuggling, infrastructure and logistics costs, tax uncertainty, capital of work, legislation and portfolio (ANDI and La República, 2019; National Trade Council, 2018; DNP, 2017; Corporación Financiera Colombiana SA, 2017; Banco de la República, 2018).

The largest number of companies in Bogotá is in the activities of personal and business services (47%), commerce (32%), and manufacturing (12%). In 2018, 7995 industrial companies were created in Bogotá and the region, of which 99.2% microenterprises, 0.7 small, and 0.1% medium. 4.3 million people were employed in the same area. These jobs are generated in service activities (50.9%), in commerce (27.7%), in the industry (14.9%), and construction (5.6%); 59.6% of employment is salaried. In 2018, the liquidation of companies was concentrated in three sectors (82%), services (48%), commerce (34%), and industry (10%). 2,346 companies in the industry were liquidated, including microenterprises (94.3%), small (4.6%), medium (0.8%), large (0.3%) (Bogota Chamber of Commerce, 2019). Exports in 2018 were 35,000 million dollars, of which the industry made 15,483 million; The United States is the leading export destination (25.8%) of the total exported. The sector with the most significant increase in jobs was the manufacturing industry (58,000). The activities that increased the most were electricity, gas and water supply

(14.7%), mining and quarrying (10.6%), manufacturing industry (2.2%), community, social and personal services (1.1%), construction (0.9%), and financial intermediation (0.3%) (ANDI and La República, 2019, p. 45; Banco de la República, 2019).

According to GEM (2017), 18% of startups are being created by people aged between 50 and 64 years (13% by entrepreneurs aged between 65 and 80 years; 11% of young people aged between 18 and 29; and 18% of young adults aged between 30 and 49 years). Intention rates and entrepreneurial activity in their initial stages are higher in Africa (between 19% and 35%), followed by Latin America and the Caribbean (between 14% and 27%), and Europe (between 4% and 6%). These results are being explained by the differences between public policies to support entrepreneurship since, in countries with economies driven by production factors, fewer resources and investment are required compared to economies driven by efficiency or innovation supported by innovation and entrepreneurship ecosystems. The higher the country's development, the lower the rates of business creation, although its sustainability over time is more outstanding. Today, public policies to support entrepreneurship focus preferentially towards the younger population, although the results of GEM (2017) show an increase in new companies by senior and older people.

The creation of a company requires the entrepreneur to discover useful knowledge and its limits, in addition to using the information to face market imperfections (Kirzner, 1986). Management implies technical knowledge accompanied by soft skills - creativity, ability to work in multidisciplinary teams, and associative thinking to acquire new knowledge quickly and communication skills (Avvisati, Jacotin, and Vincent-Lancrin, 2013). Colombia is below the average for Latin America and below Mexico, Chile, Argentina, and Brazil in management practices (Center for Economic Performance, 2015). Particularly low is the performance of management in terms of operations management. This fact is reaffirmed in the IMD World Talent Ranking 2017, in which Colombia ranks 55th out of 63 economies. (Private Competitiveness Council, 2018, p. 363; DNP, 2013; DNP, 2018). One of the weaknesses of companies includes low innovation rates due to the poor quality of management (Private Competitiveness Council, 2018, p. 363). This weakness does not allow us to take advantage of the opportunities to incorporate technology and manage the changes necessary to adapt to various forms of competition (National Trade Council, 2018; DNP, 2013).

Management Operations

Management practices involve moving from an initial balance of forces to a specific situation that has been foreseen (Lykke, 1989: pp. 3-8). For Machiavelli, a great captain must take away fear, inflame the spirits, increase the determination, reveal the deceptions, promise rewards, raise the spirit with hopes, prayers, reproaches, and threats (Macciavelli, 2003: pp. 97-98). This fact implies that the strategy is a process that maintains a certain balance between ends, methods, and means; This means the identification of the objectives - the resources and methods available - to achieve them. The tactic, at some point, referred to the order, organization, and maneuvering of the troops (Freedman, 2016).

The management of power means using the influence of cunning and deception when it comes to business or small-scale business or personal matters. Freedman (2016). It also implies that while the competition plans and their responses to certain situations cannot be known precisely, only the laws of probability can be applied. For example, Churchill did not think of strategy as a blueprint for victory. He knew that the course of the war was unpredictable and that the steps towards success could not be visualized or clarified or discerned until they had to be taken. He distrusted concrete and perfectly defined calculations about how the war was going to be won. (Cohen, 1991: p. 66).

In the business context, it is difficult to identify or point out the reliable foundations for sustainable growth, not even for business survival (Carrol, 1983: pp. 78-88). The strategies involve improvising as in chess, which for some, is not a game but a well-defined form of computing. Although not all the answers are theoretically available, there must be a solution for each position. When the strategy is handled in real life, small tactics and tricks are used, in addition to asking what the other one that I want to do will think (Poundstone, 1992: p. 6). Boyd (1976), in his model of the strategic theory, presented as the OODA loop, which translates observation, orientation, decision, and action.

Freedman (2016) assimilates the strategies and, by extension, the management practices with the chaos theory, where one cannot assume the knowledge of cause and effect of a phenomenon nor allow reliable strategic calculations. Thus, the management practice seems a disorderly system marked by developments. As a result, people, society, culture, politics, ethics, economics and logistics, organization, administration, information and intelligence, strategic theory, business, technology, operability, command, geography, friction, chance, uncertainty, adversary, and time are considered doctrine (Gray, 1999: p. 23-43).

One way of exercising management practices, according to Kahneman (2003: pp. 697-720), implies that the manager operates with a certain number of heuristic principles that reduce the complex tasks of assessing probabilities and predicting values to simplify the operations of the trial. You can trust that, in general, heuristics are quite useful, but sometimes it leads to severe and systematic errors. Drucker also foresaw the management by objectives that are useful in the company along with the SWOT analysis and the Boston matrix. Henry Mintzberg had also questioned the so-called fixed model (design model) of the strategy, and he predicted the possibility that company managers would offer a continuous, attentive, and intelligent response to changing contexts. (Freedman, 2016).

Management practices have risks, including allowing business management models to replace analysis and common sense (Seeger, 1984: pp. 93-97). Mintzberg (1994) criticized and ended the reign of strategic planners, with few achievements, according to him, behind him and many dislikes and frustrations. Finally, a bad strategy expressed in bad management practice is just gibberish disguised as strategic concepts, referring to the inability to define the challenges that should be pursued, to mislead the strategic objectives, presenting only one desire without the means to achieve it, and explaining goals without considering their practical capacities (Rumelt, 2011: p. 77)

Blackman (2003) proposed relationships between entrepreneurs 'characteristics, values, and expectations, between their values and expectations and management practices, and between their management practices and business performance in the context of the SME in the industry.

Figure 1. The Management Practices of Blackman (2003)
Source: own elaboration from Blackman (2003)

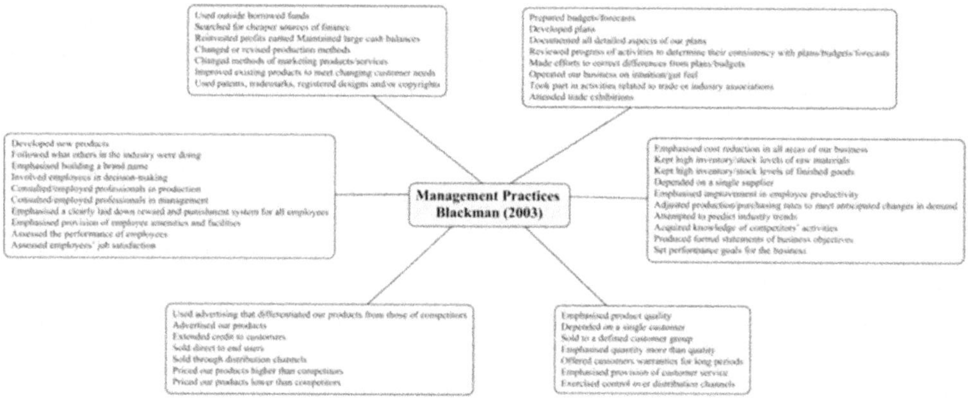

This research is based on the proposal of Blackman's model (2003). However, it focuses on age and management practices proposed and its relationship with the performance of senior entrepreneurs.

This model proposes other management variables that contribute to the durability of the organizations, such as personal attributes, the characteristics of entrepreneurs, their values, to relate them to the performance of SMEs. It is an exciting model that has not been applied in Colombia, although the measurement of the values, expectations, and even the performance of the entrepreneurs proposed is complex.

Figure 2. A theoretical model of the performance of SMEs based on values and expectations, characteristics, and practices of the entrepreneur
Source: Blackman (2003)

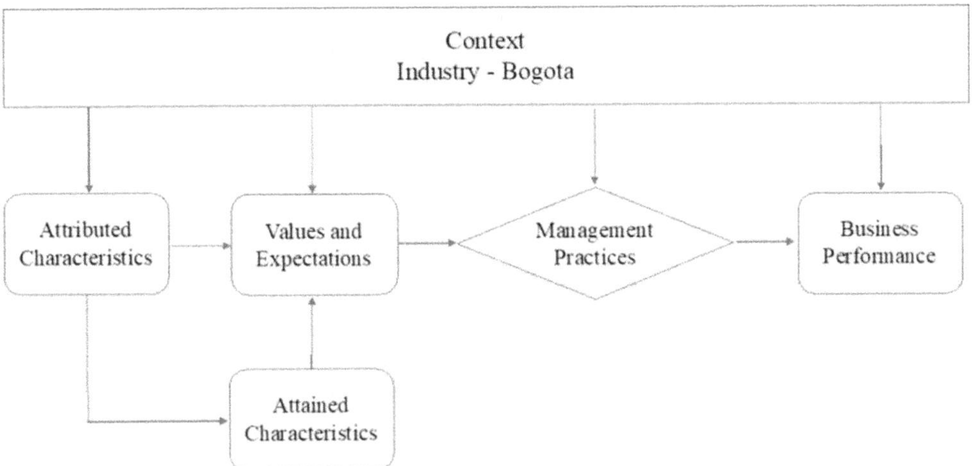

Methodological Design

The development of the research aims to determine the relationship between some beliefs, individual values, and management practices that the entrepreneurial population of Bogotá has analyzed from the possibilities of generational classification by their date of birth. Although theorizing around the behavior of generations could give important clues as to the differences that may exist between Baby Boomers, X-Gen, Millennials, and Centennials, it is possible to identify family, personal, and couple development. Few investigations have focused on determining the influence generations have on entrepreneurship. In this way, a descriptive design has been developed, taking into account what was raised by Hernández Sampieri, Férnandez Collado, and Baptista Lucio (2010). These investigations seek to specify the properties, characteristics, and profiles of people, groups, communities, processes, objects, or any phenomenon that is subjected to analysis.

With this definition and since the research had no pretensions to manipulate variables or the phenomenon of entrepreneurship, it is considered that this type of methodological design appropriately characterizes and articulates the study. However, establishing the relationship between categories, properties, or variables attributable to a population or a specific phenomenon can be done from many perspectives. For the particular case of the relationship between the characteristics identified in the scientific literature of generational studies and entrepreneurship in Bogotá, a statistical model was applied that allows to establish the statistical correlation between the two variables globally and to take into account specific characteristics for the characterization of generations as shown in Table 4.

Table 4. Variables, analysis categories, and sub-variables

Variable	Categoría de Análisis	Subcategorías de Análisis
Characteristics associated with Entrepreneurship	Value scale	Competencies y Capabilities Risk Honest Responsibility
	Managerial Practices Scale	Work in the provision of services and facilities.
Generation	Baby Boomers	Born from 1945 and 1964
	X-Gen	Born from 1965 and 1979
	Y-Gen (Millennials)	Born from 1980 and 2000

Source: own elaboration.

Results

The investigation includes secondary information recorded in various reports of the Chamber of Commerce, Ministry of Commerce, Industry and Tourism, Ministry of Finance, DANE, and ANDI, among others. The primary sources are surveys of 383 companies in the industry (see Table 5) from a database of the National Administrative Department of Statistics DANE, with 976,987 records of companies throughout the country. In 2018, Bogotá and the region had 487,141 companies, of which 58,600 (12%) are in the industry (Bogotá Chamber of Commerce, 2017; Unipymes, 2019).

The questionnaire is divided into four parts and has 45 questions. The first part collects information about the entrepreneur, country of origin, how his family nucleus and degree of schooling are formed. The second part asks for the basic knowledge of the company in aspects such as the year of creation, type of industry, the number of family members working in the company, and some necessary information about the planning activities that the company does. The third part evaluates with different scales the entrepreneurial perception on issues such as business goals and success, family, and business values. The fourth part examines the entrepreneur's management style and performance.

Table 5. Sample by sectors, number, and relative participation

International Standard Industrial Classification of All Economic Activities (ISIC)	Number	Relative participation
1300 Manufacture of knitted and crocheted fabrics / Manufacture of floor mats and carpets / Manufacture of ropes, cords, cables, bracelets, and nets / Manufacture of other textile articles n.c.p.	41	10.7%
1400 Manufacture of leather goods /Manufacture of knitted and crocheted items.	19	5.0%
1511 Tanning and retanning of leather; retanned and dyed skins	31	8.1%
1512 Manufacture of travel items, handbags, and similar items made of leather, and manufacture of saddlery and saddlery items	75	19.6%
1521 Manufacture of leather and leather footwear, with any type of sole	68	17.8%
1600 Transformation of wood and manufacture of wood and cork products, except furniture; manufacture of basketwork and wickerwork	47	12.3%
1800 Printing and copy production activities from original recordings	72	18.8%
2023 Manufacture of soaps and detergents, prepared for cleaning and polishing; perfumes and toilet preparations	5	1.3%
2500 Manufacture of fabricated metal products, except machinery and equipment	25	6.5%
Total	383	100.0%

Source: Own elaboration

Regarding the characterization of the sample, it was found:

1. Of the 383 entrepreneurs, 199 are men (52.0%) and 184 women (48.0%). It is noted that the presence of women has grown in the business world in the last ten years (Varela, Moreno, and Bedoya, 2015)
2. There are 382 Colombians and one Venezuelan, two with a foreign father (one from Ecuador and one from Venezuela), one from a Venezuelan mother. Colombia is a country of low migration (Yunis, 2009).
3. One hundred seventeen entrepreneurs had separate parents' homes.
4. Thirty-one of the entrepreneurs have an entrepreneurial father and 32 an entrepreneurial mother.
5. Sixty-one entrepreneurs finished high school in public school.

Regarding the way they are business owners, 105 bought it (27.5%), 219 founded it (57.5%), 55 inherited it (14%), and 4 acquired it in another way (1%). Generational studies are born from the perceived differences that have emerged in labor contexts, taking into account the age differences between different members of the same company. However, the analysis and curiosity that has arisen in researchers from different countries have allowed the development of various studies that have studied, among others, historical factors that directly influence social dynamics. In this way, it is possible to identify that political, social phenomena and, above all, those that are associated with the emergence of what some authors have called the fourth revolution and the digital age, play a determining role in human behavior. Information and communication technologies, the emergence and democratization of the internet, and all the phenomena that this has generated, increasingly make their influence on people's behaviors evident. From this perspective, García de Lombardía, Stein and Pin (2008), Inglehart (1997), Howe and Strauss (2000), Keeling (2003), Schneider and Stevenson (1999), and Vallejo Peña (2017) affirm political positions, religious beliefs, perception of the development of a life project, social ideals, and labor behavior are determined by the birthplace, childhood, and adolescence. This fact does not mean or imply that other cultural factors establish significant differences between young people, young adults, older adults, and people in old age. Comparing the establishment of couples between young people and young adults in the United States and Latin America, young people show a marked tendency to structure more reliable and durable family nuclei. At the same time, young adults take a little more time to decide to assume a couple of commitments mediated by religious institutions.

Based on the analysis categories of generations, the authors have classified the populations by taking into account the historical and cultural milestones that have marked the generational development. The entrepreneurs of the Bogotan industry, classified as SMEs, are characterized, as shown in Table 6.

Table 6. Categories of generations

Generation	Man	Woman	Total	% of population
Baby Boomer	22	26	48	13%
X-Gen	85	69	154	40%
Millennial	92	89	181	47%
TOTAL	199	184	383	100%

Source: own elaboration

The competences and capacities that an entrepreneur or manager of a company must have are differentially valued, taking into account the results found when analyzing the value that competencies and capabilities have for entrepreneurs, associated with specific areas of knowledge. In this way, there are perceptions for this subcategory of analysis that shows the following trend: the higher the age of the entrepreneurs, these competencies tend to be given less value than, although they are not directly related to the educational level. Yes, it could be associated with interest in learning processes. Consistent with what was found by (Bonelli 2015), Millennials tend to provide high levels of importance to the development of performance skills in the context of organizations. "Starting with the issues that concern them most and consider them important, young people ... ... first mention the study because it offers better job opportunities, then works because it allows you to earn money for greater economic stability, access to things you want and because it gives independence" (Bonelli, 2015).

Figure 3. Correspondence diagram: Skills / Generation
Source: own elaboration

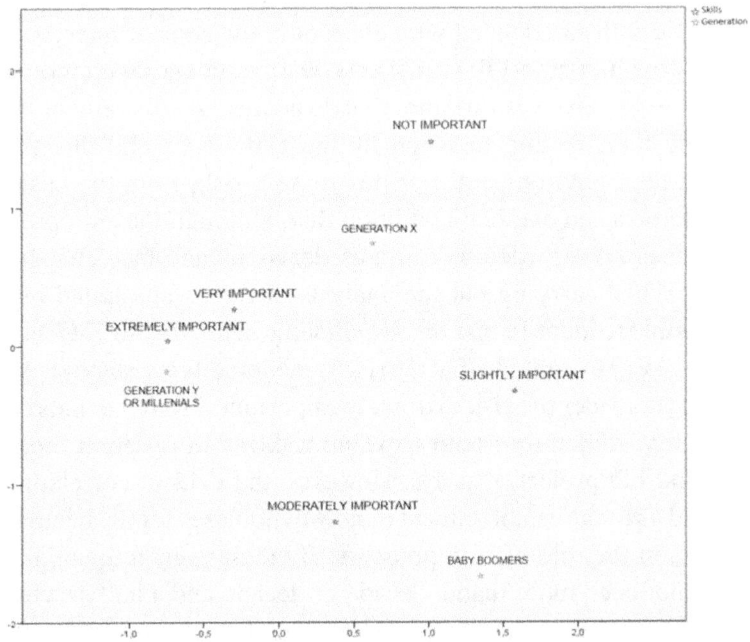

In the business context, it is difficult to identify or point out the reliable foundations for sustainable growth, even business survival. The age of the entrepreneur and his experience determine the success to reach the goals (Carroll, 1983).

Table 7. Goals and generations

Generation	Extremely Important	Very Important	Moderately Important	Slightly Important	Not Important	Total
Baby Boomer	19%	21%	23%	25%	13%	100%
X-Gen	34%	23%	16%	13%	14%	100%
Millennial	45%	28%	14%	6%	8%	100%

Source: own elaboration

As shown in Table 7, the results show that while 72% of millennials value competencies and skills as "Very Important" and "Extremely Important," only 56% of X-Gen entrepreneurs value them in the same way, and 40% of the Baby Boomers. This fact makes it possible to argue and strengthen the theoretical approaches that shape the idea that millennials differentially value work contexts that promote the development of specific skills associated with areas of knowledge of interest.

The development of managerial skills and the values associated with entrepreneurship can be conceived as variables that do not necessarily remain stable over time, considering their nature mediated by the experience and interaction that people have with their environment. For this reason, risk, from the business perspective, is considered as an external condition that, although the entrepreneur cannot control it, it must be regarded as to make decisions and face changes in the business context. When carrying out the analysis of the results found in this investigation, it is possible to identify that the respondents belonging to X-Gens and the Baby Boomers are closer to thinking that the risk is moderately substantial. At the same time, Millennials consider the risk extremely important. From the theoretical and empirical generality, millennials tend to value riskless in different areas of performance (labor and life project, mainly). However, the evident correlation in these results could lead us to the establishment of new hypotheses for the behavioral analysis of millennials in the role of entrepreneurs. By their ages, millennials are a generation that has not been more than a decade or decade and a half serving as head, owner, manager, or head of an organization. This fact could indicate that, unlike the generation of the baby boomers and the X Generation, Millennials so far are facing the consequences of improper risk management. In contrast, the people of the other two ages, with a high probability, they have had to face moments of crisis generated by internal and external factors to the organizations, thus developing skills to deal with these situations.

In practice, the strategy is based on negotiation, persuasion, words, and deeds, as well as physical and philosophical facts (Freedman, 2016).

Figure 4. Correspondence diagram: Risk / Generation
Source: own elaboration

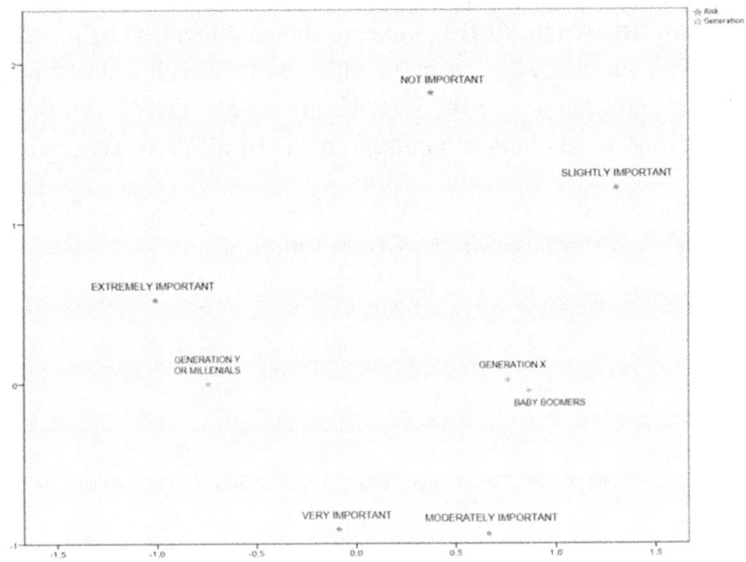

Management practices have risks, including allowing business management models to replace analysis and common sense (Seeger, 1984). Mintzberg (1994) criticized the reign of the planners. In this sample, it is evident that risk management is complex and seems to be related to age and experience that can become frustration according to the stage of life in which the small business owner locates.

Table 8. Management practices and Generations

Generation	Extremely Important	Very Important	Moderately Important	Slightly Important	Not Important	Total
Baby Boomer	21%	29%	23%	15%	13%	100%
X-Gen	25%	31%	22%	13%	10%	100%
Millennial	34%	31%	17%	9%	9%	100%

Source: own elaboration

The results show in Table 8 that, while 65% of millennials value risk as "Very Important" and "Extremely Important," only 55% of X-Gen entrepreneurs value them in the same way, and 50% of The Baby Boomers

The results found by Blackman (2013) indicate that the level of helplessness that entrepreneurs give to honesty and responsibility is negatively related to the occupational skill levels of the parents. In this way, it is possible to identify differences between the valuation that occurs between entrepreneurs of different generations.

Figure 5. Correspondence diagram: Honesty / Generation
Source: own elaboration

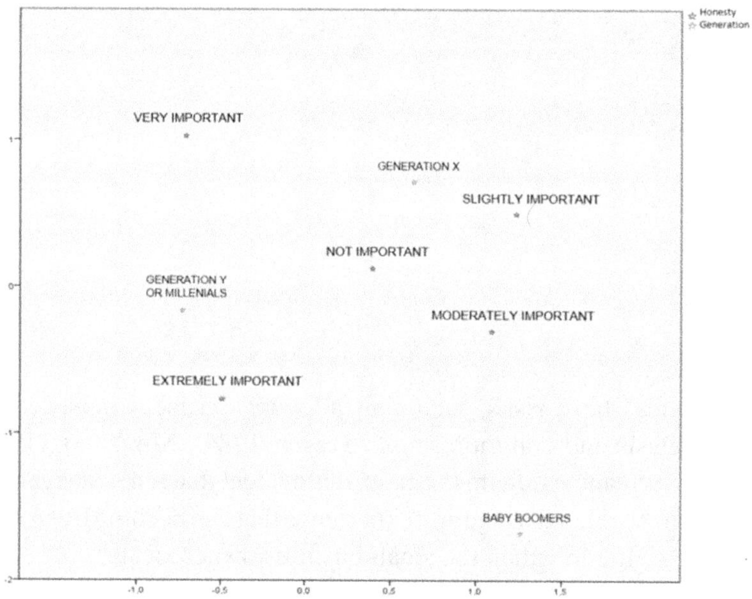

According to Kahneman (2003: P. 697-720), the manager operates with a certain number of heuristic principles that reduce the complex tasks of assessing probabilities and predicting values to simplify the operations of the business.

As seen in Table 9, X-Gen entrepreneurs are closer to those who consider honesty unimportant, while Millennials and Baby Boomers are closer to feeling it extremely important. In this way, it is possible to infer that Millennials are a generation that significantly values transparency in coherence with what is stated in the theoretical framework.

Management practices could be considered friction and uncertainty (Gray, 1999).

Table 9. Values and Generations

Generation	Extremely Important	Very Important	Moderately Important	Slightly Important	Not Important	Total
Baby Boomer	35%	15%	21%	17%	13%	100%
X-Gen	32%	22%	18%	17%	11%	100%
Millennial	42%	29%	10%	9%	10%	100%

Source: own elaboration

Figure 6. Correspondence diagram: Responsability / Generation
Source: own elaboration

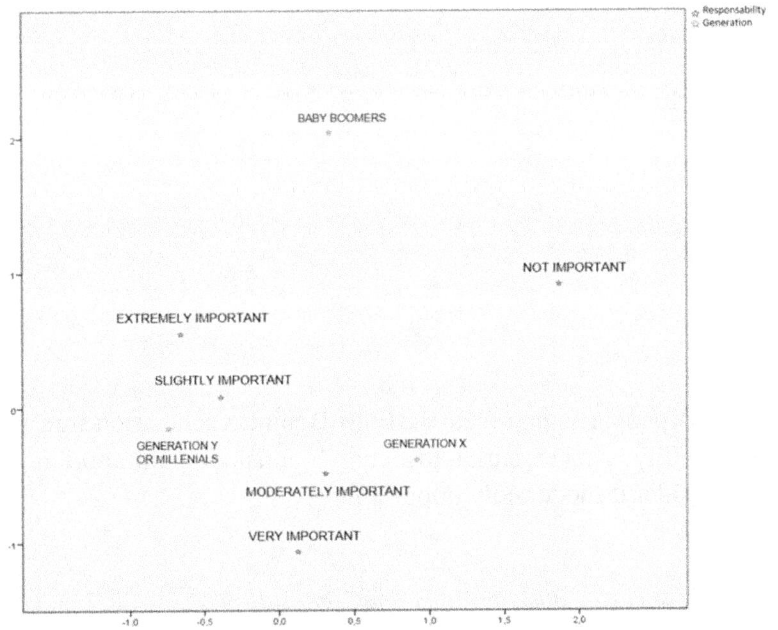

Table 10. Generations and Management practices

Generation	Extremely Important	Very Important	Moderately Important	Slightly Important	Not Important	Total
Baby Boomer	38%	19%	13%	13%	19%	100%
X-Gen	34%	27%	16%	6%	16%	100%
Millennial	44%	24%	14%	12%	6%	100%

Source: own elaboration

Figure 7. Correspondence diagram: Provision of services and facilities / Generation
Source: own elaboration

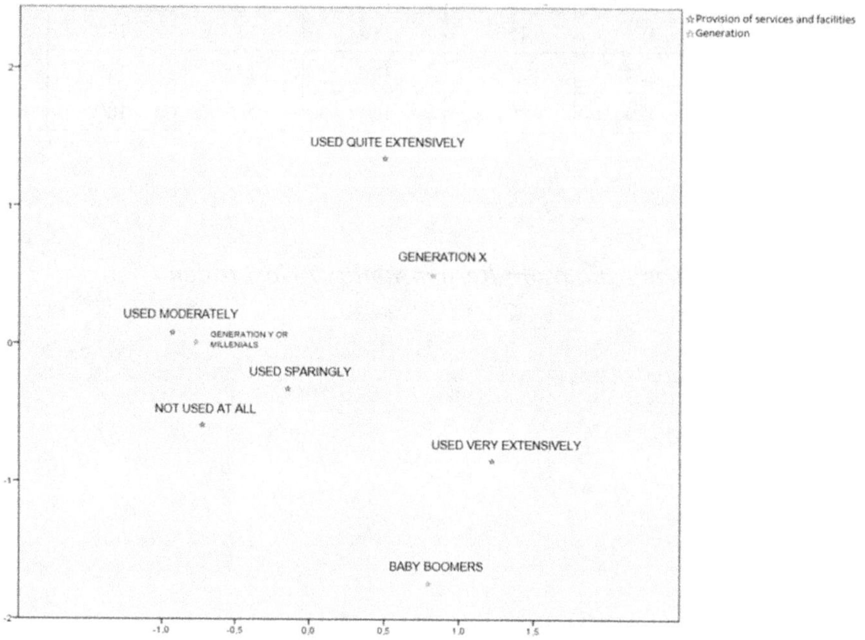

As seen in Table 10, people belonging to the Baby Boomers generation are among critical, and responsibility is not essential, Millennials consider it unimportant, and people of X-Gen consider it moderately important.

Table 11. Provision of services and facilities and Generations

Generation	Not Used at All	Use Extensively	Use Moderately	Use Very Intensively	Use Sparingly	Total
Baby Boomer	13%	21%	15%	29%	23%	100%
X-Gen	10%	27%	18%	26%	19%	100%
Millennial	18%	18%	30%	12%	22%	100%

Source: own elaboration

As seen in Table 11, people belonging to X-Gen worked extensively in the provision of services and facilities. Millennials worked moderately in this provision. In contrast, Baby Boomers worked hard to provide services and facilities.

Discussion of Results

Accompanied by an adequate policy framework, these companies, and in particular, their potentially more dynamic segments, could become a factor of change in Latin American economies carrying out tasks such as: contributing to increasing productivity through the introduction of technological changes and organizational. That way, they would act as agents that foster structural growth by helping to create and disseminate innovations and develop new markets (CEPAL/OCDE, 2012).

The State has to promote the entry of new companies encourages competition, as new business models that challenge the traditional ones are introduced by creating healthy turbulence that leads to the constant search for more productive use of resources (Altenburg and Eckhardt, 2006). It must also promote productive agglomerations, conceived as a collaboration between economic agents and institutions at the local level, to generate a competitive benefit (Ferraro, 2010; Dini and Stumpo, 2004). Well-managed SMEs contribute to social inclusion by increasing the income of microenterprises and reducing their vulnerability (Dini and Stumpo, 2019).

There is still little research with approaches and tools of company history and generations, especially in family businesses (see Lomnitz and Pérez-Lizaur 1987).

CONCLUSION

This study found a tendency to decrease jobs in the provision of services and facilities for generations, associated with current changes in the economic sectors.

Generations of Baby Boomers and X tend to value responsibility more than millennials, consistent with what is identified in the general literature.

Millennials value risk significantly, which could be because they are the youngest business generation that is leading organizations, and this means less experience in dealing with crises.

The development of skills and competencies tends to be most valued by millennials, concerning the generations of Baby Boomers and X, taking into account that markets increasingly demand higher levels of knowledge for the development of goods and products.

Integral analyzes of generations are essential for the design and implementation of strategies that facilitate generational transitions in family businesses, taking into account that these processes are affected in a multivariate way by many factors—one of them the differences between one generation and another.

REFERENCES

Allende, F. (2009). Poor Thomas Buddenbrook! Family business in literature. *Business & Economic History Online*, 1-27.

Begazo Villanueva, J., & Fernández Baca, W. (2015). Peruvian Millennials: Features and projections of life (Vols. 18-II). Lima, Perú: Gestión en el Tercer Milenio.

Blackman, A. J. (2003). *Entrepreneurs: Interrelationships between their characteristics, values, expectations, management practices, and SME performance*. Griffith University.

Bonelli, A. N. (2015). *Juventud Actual: ¿Tendencias egoístas o cuidar "lo propio" en un contexto marcado por la incertidumbre?* Buenos Aires: IX Congreso Argentino de Salud Mental – Lecturas de la memoria – Ciencia, clínica y política.

Boschma, J. (2008). *Generación Einstein. Más listos, más rápidos y más sociables*. Barcelona: Ediciones Gestión 2000.

Boyd, J. (1976). Destruction and Creation. In A Discourse of Winning and Losing. PN Editions.

Busenitz, L., West, G. P., Shepherd, D., Nelson, T., Chandler, G. N., & Zacharakis, A. (2001). *Entrepreneurship in emergence: Fifteen years of entrepreneurship research in management journals*. Paper presented at the Academy of Management meetings, Washington, DC.

Cabra-Torres, F., & Marciales-Vivas, G. (2009). Mitos, realidades y preguntas de investigación sobre los 'nativos digitales': Una revisión. *Universitas Psychologica*, *8*(2), 323–338.

Cámara de Comercio de Bogotá. (2017). *Balance de la economía de la región Bogotá- Cundinamarca 2016*. Cámara de Comercio.

Carrol, D. (1983). A disappointing Search for Excellence. *Harvard Business Review*, (November-December), 78–88.

Castro, W. (2017). *Factores que inciden en la quiebra de las pymes en Colombia basado en la administración del emprendimiento*. Universidad Militar Nueva Granada.

Cohen, E. (1991). Churchill and Coalition Strategy. In Grand Strategies in War and Peace. New Haven, CT: Yale University Press.

Colombia ANIF. (2017). *La Gran encuesta PYME Informe de Resultados 2do Semestre 2017*. Author.

Confecámaras. (2016). *Determinantes del crecimiento acelerado de las empresas en Confecámaras (2016)*. Nacimiento y supervivencia de las empresas en Colombia.

Confecámaras. (2017). *Determinantes de la supervivencia empresarial en Colombia*. Author.

Confecámaras. (2018). *7,3% incrementó la creación de empresas en el país en 2017*. Confecámaras.

Consejo Privado de Competitividad. (2018). *Informe Nacional de Competitividad 2018-2019*. Zetta Comunicadores.

Cuevas, H. (2007). *La empresa y los empresarios en la teoría económica*. Universidad Externado de Colombia.

DANE. (2018). *Estadisticas por tema industria*. Obtenido de https://www.dane.gov.co/index.php/estadisticas-por-tema/industria

DANE. (2018). *Indice de producción industrial*. Recuperado el 2018, de https://www.dane.gov.co/index.php/estadisticas-por-tema/industria/indice-de-produccion-industrial-ipi

Davila, M., Layrisse F., Lozano G., Rojas E., & Urbina, H. (2014). Las principales causas de fracaso de los negocios en México. *En el libro del fracas*, 140-159.

Dinero. (2016). *Mipymes generan alrededor del 67% del empleo en Colombia*. Dinero.

Dinero. (2017). *Una pyme colombiana genera 5 veces menos valor agregado que una gran empresa*. Dinero.

Dinero. (2018). *Los desafíos estructurales de las pymes en Colombia*. Dinero.

Dini, M., & Stumpo G. (2019). *Mipymes en América Latina: un frágil desempeño y nuevos desafíos para las políticas de fomento. Síntesis*. Documentos de Proyectos (LC/TS.2019/20), Santiago, Comisión Económica para América Latina y el Caribe (CEPAL).

Escandón-Barbosa, D., Arias, A., Medina, L., Gómez, L. V., & Parra, L. (2015). *Reporte GEM Colombia 2015/2016*. Ediciones Sello Javeriano.

Fernández Pérez, P. (2003). Reinstalando la empresa familiar en la Economía y la Historia Económica. Una aproximación a debates teóricos recientes. *Cuadernos de Economía y Dirección de la Empresa*, *17*, 45–66.

Ferrer, A. (2010). Millennials, la generación del siglo XXI. *Nueva Revista*, 130 (5).

Finra. (2018). *Uncertain Futures: 7 Myths about Millennials and Investing*. Charlottesville, VA: CFA Institute.

Franco, M., & Urbano, D. (2010, January). El Éxito de Las Pymes en Colombia. Un estudio de casos en el sector salud. *Estudios Gerenciales*, *26*(114), 77–96. doi:10.1016/S0123-5923(10)70103-0

Freedman, L. (2016). *Estrategia (Historia)* [Kindle iOS version]. Retrieved from Amazon.com.

Gámez, J. (2013). *Emprendimiento y creación de empresa. Teorías, modelos y casos*. Unisalle.

GEM. (2018). *Global Entrepreneurship Monitor. GLobal report 2017-2018*. GEM.

Geroski, P., Mata, J., & Portugal, P. (2007). *Founding Conditions and the Survival of New Firms*. Danish Research Unit for Industrial Dynamics.

Gértrudix, F., Durán, J., Gamonal, R., Galvez de la Cuesta, M., & García, F. (2010). *Una taxonomía del término "nativo digital". Nuevas formas de relación y de comunicación. Congreso Euro-Iberoamericano de Alfabetización Mediática y Culturas Digitales*. Universidad de Sevilla.

Global Entrepreneurship Monitor. (2015). *Leveraging Entrepreneurial Ambition and Innovation: A Global Perspective on Entrepreneurship, Competitiveness, and Development*. GEM.

González Domínguez, F. (2007). *Creación de empresas. Guía del emprendedor*. Pirámide.

Gray, C. (1999). *Modern Strategy*. Oxford University Press.

Green, A., & McClelland, C. (2019). Male Gender Expression Conflict Between Baby Boomers and Millennials. *Pepperdine Journal of Communication Research*, *7*(6), 1–15.

Gurd, B., & Thomas, J. (2012). Family business management: Contribution of the CFO. *International Journal of Entrepreneurial Behaviour & Research*, *18*(3), 286–304. doi:10.1108/13552551211227684

Guzmán, J., & Liñán, F. (2005). *Perspectives on Entrepreneurial Education: A US-Europe Comparison*. Jean Monnet European Studies Centre and Universidad Antonio de Nebrija.

Hayek, F. A. (1991). *The trend of economic thinking. Essays on political economists and economic history*. Taylor & Francis. doi:10.7208/chicago/9780226321363.001.0001

Hernández, I. (2008). *Empresa, innovación y desarrollo*. Universidad Nacional de Colombia.

Hernández Sampieri, R., Férnandez Collado, C., & Baptista Lucio, P. (2010). *Metodología de la Investigación*. McGraw-Hill.

Institute of Child Nutrition. (2018). *Managing Personalities and Conflict. Participant's Workbook*. The University of Mississippi, School of Applied Sciences.

Kahneman, D. (2003). A Perspective on Judgment and Choice: Mapping Bounded Rationality. *The American Psychologist*, *56*(9), 697–720. doi:10.1037/0003-066X.58.9.697

Kautonen, T. (2013). *Senior entrepreneurship*. OECD.

Kim, K., Knotts, T., & Jones, S. (2008). Characterizing viability of small manufacturing enterprises (SME) in the market. *Expert Systems with Applications*, *34*(1), 128–134. doi:10.1016/j.eswa.2006.08.009

Kirzner, I. (1986). Entrepreneurial Discovery and the Competitive Market Process: An Austrian Approach. *Journal of Economic Literature*, *35*(1), 60–85.

Knight, F. (1942). Profit and Entrepreneurial Functions. *The Journal of Economic History*, *2*, 126-132.

Koc, T., & Bozdag, E. (2007). Empirical research for CNC technology implementation in manufacturing SMEs. *International Journal of Advanced Manufacturing Technology*, *34*(11-12), 1144–1152. doi:10.100700170-006-0681-5

Kraus, S., Harms, R., & Schwarz, E. (2006). Strategic planning in smaller enterprises - new empirical findings. *Management Research News*, *29*(6), 334–344. doi:10.1108/01409170610683851

Lansberg, I. (1983). Managing Human Resources in Family Firms: The Problem of Institutional Overlap. *Organizational Dynamics*, *12*(1), 39–46. doi:10.1016/0090-2616(83)90025-6

Luna Correa, J. (2013). *Influencia del capital humano para la competitividad de las PYMES en el sector manufacturero de Celaya Guanajuato* (Tesis Doctoral). Universidad de Celaya, Mexico.

Lykke, A. (1989). *Toward an Understanding of Military Strategy. Military Strategy: Theory and Application*. US Army War College.

Macciavelli, N. (2003). The prince. University of Chicago Press. doi:10.7208/chicago/9780226500324.001.0001

Manrique, G. (2013). Revisión conceptual y definición del término emprendimiento para la tecnología en gestión industrial. *Revista Estrategia Organizacional, 21*, 181–192.

Mauno, S., Kinnunen, U., Makikangas, A., & Natti, J. (2005). Psychological Consequences of Fixed-Term Employment and Perceived Job Insecurity among Health Care Staff. *European Journal of Work and Organizational Psychology, 14*(3), 209–237. doi:10.1080/13594320500146649

Microempresas–OCM. (2007). Estadísticas de la Microempresa en Colombia. Análisis comparativo 1990 – 2005, Bogota, Colombia.

Mintzberg, H. (1994). *The Rise and Fall of Strategic Planning*. Prentice-Hall.

Misanková, M., & Kocisová, K. (2012). Strategic Implementation as a Part of Strategic Management. *Procedia: Social and Behavioral Sciences, 110*, 861–870. doi:10.1016/j.sbspro.2013.12.931

MontenegroA. (2019). *ANIF*. Retrieved from http://www.anif.co/Biblioteca/politica-fiscal/notas-sobre-la-reforma-tributaria

Montilla Carmon, M., & Montero Caro, M. (2011). *Fudepa*. Desarrollo Empresarial y Emprendedores.

Moriano, J. (2005). El perfil psicosocial del emprendedor. Madrid, Spain: CES (Consejo Económico y Social).

Mouján, H. (2006). *Cómo desarrollar microemprendimientos*. Longseller.

Ooghe, H., & Prijcker, S. (2007). Failure processes and causes of company bankruptcy: A typology. *Management Decision, 46*(2), 223–232. doi:10.1108/00251740810854131

Pardo, C., & Alfonso, W. (2018). Por qué los negocios fracasan en Colombia? (U. d. Colciencias, Ed.). Academic Press.

Pereira, F. (2007). *La evolución del espíritu empresarial como campo del conocimiento. Hacia una visión sistémica y humanista. Cuadernos de Administración*. Universidad Javeriana.

Poundstone, W. (1992). Prisoner's Dilemma. Academic Press.

Quinn, R., & Rohrbaugh, J. (1983). A spatial model of effectiveness criteria: Towards a competing values approach to organizational analysis. *Management Science, 29*(3), 363–377. doi:10.1287/mnsc.29.3.363

Rabellotti, R. (1997). *External Economies and Cooperation in Industrial Districts: a Comparison of Italy and Mexico*. Macmillan. doi:10.1007/978-1-349-25794-2

Rumelt, R. (2011). *Good Strategy, Bad Strategy: The Difference and Why it Matters*. Profile Books.

Sanabria, N. (2012). *Perdurabilidad empresarial. Anotaciones teóricas*. Universidad Autónoma del Caribe.

Sánchez, R. (2018). *Panorama laboral en Colombia: situación reciente y desafíos*. UN Periódico, Bogota, Colombia.

Schumpeter, J. (1939). *Ciclos económicos. Análisis teórico, histórico y estadístico del proceso capitalista*. Prensas Universitarias de Zaragoza.

Seco, C. (2018). *Aging and Entrepreneurship: Firm Creation and Performance among Older Individuals*. Universidade de Lisboa.

Seeger, J. A. (1984). Reversing the Images of BCG's Growth/Share Matrix. *Strategic Management Journal, 5*(1), 93–97. doi:10.1002mj.4250050107

Tapscott, D. (1998). *Growing up digital: The rise of the Net generation*. McGraw-Hill.

Tavizón, A., & Cortes, K. (2016). *Vinculación estratégica en las organizaciones*. Pearson.

UN-Cepal. (2004). *Pequeñas y medianas empresas y eficiencia colectiva: estudios de caso en América Latina*. Mexico: Siglo veintiuno editores.

Vallejo Peña, A. (2017). *La Generación Y ante el desafío de su incersión laboral: Realidades frente a estereotipos*. Arbor.

Varela, R., Moreno, J., & Bedoya, M. (2014). *Colombian Entrepreneurial Dynamics*. Global Entrepreneurship Monitor.

Zapata Guerrero, E. (2004). Las Pymes y su problemática empresarial. Analisis de Casos. *Revista EAN, 52*, 119–135.

KEY TERMS AND DEFINITIONS

Baby Boomers: It is the population born between 1946 and 1964.

Boston Matrix: Also called the BCG Matrix, it is a graphical method of business portfolio analysis used to analyze portfolios and brands.

Family Business: It is a type of enterprise defined by having at least two partners with the same consanguinity up to the second degree, or partners being married.

Supply Chain: It is an industrial or a commercial network between a company and its suppliers to produce and distribute a specific product o service to the final consumer.

SWOT Analysis: It is a tool for studying the situation of a company, institution, project, or person, analyzing its internal characteristics and its external position.

X-Gen: It is the population born between 1965 and 1976.

Y-Gen: Also known as Millennials, they integrate the population born between 1977 and 1995.

Z-Gen: Also known as Centennials, they are the population born between 1995 and 2012. The Alpha generation follows them.

Compilation of References

Abramo, P. (2012). La ciudad confusa: Mercado y producción de la estructura urbana en las grandes metrópolis latinoamericanas. *EURE. Revista Latinoamericana de Estudios Urbano Regionales*, *38*(114), 35–69. doi:10.4067/S0250-71612012000200002

Acharya, A., Singh, S. K., Pereira, V., & Singh, P. (2018). Big data, knowledge co-creation, and decision making in the fashion industry. *International Journal of Information Management*, *42*, 90–101. doi:10.1016/j.ijinfomgt.2018.06.008

Acosta Véliz, M. M., Coronel Pérez, V., & Jiménez Cercado, M. (2018). Emprendimiento Social Y Su Relación Con La Base De La Pirámide En Latinoamérica. *3C Empresa. Investigación y Pensamiento Crítico*, *7*(4), 50–67. doi:10.17993/3cemp.2018.070436.50-67/

Agencia Nacional del Espectro. (2010). *Cartilla #1*. Conceptos del Espectro Radioeléctrico.

Agencia Nacional del Espectro. (2010). *Cartilla #2*. Gestión del Espectro.

Agencia Nacional del Espectro. (2010). Cartilla #3. Uso eficiente del Espectro Radioeléctrico. Author.

Agencia Nacional del Espectro. (2016). *Cuadro Nacional de Atribución de Bandas de Frecuencia*. Author.

Agencia Nacional del Espectro. (2017). *Manual de Calidad*. Author.

Ahmad, Z., Menon, A. S., Mason, C., Shamsudin, M. F., & Sentosa, I. (2020). Does social media engagement moderate brand engagement and brand loyalty? Evidence from young consumers of Malaysian modest fashion industry. *International Journal of Psychosocial Rehabilitation*, *24*(2), 2500–2508. doi:10.37200/IJPR/V24I2/PR200546

Alali, F., Elder, R., & Zhou, J. (2019). An Analysis of Big 4 Pricing and Firm Size: The Differential Impact of Demand and Supply Shocks on Large and Small Clients. *Journal of Accounting, Auditing & Finance*, *34*(2), 204–230. doi:10.1177/0148558X17704555

Allende, F. (2009). Poor Thomas Buddenbrook! Family business in literature. *Business & Economic History Online*, 1-27.

Allon, G., Bassamboo, A., & Çil, E. B. (2019). Large-Scale Service Marketplaces: The Role of the Moderating Firm. In M. Hu (Ed.), *Sharing Economy. Making Supply Meet Demand* (pp. 165–192). Springer Nature Switzerland. doi:10.1007/978-3-030-01863-4_9

Álvarez-Aros, E., & Bernal-Torres, C. (2017). Modelo de Innovación Abierta: Énfasis en el Potencial Humano. *Información Tecnológica*, *28*(1), 65–76. doi:10.4067/S0718-07642017000100007

Alvira, M. F. (2011). La encuesta: una perspectiva general metodológica. Madrid, Spain: Centro de Investigaciones Sociologicas (CIS)

Amed, I., Berg, A., Brantberg, L., & Hedrich, S. (2016). *The state of fashion 2017*. Retrieved from https://www.mckinsey.com/industries/retail/our-insights/the-state-of-fashion

Aoaeh, B. L., & Morales-Hellebo, L. (2018). *Where will technological disruption in the fashion supply chain come from?* Retrieved from http://www.refashiond.com/blog/2018/10/25/where-will-technological-disruption-in-the-fashion-supply-chain-come-from

Artesanías de Colombia. (n.d.). *Canasto Werregue Mediano*. https://artesaniasdecolombia.com.co/PortalAC/Productos/canasto-Werregue-mediano_284

Assenova, V. A., & Sorenson, O. (2017). Legitimacy and the benefits of firm formalization. *Organization Science*, *28*(5), 804–818. doi:10.1287/orsc.2017.1146

Audretsch, D. B., & Keilbach, M. (2004). Does entrepreneurship capital matter? *Entrepreneurship Theory and Practice*, *28*(5), 419–429. doi:10.1111/j.1540-6520.2004.00055.x

Austin, J., Stevenson, H., & Wei-Skillern, J. (2012). Social and commercial entrepreneurship: Same, different, or both? *Revista ADM*, *47*(3), 370–384. doi:10.5700/rausp1055

Austin, J., Svenson, H., & Skilem, J. (2006). Social and commercial entrepreneurship: Some, different, or both. *Entrepreneurship Theory and Practice*, *30*(1), 1–22. doi:10.1111/j.1540-6520.2006.00107.x

B., J., Cantillon, R., & Higgs, H. (1932). Essai sur la Nature du Commerce en General. *Journal of the Royal Statistical Society, 95*(1), 131. doi:10.2307/2341977

Bailey, S., & Baker, J. (2014). *Moda y visual merchandising*. Gustavo Gili.

Balachandra, P., Kristle Nathan, H. S., & Reddy, B. S. (2010). Commercialization of sustainable energy technologies. *Renewable Energy*, *35*(8), 1842–1851. doi:10.1016/j.renene.2009.12.020

Ballard, G. (2008). *Our History - Power to Change the World | Ballard Power*. Retrieved January 16, 2020, from https://www.ballard.com/about-ballard/our-history

Balsam, S., Krishnan, J., & Yang, J. S. (2003). Auditor industry specialization and earnings quality. *Auditing*, *22*(2), 71–97. doi:10.2308/aud.2003.22.2.71

Barbosa-Póvoa, A. P., da Silva, C., & Carvalho, A. (2018). Opportunities and challenges in sustainable supply chain: An operations research perspective. *European Journal of Operational Research*, *268*(2), 399–431. doi:10.1016/j.ejor.2017.10.036

Bargsted, A. M. (2013). El emprendimiento social desde una mirada psicosocial. *Civilizar*, *13*(25), 121–132. doi:10.22518/16578953.133

Barkova, N. (2018). Mass customization in the fashion industry. *Vestnik Universiteta*, *5*(5), 85–90. doi:10.26425/1816-4277-2018-5-85-90

Basak, A., Seddiqe, M. I. S., Islam, M. R., & Akanda, M. O. F. (2014). Supply chain management in garments industry. *Global Journal of Management and Business Research*, *14*(11), 23–28.

Becker, S., Kunze, C., & Vancea, M. (2017). Community energy and social entrepreneurship: Addressing purpose, organisation and embeddedness of renewable energy projects. *Journal of Cleaner Production*, *147*, 25–36. doi:10.1016/j.jclepro.2017.01.048

Begazo Villanueva, J., & Fernández Baca, W. (2015). Peruvian Millennials: Features and projections of life (Vols. 18-II). Lima, Perú: Gestión en el Tercer Milenio.

Bello, H. S. (2019). Female Entrepreneurship in the African Fashion Industry: A Review of Its Determinants and Characteristics. In C. Moreno-Gavara & A. I. Jiménez-Zarco (Eds.), *Sustainable Fashion*. Palgrave Studies of Entrepreneurship in Africa., doi:10.1007/978-3-319-91265-3_5

Benegas, L. A. (2002). *Telecomunicaciones para comunicarse eficientemente - Libertas 19*. Eseade.

Benjaafar, S., Kong, G., Li, X. X., & Courcoubetis, C. (2019). Peer-to-Peer Product Sharing (pp. 11-36). In Sharing Economy. Making Supply Meet Demand. Springer Nature Switzerland.

Benton, D. (2018). *Exclusive interview: Bolloré logistics, sustainability development manager, mathilde dumoulin*. Retrieved from https://www.supplychaindigital.com/company/exclusive-interview-bollore-logistics-sustainability-development-manager-mathilde-dumoulin#

Bernal-Torres, C. A., & Frost-González, S. (2015). Innovación abierta en empresas colombianas: Reto a superar. *Revista Venezolana de Gerencia*, *13*(70), 262–267. doi:10.31876/revista.v20i70.19996

Berry, G., & Aceves, S. (2006). La Economía del Hidrógeno como Solución al Problema de la Estabilización del Clima Mundial. *Acta Universitaria*, *16*(1), 5–14. doi:10.15174/au.2006.192

Bertelsmann, F. (2019). *Emprendimiento Social Juvenil*. Academic Press.

Bertoletti, P., & Etro, F. (2017). Monopolistic Competition When Income Matters. *Economic Journal (London)*, *127*(603), 1217–1243. doi:10.1111/ecoj.12329

Björgvinsson, E., Ehn, P., & Hillgren, P. (2010). Participatory design and democratizing innovation. In *Proceedings of the 11th Biennial Participatory Design Conference* (pp. 41-50). Sydney: ACM. 10.1145/1900441.1900448

Blackman, A. J. (2003). *Entrepreneurs: Interrelationships between their characteristics, values, expectations, management practices, and SME performance*. Griffith University.

Bloom, R., & Schirm, D. (2008). An analysis of the GAO study on audit market concentration. *The CPA Journal*, *78*(4), 6.

Bockris, J. (1972). *A Hydrogen Economy*. Academic Press.

Bockris, J. (2013). The hydrogen economy: Its history. *International Journal of Hydrogen Energy*, *38*(6), 2579–2588. doi:10.1016/j.ijhydene.2012.12.026

BOF & McKinsey. (2020). *The State of Fashion Report 2019*. Available online: https://www.businessoffashion.com/articles/intelligence/the-state-of-fashion-2019

Bonelli, A. N. (2015). *Juventud Actual: ¿Tendencias egoístas o cuidar "lo propio" en un contexto marcado por la incertidumbre?* Buenos Aires: IX Congreso Argentino de Salud Mental – Lecturas de la memoria – Ciencia, clínica y política.

Boschma, J. (2008). *Generación Einstein. Más listos, más rápidos y más sociables*. Barcelona: Ediciones Gestión 2000.

Bowersox, D. J., Closs, D. J., & Drayer, R. W. (2005). The digital transformation: Technology and beyond. *Supply Chain Management Review*, *9*(1), 22–29.

Boyd, J. (1976). Destruction and Creation. In A Discourse of Winning and Losing. PN Editions.

Bravo-Ibarra, E. R., León-Arenas, A. P., & Serrano-Cárdenas, L. F. (2014). Explorando las principales ventajas y factores de éxito de la innovación abierta en las organizaciones. *Revista Entramado*, *25*, 44–59. doi:10.18041/entramado.2014v10n2.20220

Brun, A., Caniato, F., Caridi, M., Castelli, C., Miragliotta, G., Ronchi, S., Sianesi, A., & Spina, G. (2008). Logistics and supply chain management in the luxury fashion retail: Empirical investigation of Italian firms. *International Journal of Production Economics*, *114*(2), 554–570. doi:10.1016/j.ijpe.2008.02.003

Brun, A., & Castelli, C., RayeCarol, C., & Doris, K. (2015). A luxury brand management framework built from historical review and case study analysis. *International Journal of Retail & Distribution Management*, *43*(10/11), 1083–1100. doi:10.1108/ijrdm-07-2014-0103

Busenitz, L., West, G. P., Shepherd, D., Nelson, T., Chandler, G. N., & Zacharakis, A. (2001). *Entrepreneurship in emergence: Fifteen years of entrepreneurship research in management journals*. Paper presented at the Academy of Management meetings, Washington, DC.

Cabra-Torres, F., & Marciales-Vivas, G. (2009). Mitos, realidades y preguntas de investigación sobre los 'nativos digitales': Una revisión. *Universitas Psychologica*, *8*(2), 323–338.

Cadena, E. (2013). *Gestión del Espectro Radioeléctrico en Colombia*. Universidad Distrital Francisco José de Caldas.

Cajaiba, G. (2014). Social innovation: Moving the field forward. A conceptual framework. *Technological Forecasting and Social Change*, *82*, 42–51. doi:10.1016/j.techfore.2013.05.008

Calvo-Porral, C., & Calvo-Dopico, D. (2011). "Carolina Herrera" Internationalization Strategy: Democratic Luxury or Maximum Exclusiveness? *European Research Studies*, *14*(2), 3–25.

Cámara de Comercio de Bogotá. (2017). *Balance de la economía de la región Bogotá-Cundinamarca 2016*. Cámara de Comercio.

Camarena, D. E. S. (2002). La intervención institucional en las micro y pequeñas empresas de la industria del calzado de Guadalajara. *México y la Cuenca del Pacífico*, (17), 53–59. doi:10.32870/mycp.v5i17.178

Carrol, D. (1983). A disappointing Search for Excellence. *Harvard Business Review*, (November-December), 78–88.

Cassagnard, P., & Regibeau, P. (2018). *Collective Entry Deterrence and Free Riding: Airbus and Boeing in China*. https://hal-univ-pau.archives-ouvertes.fr/hal-02141056

Castro, W. (2017). *Factores que inciden en la quiebra de las pymes en Colombia basado en la administración del emprendimiento*. Universidad Militar Nueva Granada.

CB Insights Research. (2019). *Fashion forward: How tech is targeting waste & pollution in the $2.4t fashion industry*. Retrieved from https://www.cbinsights.com/research/fashion-sustainable-technology/

Cerruti, C., Mena, C., Skipworth, H., & Tavoletti, E. (2016). Characterizing agile supply partnerships in the fashion industry. *International Journal of Operations & Production Management, 36*(8), 923–947. doi:10.1108/IJOPM-03-2015-0181

Chandler, G. N., DeTienne, D. R., McKelvie, A., & Mumford, T. V. (2011). Causation and effectuation processes: A validation study. *Journal of Business Venturing, 26*(3), 375–390. doi:10.1016/j.jbusvent.2009.10.006

Cheng, Y.-L., & Tabuchi, T. (2019). First mover advantage by product proliferation in multiproduct duopoly. *International Journal of Economic Theory*. doi:10.1111/ijet.12242

Chen, Y. T., & Hsu, C. W. (2018). The key factors affecting the strategy planning of Taiwan's hydrogen economy. *International Journal of Hydrogen Energy*, 3290–3305. doi:10.1016/j.ijhydene.2018.07.159

Chesbrough, H. (2006). *Open Innovation. The new imperative for creating and profiting from technology*. Harvard Business School Press.

Chu, L., Simunic, D. A., Ye, M., & Zhang, P. (2018). Transaction costs and competition among audit firms in local markets. *Journal of Accounting and Economics, 65*(1), 129–147. doi:10.1016/j.jacceco.2017.11.004

Cillo, P., De Luca, L. M., & Troilo, G. (2010). Market information approaches, product innovativeness, and firm performance: An empirical study in the fashion industry. *Research Policy, 39*(9), 1242–1252. doi:10.1016/j.respol.2010.06.004

Claxton, S., & Kent, A. (2020). The management of sustainable fashion design strategies: An analysis of the designer's role. *Journal of Cleaner Production, 268*, 122112. doi:10.1016/j.jclepro.2020.122112

Cohen, E. (1991). Churchill and Coalition Strategy. In Grand Strategies in War and Peace. New Haven, CT: Yale University Press.

Cohen, B., & Winn, M. I. (2007). Market imperfections, opportunity and sustainable entrepreneurship. *Journal of Business Venturing, 22*(1), 29–49. doi:10.1016/j.jbusvent.2004.12.001

Collis, J. (2012). Determinants of voluntary audit and voluntary full accounts in micro-and non-micro small companies in the UK. *Accounting and Business Research, 42*(4), 441–468. doi:10.1080/00014788.2012.667969

Colombia ANIF. (2017). *La Gran encuesta PYME Informe de Resultados 2do Semestre 2017.* Author.

Colucci, M., Tuan, A., & Visentin, M. (2020). An empirical investigation of the drivers of CSR talk and walk in the fashion industry. *Journal of Cleaner Production, 248*, 119200. doi:10.1016/j.jclepro.2019.119200

Confecámaras. (2016). *Determinantes del crecimiento acelerado de las empresas en Confecámaras (2016).* Nacimiento y supervivencia de las empresas en Colombia.

Confecámaras. (2017). *Determinantes de la supervivencia empresarial en Colombia.* Author.

Confecámaras. (2018). *7,3% incrementó la creación de empresas en el país en 2017.* Confecámaras.

Consejo Privado de Competitividad. (2018). *Informe Nacional de Competitividad 2018-2019.* Zetta Comunicadores.

Craswell, A. T., Francis, J. R., & Taylor, S. L. (1995). Auditor brand name reputations and industry specializations. *Journal of Accounting and Economics, 20*(3), 297–322. doi:10.1016/0165-4101(95)00403-3

Cravens, D. W., Lassk, F. G., Low, G. S., Marshall, G. W., & Moncrief, W. C. (2004). Formal and informal management control combinations in sales organizations: The impact on salesperson consequences. *Journal of Business Research, 57*(3), 241–248. doi:10.1016/S0148-2963(02)00322-3

Cuevas, H. (2007). *La empresa y los empresarios en la teoría económica.* Universidad Externado de Colombia.

Cuevas, J. G. (1994). Towards a Taxonomy of Entrepreneurial Theories. *International Small Business Journal, 12*(4), 77–88. Advance online publication. doi:10.1177/0266242694124005

Curwen, P., & Whalley, J. (2017). The evolution of US mobile operators within a multi-play world. *Digital Policy, Regulation and Governance.*

D'Avolio, E., Bandinelli, R., & Rinaldi, R. (2016). How Product Development Can Be Improved in Fast Fashion Industry: An Italian Case. *IFIP International Conference on Product Lifecycle Management (PLM) 2015: Product Lifecycle Management in the Era of Internet of Things*, 718-728. 10.1007/978-3-319-33111-9_65

Da Giau, A., Foss, N. J., Furlan, A., & Vinelli, A. (2020). Sustainable development and dynamic capabilities in the fashion industry: A multi-case study. *Corporate Social Responsibility and Environmental Management*, *27*(3), 1509–1520. doi:10.1002/csr.1891

Dacin, P. A., Dacin, M. T., & Matear, M. (2010). Social entrepreneurship: Why we don't need a new theory and how we move forward from here. *The Academy of Management Perspectives*, *24*(3), 37–57.

DANE. (2018). *Estadísticas por tema industria*. Obtenido de https://www.dane.gov.co/index.php/estadisticas-por-tema/industria

DANE. (2018). *Indice de producción industrial*. Recuperado el 2018, de https://www.dane.gov.co/index.php/estadisticas-por-tema/industria/indice-de-produccion-industrial-ipi

Davila, M., Layrisse F., Lozano G., Rojas E., & Urbina, H. (2014). Las principales causas de fracaso de los negocios en México. *En el libro del fracas*, 140-159.

Davila, A., & Foster, G. (2005). Management accounting systems adoption decisions: Evidence and performance implications from early-stage/startup companies. *The Accounting Review*, *80*(4), 1039–1068. doi:10.2308/accr.2005.80.4.1039

Davila, T., Epstein, M., & Shelton, R. (2008). *Making Innovation Work, How to Manage It, Measure It, and Profit from It*. Seventh Printing & Pearson Education.

De Pablo, V., & Uribe, J. (Coords.). (2017). Experiencias de emprendimiento social en Iberoamérica. Almeria, Spain: Universidad de Almería.

Dee, C. C., Lulseged, A. A., & Zhang, T. (2010). *Client Stock Market Reaction to PCAOB Sanctions Against a Big Four Auditor* (SSRN Scholarly Paper ID 1598401). Social Science Research Network. https://papers.ssrn.com/abstract=1598401

Dees, J. G. (1998). *The Meaning of "Social Entrepreneurship."* Academic Press.

Dees, J. G. (1998). Enterprising non-profits. *Harvard Business Review*, *76*, 54–69.

Deloitte. (2019). *Global Powers of Luxury Goods 2019. Bridging the gap between the old and the new*. Author.

Díaz-Foncea, M., & Marcuello, C. (2014). Las empresas sociales en España: Concepto y características. *Gizarte Ekonomiaren Euskal Aldizkaria-Revista Vasca de Economía Social*, *8*, 23–36.

Díaz, P. (2014). *Comunicación y gestión de marcas de moda*. Gustavo Gili.

Dinero. (2016). *Mipymes generan alrededor del 67% del empleo en Colombia*. Dinero.

Dinero. (2017). *Una pyme colombiana genera 5 veces menos valor agregado que una gran empresa*. Dinero.

Dinero. (2018). *Los desafíos estructurales de las pymes en Colombia*. Dinero.

Dini, M., & Stumpo G. (2019). *Mipymes en América Latina: un frágil desempeño y nuevos desafíos para las políticas de fomento. Síntesis*. Documentos de Proyectos (LC/TS.2019/20), Santiago, Comisión Económica para América Latina y el Caribe (CEPAL).

Duke, J. D. (1990). Accountants' Liability to Third Parties for Negligent Misrepresentation: Should There Be a Uniform Standard. *The American Journal of Trial Advocacy*, *14*, 133.

Dunn, K. A., & Mayhew, B. W. (2004). Audit Firm Industry Specialization and Client Disclosure Quality. *Review of Accounting Studies*, *9*(1), 35–58. doi:10.1023/B:RAST.0000013628.49401.69

Duong, L. (2013). *Effective Risk Management Strategies for Small-Medium Enterprises and Micro Companies: A case study*. Viope Solutions Ltd.

Eder-Hansen, J., Chalmer, C., Tärneberg, S., & Jäger, K. (2017). *Pulse of the Fashion Industry*. Global Fashion Agenda and The Boston Consulting.

Edge Fashion Intelligence. (2018). *Fashion industry waste statistics*. Retrieved from https://edgexpo.com/fashion-industry-waste-statistics/

El Ghoul, S., Guedhami, O., & Pittman, J. (2016). Cross-country evidence on the importance of Big Four auditors to equity pricing: The mediating role of legal institutions. *Accounting, Organizations and Society*, *54*, 60–81. doi:10.1016/j.aos.2016.03.002

Elert, N., & Henrekson, M. (2016). Evasive entrepreneurship. *Small Business Economics*, *47*(1), 95–113. doi:10.100711187-016-9725-x

Escamilla, S., Alonso, N., & Plaza, P. (2017). Emprendimiento social. *Revista de Estudios de Juventud*, *118*, 240. doi:10.1017/CBO9781107415324.004

Escandón-Barbosa, D., Arias, A., Medina, L., Gómez, L. V., & Parra, L. (2015). *Reporte GEM Colombia 2015/2016*. Ediciones Sello Javeriano.

Espitia, P. E., & Cedeño, M. (2017). Formulación de una línea de investigación en Diseño sostenible para la innovación y el emprendimiento en Colombia, a partir del análisis de las líneas y grupos de investigación registrados en el Sistema de Ciencia Tecnología e Innovación (CTI). *ArDin. Arte. Diseño e Ingeniería*, *6*, 24–45.

Esty, B., & Fisher, D. (2019). *Gillette: Cutting Prices to Regain Share* (SSRN Scholarly Paper ID 3481513). Social Science Research Network. https://papers.ssrn.com/abstract=3481513

Fedesarrollo. (2013). *El sector TIC: la nueva locomotora de la economía colombiana. Informe trimestral TIC*. Author.

Feijoó, J.L. (2012). *El planeamiento estratégico en hotelería*. Buenos Aires, Argentina: Ugerman Editor.

Fernández Pérez, P. (2003). Reinstalando la empresa familiar en la Economía y la Historia Económica. Una aproximación a debates teóricos recientes. *Cuadernos de Economía y Dirección de la Empresa*, *17*, 45–66.

Fernández, N. J. (2007). *El universo de las radiaciones*. Eudeba.

Fernández, Z., & Nieto, M. J. (2005). Internationalization strategy of small and medium-sized family businesses: Some influential factors. *Family Business Review*, *18*(1), 77–89. doi:10.1111/j.1741-6248.2005.00031.x

Ferrer, A. (2010). Millennials, la generación del siglo XXI. *Nueva Revista*, 130 (5).

Ferruzca, M., & Rodríguez, J. (2011). Diseño sostenible: Herramienta estratégica de innovación. *Revista Legislativa de Estudios Sociales y de Opinión Pública*, *4*(8), 47–87.

Filion, L., Cisneros, L., & Mejía, M. J. (2011). *Administración de PYMES. Emprender, dirigir y desarrollar empresas*. Pearson Educación.

Finra. (2018). *Uncertain Futures: 7 Myths about Millennials and Investing*. Charlottesville, VA: CFA Institute.

Fischer, C., & Normann, H.-T. (2019). Collusion and bargaining in asymmetric Cournot duopoly—An experiment. *European Economic Review*, *111*, 360–379. doi:10.1016/j.euroecorev.2018.10.005

Formichella, M. M. (2015, Sept.). "La Administración en un mundo complejo" "La recuperación de la Competitividad, el Crecimiento y el Trabajo." *Monografia*.

Francis, J. R., & Michas, P. N. (2012). The Contagion Effect of Low-Quality Audits. *The Accounting Review*, *88*(2), 521–552. doi:10.2308/accr-50322

Franco, M., & Urbano, D. (2010, January). El Éxito de Las Pymes en Colombia. Un estudio de casos en el sector salud. *Estudios Gerenciales*, *26*(114), 77–96. doi:10.1016/S0123-5923(10)70103-0

Freedman, L. (2016). *Estrategia (Historia)* [Kindle iOS version]. Retrieved from Amazon.com.

Fritsch, M. (2017). The theory of economic development – An inquiry into profits, capital, credit, interest, and the business cycle. *Regional Studies*, *51*(4), 654–655. doi:10.1080/00343404.2017.1278975

Frunza, M. (2013). *Market Manipulation and Moral Hazard: Can the LIBOR be Fixed?* (SSRN Scholarly Paper ID 2207703). Social Science Research Network. https://papers.ssrn.com/abstract=2207703

Gámez G.J., & Garzón, J. (2016). Teaching entrepreneurship: towards a proposal of an educational program in the third level (tertiary) education. *i*, 458.

Gámez Gutiérrez, J., & Garzón Baquero, J. E. (2017). Nueva propuesta transversal de emprendimiento e innovación para programas educativos en el tercer nivel de educación. *Contaduría y Administración*, *62*(1), 239–261. doi:10.1016/j.cya.2016.10.005

Gámez, J. (2013). *Emprendimiento y creación de empresa. Teorías, modelos y casos*. Unisalle.

Gámez, J. (2017). Aproximación al emprendimiento social. *Revista Gestión y Finanzas*, *1*(1), 21–28.

Gámez, J., & Saiz-Álvarez, J. M. (2012). Microcredits for Women Entrepreneurship: Are They an Effective Tool to Avoid Family Impoverishment? In M. A. Galindo & D. Ribeiro (Eds.), *Women's Entrepreneurship and Economics. New Perspectives, Practices, and Policies* (pp. 167–177). Springer. doi:10.1007/978-1-4614-1293-9_11

Gámez, J., & Saiz-Álvarez, J. M. (2016). A Model of Social Entrepreneurship based on Distance Education y ICT. In A. Cotte, A. G. Muñoz, & G. Correa (Eds.), *Development, Growth, Environment and Social Equity* (pp. 1–25). Nova Science Publishers.

Ganeshan, R., Jack, E., Magazine, M. J., & Stephens, P. (1999). A taxonomic review of supply chain management research. *International Series In Operations Research And Management Science*, *17*, 839–879. doi:10.1007/978-1-4615-4949-9_27

Ganne, B. (1989). Regional Dynamics of Innovation: A Look at the Rhône-Alpes región. *Entrepreneurship and Regional Development*, *1*(2), 147–154. doi:10.1080/08985628900000013

Gazzola, P., Pavione, E., Pezzetti, R., & Grechi, D. (2020). Trends in the Fashion Industry. The Perception of Sustainability and Circular Economy: A Gender/Generation Quantitative Approach. *Sustainability*, *12*(7), 2809. doi:10.3390u12072809

GEM. (2018). *Global Entrepreneurship Monitor. GLobal report 2017-2018*. GEM.

Geroski, P., Mata, J., & Portugal, P. (2007). *Founding Conditions and the Survival of New Firms*. Danish Research Unit for Industrial Dynamics.

Gértrudix, F., Durán, J., Gamonal, R., Galvez de la Cuesta, M., & García, F. (2010). *Una taxonomía del término "nativo digital". Nuevas formas de relación y de comunicación. Congreso Euro-Iberoamericano de Alfabetización Mediática y Culturas Digitales*. Universidad de Sevilla.

GESP. (2010). *Introducción a la gestión del espectro radioeléctrico. Grupo del Espectro*. Colegio Oficial Ingenieros de Telecomunicación.

Global Entrepreneurship Monitor. (2015). *Leveraging Entrepreneurial Ambition and Innovation: A Global Perspective on Entrepreneurship, Competitiveness, and Development*. GEM.

Godart, F. (2010). *Sociologie de la Mode*. Editions La Découverte.

Gómez R., H. J., & Mitchell, D. (2014). Innovación y emprendimiento en Colombia: alcance, perspectivas y recomendaciones de política, 2014-2018. *Cuadernos de Fedesarrollo*, 82.

González Domínguez, F. (2007). *Creación de empresas. Guía del emprendedor*. Pirámide.

González, R. Y., & García, F. E. (2011). Innovación abierta: Un modelo preliminar desde la gestión del conocimiento. *Intangible Capital*, *7*(1), 82–115.

Gray, C. (1999). *Modern Strategy*. Oxford University Press.

Green, A., & McClelland, C. (2019). Male Gender Expression Conflict Between Baby Boomers and Millennials. *Pepperdine Journal of Communication Research*, *7*(6), 1–15.

Guang-wen, Y. H. F. H. (2012). Can Commercial Micro Credit Companies Benefit Small Customers? *Finance and Trade Research*, (1), 8.

Guo, Q., Koch, C., & Zhu, A. (2017). Joint audit, audit market structure, and consumer surplus. *Review of Accounting Studies*, *22*(4), 1595–1627. doi:10.100711142-017-9429-8

Gurd, B., & Thomas, J. (2012). Family business management: Contribution of the CFO. *International Journal of Entrepreneurial Behaviour & Research*, *18*(3), 286–304. doi:10.1108/13552551211227684

Guzmán, A., & Trujillo, M. (2008). Emprendimiento social - revisión de literatura. *Estudios Gerenciales*, *24*, 20.

Guzmán, J., & Liñán, F. (2005). *Perspectives on Entrepreneurial Education: A US-Europe Comparison*. Jean Monnet European Studies Centre and Universidad Antonio de Nebrija.

Hajej, Z., Rezg, N., & Gharbi, A. (2017). Ecological optimization for forecasting production and maintenance problem based on carbon tax. *International Journal of Advanced Manufacturing Technology*, *88*(5-8), 1595–1606. doi:10.100700170-016-8877-9

Hamilton, J. T. (1997). Taxes, torts, and the toxics release inventory: Congressional voting on instruments to control pollution. *Economic Inquiry*, *35*(4), 745–762. doi:10.1111/j.1465-7295.1997.tb01961.x

Harding, R. (2004). Social Enterprise: The New Economic Engine? *Business Strategy Review*, *15*(4), 539-43.

Hayek, F. A. (1991). *The trend of economic thinking. Essays on political economists and economic history*. Taylor & Francis. doi:10.7208/chicago/9780226321363.001.0001

Hernández Sampieri, R., Fernández Collado, C., & Baptista Lucio, P. (2010). *Metodología de la investigación*. McGraw-Hill.

Hernandez Sampieri, R., Fernandez Collazo, C., & Baptista Lucio, P. (2006). *Metodología de la Investigación* (4th ed.). Mc Graw Hill.

Hernández, G., Yescas, L., & Domínguez, H. (2007). Factores de éxito en los negocios de artesanía en México. *Estudios Gerenciales*, *23*(104), 77–99. doi:10.1016/S0123-5923(07)70018-9

Hernández, I. (2008). *Empresa, innovación y desarrollo*. Universidad Nacional de Colombia.

Hernández, J. C. (2016). *Hogar de Cristo en Monte Sinaí: La herencia de los Vulnerados*. Guayaquil.

Herrera, R., Araujo, D., Guerrero, G., & Tapia, F. (2020). Time optimization using augmented reality for the fashion industry [Optimización de tiempos utilizando realidad aumentada para la industria de la moda]. *RISTI-Revista Ibérica de Sistemas e Tecnologías de Informacao*, *2020*(E28), 806–815.

He, S., Hipel, K. W., & Kilgour, D. M. (2017). Analyzing market competition between Airbus and Boeing using a duo hierarchical graph model for conflict resolution. *Journal of Systems Science and Systems Engineering*, *26*(6), 683–710. doi:10.100711518-017-5351-7

Heß, B., & Stefani, U. (2012). *Audit market regulation and supplier concentration around the world: Empirical evidence*. Academic Press.

Hines, T., & Bruce, M. (2007). *Fashion marketing: Contemporary issues* (2nd ed.). Butterworth–Heinemann. doi:10.4324/9780080468174

Hitomi, K. (2017). *Manufacturing systems engineering: A unified approach to manufacturing technology, production management and industrial economics*. Routledge. doi:10.1201/9780203748145

Hoffmann, P., & Mirza, U. K. (2002). Tomorrow's energy: Hydrogen, fuel cells, and the prospects for a cleaner planet. *Electronic Green Journal*, *37*(16), 95521. doi:10.2307/20050353

House of Commons Environmental Audit Committee. (2019). *Fixing fashion: clothing consumption and sustainability*.

Hsu, W.-Y., Troy, C., & Huang, Y. (2015). The determinants of auditor choice and audit pricing among property-liability insurers. *Journal of Accounting and Public Policy*, *34*(1), 95–124. doi:10.1016/j.jaccpubpol.2014.09.001

Huddart, S. (2013). Discussion of Empirical Evidence on the Implicit Determinants of Compensation in Big 4 Audit Partnerships. *Journal of Accounting Research*, *51*(2), 389–397. doi:10.1111/1475-679X.12010

Hult, G. T. M., Hurley, R. F., & Knight, G. A. (2004). Innovativeness: Its antecedents and impact on business performance. *Industrial Marketing Management*, *33*(5), 429–438. doi:10.1016/j.indmarman.2003.08.015

Hu, M., Shi, M., & Wu, J. (2019). Online Group Buying and Crowdfunding: Two Cases of All-or-Nothing Mechanisms. In M. Hu (Ed.), *Sharing Economy. Making Supply Meet Demand* (pp. 319–346). Springer Nature Switzerland. doi:10.1007/978-3-030-01863-4_14

Hyundai Motor. (2009). *Hyundai motor company I 2009 Annual Report Table of Contents*. Hyundai Motor Company Annual Report.

Ignaciuk, P. (2013). LQ optimal and robust control of perishable inventory systems with multiple supply options. *IEEE Transactions on Automatic Control*, *58*(8), 2108–2113. doi:10.1109/TAC.2013.2246093

INEC. (2017). *Encuesta de Superficie y Producción Agropecuaria Continua ESPAC 2016*. Quito.

INEC. (2019). Reporte de Pobreza - Marzo 2019. Quito.

INEC. (2019). Reporte de Pobreza y Desigualdad- Junio 2019. Quito.

Institute of Child Nutrition. (2018). *Managing Personalities and Conflict. Participant's Workbook.* The University of Mississippi, School of Applied Sciences.

Instituto Nacional de Economía Popular y Solidaria (IEPyS). (2017). http://www.socioeco.org/bdf_organisme-558_es.html

Jain, S., & Mishra, S. (2020). Luxury fashion consumption in sharing economy: A study of Indian millennials. *Journal of Global Fashion Marketing, 11*(2), 171–189. doi:10.1080/20932685.2019.1709097

Jaouen, A., & Lasch, F. (2015). A new typology of micro-firm owner-managers. *International Small Business Journal, 33*(4), 397–421. doi:10.1177/0266242613498789

Jiang, J., Wang, I. Y., & Wang, K. P. (2018). Big N Auditors and Audit Quality: New Evidence from Quasi-Experiments. *The Accounting Review, 94*(1), 205–227. doi:10.2308/accr-52106

Jiménez, J. E. (2017). *Análisis y desarrollo de un modelo de tutorización integral basado en el Design Thinking orientado a la innovación estratégica en empresas colombianas* (Tesis Doctoral). Valencia, España: Universidad Politécnica de Valencia.

Jin, B. E., & Cedrola, E. (Eds.). Product Innovation in the Global Fashion Industry. Palgrave Studies in Practice: Global Fashion Brand Management. doi:10.1057/978-1-137-52349-5

Jin, B. E., & Shin, D. C. (2020). Changing the game to compete: Innovations in the fashion retail industry from the disruptive business model. *Business Horizons, 63*(3), 301–311. doi:10.1016/j.bushor.2020.01.004

Kahneman, D. (2003). A Perspective on Judgment and Choice: Mapping Bounded Rationality. *The American Psychologist, 56*(9), 697–720. doi:10.1037/0003-066X.58.9.697

Kaiser, S. B. (2012). *Fashion and cultural studies.* Berg Publishers.

Kakihara, T. (2010). *The Small and Medium Sized Enterprises (SMEs) in Mexico: the Case of Jalisco State.* Institute for Economic Studies, Seijo University.

Kautonen, T. (2013). *Senior entrepreneurship.* OECD.

Kazlacheva, Z., Stoykova, V., Georgieva, K., & Ilieva, J. (2018). Application of innovative technologies in fashion design education. *IOP Conference Series. Materials Science and Engineering, 459*(1), 012080. doi:10.1088/1757-899X/459/1/012080

Kelliher, F., & Reinl, L. (2009). A resource-based view of micro-firm management practice. *Journal of Small Business and Enterprise Development, 16*(3), 521–532. doi:10.1108/14626000910977206

Kend, M., Houghton, K. A., & Jubb, C. (2014). Competition issues in the market for audit and assurance services: Are the concerns justified? *Australian Accounting Review, 24*(4), 313–320. doi:10.1111/auar.12063

Kim, K., Knotts, T., & Jones, S. (2008). Characterizing viability of small manufacturing enterprises (SME) in the market. *Expert Systems with Applications*, *34*(1), 128–134. doi:10.1016/j.eswa.2006.08.009

Kirzner, I. (1986). Entrepreneurial Discovery and the Competitive Market Process: An Austrian Approach. *Journal of Economic Literature*, *35*(1), 60–85.

Knechel, W. R., Niemi, L., & Zerni, M. (2013). Empirical Evidence on the Implicit Determinants of Compensation in Big 4 Audit Partnerships. *Journal of Accounting Research*, *51*(2), 349–387. doi:10.1111/1475-679X.12009

Knight, F. (1942). Profit and Entrepreneurial Functions. *The Journal of Economic History*, *2*, 126-132.

Koc, T., & Bozdag, E. (2007). Empirical research for CNC technology implementation in manufacturing SMEs. *International Journal of Advanced Manufacturing Technology*, *34*(11-12), 1144–1152. doi:10.100700170-006-0681-5

Kornberger, M., Justesen, L., & Mouritsen, J. (2011). "When you make manager, we put a big mountain in front of you": An ethnography of managers in a Big 4 Accounting Firm. *Accounting, Organizations and Society*, *36*(8), 514–533. doi:10.1016/j.aos.2011.07.007

Kotur, A. (2004). *Carolina Herrera: Portrait of a Fashion Icon*. Assouline.

Koumbis, D. (2015). *Moda y retail: de la gestión al merchandising*. Gustavo Gili.

Kraus, S., Harms, R., & Schwarz, E. (2006). Strategic planning in smaller enterprises - new empirical findings. *Management Research News*, *29*(6), 334–344. doi:10.1108/01409170610683851

Krois, K. (2015). *Watch & read Eco-Social Design according to Ezio Manzini*. https://designdisaster.unibz.it/watch-read-eco-social-design-according-to-eziomanzini/

Lacefield, S. K. (2018). *A pragmatist's take on sustainability: Interview with Yossi Sheffi*. Retrieved from https://www.dcvelocity.com/articles/20180607-a-pragmatists-take-on-sustainability-interview-with-yossi-sheffi/

Langert, B. (2016). *One year later: Mcdonald's supply chain, sustainability chief Francesca Debiase*. Retrieved from https://www.greenbiz.com/article/one-year-later-mcdonalds-supply-chain-sustainability-chief-francesca-debiase

Lansberg, I. (1983). Managing Human Resources in Family Firms: The Problem of Institutional Overlap. *Organizational Dynamics*, *12*(1), 39–46. doi:10.1016/0090-2616(83)90025-6

Latorre, J. I. (2019). *Ética para máquinas*. Academic Press.

Leclair, M. (2017). "Dior and I": Understanding the combination of creativity and economy in the fashion industry. *Society and Business Review*, *12*(3), 274–284. doi:10.1108/SBR-11-2016-0066

Lee, J. (2016). The Model of Fast Fashion Industry: A Case Survey of "Inditex," *Aktual' ni Problemy Ekonomiky = Actual. Problems of Economics*, *185*, 430–436.

Lennox, C., & Pittman, J. (2010). Auditing the auditors: Evidence on the recent reforms to the external monitoring of audit firms. *Journal of Accounting and Economics*, *49*(1), 84–103. doi:10.1016/j.jacceco.2009.04.002

Li, J., Moreno, A., & Zhang, D. J. (2019). Agent Pricing in the Sharing Economy: Evidence from Airbnb. In M. Hu (Ed.), *Sharing Economy. Making Supply Meet Demand* (pp. 485–503). Springer Nature Switzerland. doi:10.1007/978-3-030-01863-4_20

Linares, P. (2013). Dimensión tecnológica del emprendimiento social. In Guía del emprendedor social: inspiraciones para la creación de empresas al servicio de la sociedad. Academic Press.

Lin, E. (1980). Inventory Control Systems for Small Business. *American Journal of Small Business*, *4*(4), 11–19. doi:10.1177/104225878000400404

Li, S. (2013). Emission permit banking, pollution abatement and production–inventory control of the firm. *International Journal of Production Economics*, *146*(2), 679–685. doi:10.1016/j.ijpe.2013.08.023

Llach, J., & Alonso-Almeida, M. D. M. (2015). Integrating ICTs and Supply Chain Management: The Case of Micro-Sized Firms. *Human Factors and Ergonomics in Manufacturing & Service Industries*, *25*(4), 385–397. doi:10.1002/hfm.20559

López, J., & García, A. (2010). *Innovación abierta: Desafíos organizacionales de este modelo de gestión de innovación para las empresas, Red de redes científicas de América Latina y el Caribe, España y Portugal*. Universidad de A Coruña.

Louis, H. (2005). Acquirers' abnormal returns and the non-Big 4 auditor clientele effect. *Journal of Accounting and Economics*, *40*(1–3), 75–99. doi:10.1016/j.jacceco.2005.03.001

Low, C. (2006). A Framework for the Governance of Social Enterprises. *International Journal of Social Economics*, *33*(5/6), 376–385. doi:10.1108/03068290610660652

Lu, C. (2014). *Zara supply chain analysis—The secret behind Zara's retail success*. Retrieved from https://www.tradegecko.com/blog/supply-chain-management/zara-supply-chain-its-secret-to-retail-success

Luna Correa, J. (2013). *Influencia del capital humano para la competitividad de las PYMES en el sector manufacturero de Celaya Guanajuato* (Tesis Doctoral). Universidad de Celaya, Mexico.

Lykke, A. (1989). *Toward an Understanding of Military Strategy. Military Strategy: Theory and Application*. US Army War College.

Macchion, L., Da Giau, A., Caniato, F., Caridi, M., Danese, P., Rinaldi, R., & Vinelli, A. (2018). Strategic approaches to sustainability in fashion supply chain management. *Production Planning and Control*, *29*(1), 9–28. doi:10.1080/09537287.2017.1374485

Macchion, L., Moretto, A., Caniato, F., Caridi, M., Danese, P., & Vinelli, A. (2015). Production and supply network strategies within the fashion industry. *International Journal of Production Economics*, *163*, 173–188. doi:10.1016/j.ijpe.2014.09.006

Macciavelli, N. (2003). The prince. University of Chicago Press. doi:10.7208/chicago/9780226500324.001.0001

Mair, J., & Marti, I. (2006). Social entrepreneurship research: A source of explanation, prediction, and delight. *Journal of World Business*, *41*(1), 36–44. doi:10.1016/j.jwb.2005.09.002

Mandal, P., & Gunasekaran, A. (2002). Application of SAP R/3 in on-line inventory control. *International Journal of Production Economics*, *75*(1-2), 47–55. doi:10.1016/S0925-5273(01)00180-3

Manrique, G. (2013). Revisión conceptual y definición del término emprendimiento para la tecnología en gestión industrial. *Revista Estrategia Organizacional*, *21*, 181–192.

Manzini, E. (2015). *Design, when everybody designs. An introduction to design for social innovation*. The MIT Press. doi:10.7551/mitpress/9873.001.0001

Marginson, D. E. (2002). Management control systems and their effects on strategy formation at middle-management levels: Evidence from a UK organization. *Strategic Management Journal*, *23*(11), 1019–1031. doi:10.1002mj.271

Margolin, V., & Margolin, S. (2002). A "social model" of design: Issues of practice and research. *Design Issues*, *18*(4), 24–30. doi:10.1162/074793602320827406

Martínez Cousinou, G. (2003). El malestar en la globalización. Madrid, Taurus, 2002. *Revista Internacional de Sociologia*, *61*(34), 216–220.

Martínez, P., Barana, M., Rocha, R., & Paschoarelli, L. (2017). Innovación, design y sostenibilidad social: nuevas tendencias para el desarrollo local en la contemporaneidad. *Revista de Arquitectura*, *19*(2), 68-77.

Martins, P. M. M. da S. (2019). *Shaving as a subscription: Analysis of Portuguese male consumers interest on buying razors and blades by subscription*. https://repositorio.ucp.pt/handle/10400.14/26910

Mauno, S., Kinnunen, U., Makikangas, A., & Natti, J. (2005). Psychological Consequences of Fixed-Term Employment and Perceived Job Insecurity among Health Care Staff. *European Journal of Work and Organizational Psychology*, *14*(3), 209–237. doi:10.1080/13594320500146649

Mbonu, E. (2014). *Diseño de moda: creatividad e investigación*. Promopress.

McDean, C., Shillingford, K., & Frankel, S. (2018). *"People need reality" Alessandro Michele on his Gucci*. Retrieved from https://www.anothermag.com/fashion-beauty/10576/people-need-reality-alessandro-michele-on-his-gucci

Medina, D. (2017). ¿Qué le espera al sector. *El Espectador*.

Microempresas–OCM. (2007). Estadísticas de la Microempresa en Colombia. Análisis comparativo 1990 – 2005, Bogota, Colombia.

MIDUVI. (2011). *Intervención Urbana Integral en la Zona de Expansión del Noroeste de la Ciudad de Guayaquil.* Subsecretaría de Hábitat y Asentamientos Humanos.

Ministerio de Tecnologías de la Información y las Comunicaciones y Agencia Nacional del Espectro. (2012). Monitoreo del Espectro Radioeléctrico. Manual de Gestión Nacional del Espectro Radioeléctrico - Título V. Author.

Ministerio de Tecnologías de la Información y las Comunicaciones. (2015). *Comportamiento macroeconómico del sector TIC en Colombia.* Panorama TIC.

Ministerio de Tecnologías de la Información y las Comunicaciones. (2017). *Primera Gran Encuesta TIC 2017: Estudio de Acceso.* Usos y Retos de las TIC en Colombia.

Mintzberg, H. (1994). *The Rise and Fall of Strategic Planning.* Prentice-Hall.

Misanková, M., & Kocisová, K. (2012). Strategic Implementation as a Part of Strategic Management. *Procedia: Social and Behavioral Sciences, 110,* 861–870. doi:10.1016/j.sbspro.2013.12.931

Moliner, R., Lázaro, M. J., & Suelves, I. (2016). Analysis of the strategies for bridging the gap towards the Hydrogen Economy. *International Journal of Hydrogen Energy, 41*(43), 19500–19508. doi:10.1016/j.ijhydene.2016.06.202

MontenegroA. (2019). *ANIF.* Retrieved from http://www.anif.co/Biblioteca/politica fiscal/notas sobre-la-reforma-tributaria

Montilla Carmon, M., & Montero Caro, M. (2011). *Fudepa.* Desarrollo Empresarial y Emprendedores.

Morales, M.I. (2011). 50 Aniversarios del canje de la moneda. *Revista del Banco Central de Cuba,* 1-68.

Morales-Gutiérrez, A. C., Ariza-Montes, J., & Rodríguez, N. M. (2012). El emprendedor social y el E-empowerment de las redes virtuales. *CIRIEC – España. C.I.R.I.E.C. España, 75,* 153–177.

Moreira, P., & Urriolagoitia, L. (2011). Emprendimiento social. *Revista española del tercer sector, 17,* 19-21.

Morelli, N. (2007). Social innovation and new industrial contexts: Can designers "industrialize" socially responsible solutions? *Design Issues, 23*(4), 3–21. doi:10.1162/desi.2007.23.4.3

Moriano, J. (2005). El perfil psicosocial del emprendedor. Madrid, Spain: CES (Consejo Económico y Social).

Mouján, H. (2006). *Cómo desarrollar microemprendimientos.* Longseller.

Mueller, F., Carter, C., & Whittle, A. (2015). Can audit (still) be trusted? *Organization Studies, 36*(9), 1171–1203. doi:10.1177/0170840615585336

Mulgan, G. (2006). The process of social innovation. *Innovations, 8*(2), 145–162. doi:10.1162/itgg.2006.1.2.145

Murphy, P. J., & Coombes, S. M. (2009). A model of social entrepreneurial: Discovery. *Journal of Business Ethics*, *85*(3), 325–336. doi:10.100710551-008-9921-y

Navarrete Baez, F. E. (2015). Las prácticas de desarrollo sustentable: Un acercamiento descriptivo a las pequeñas empresas de Guadalajara, México. *Cuadernos Americanos*, *31*(53), 48–58. doi:10.25100/cdea.v31i53.16

Navarro, A. M., Climent, V. C., & Palacio, J. R. S. (2011). Emprendimiento social y empresas de inserción en España. Aplicación del método delphi para la determinación del perfil del emprendedor y las empresas sociales creadas por emprendedores. *Revesco: Revista de Estudios Cooperativos*, *106*, 150–172.

Newbold, M. (2018). *Ethical footwear brand Po-Zu calls for consumers to 'Champion an Alternative Black Friday*. Fantha Tracks.

Nicoletti, G., Arcuri, N., Nicoletti, G., & Bruno, R. (2015). A technical and environmental comparison between hydrogen and some fossil fuels. *Energy Conversion and Management*, *89*, 205–213. doi:10.1016/j.enconman.2014.09.057

Nikunen, T., Saarela, M., Oikarinen, E. L., Muhos, M., & Isohella, L. (2017). Micro-Enterprise's Digital Marketing Tools for Building Customer Relationships. *Management*, *12*(2).

Nyathi, M., & Benedict, O. H. (2017). An Analysis of Bookkeeping Practises of Micro-Entrepreneurs in the Retail Clothing Industry in Cape Town, South Africa. *J Entrepren Organiz Manag*, *6*(216), 2.

O'Dwyer, M., & Ryan, E. (2000). Management development issues for owners/managers of micro-enterprises. *Journal of European Industrial Training*, *24*(6), 345–353. doi:10.1108/03090590010373334

OIT. (2015). *Derecho de los pueblos indígenas y tribales a un desarrollo incluyente sostenible*. ILO.

Ojala, H., Collis, J., Kinnunen, J., Niemi, L., & Troberg, P. (2016). The demand for voluntary audit in micro-companies: Evidence from Finland. *International Journal of Auditing*, *20*(3), 267–277. doi:10.1111/ijau.12070

Olarte, C., Sierra, Y., & Mosquera, A. (2016). *Venta de moda femenina: una guía muy práctica*. ESIC.

ONU. (2010). State of the world's indigenous people. New York: Department of Public Information & Center for Indigenous People's Autonomy and Development (CADPI).

ONU. (2015). *Convención Marco sobre el Cambio Climático, 21930*. Retrieved from file:///C:/Users/W7/Desktop/ufc.pdf

Ooghe, H., & Prijcker, S. (2007). Failure processes and causes of company bankruptcy: A typology. *Management Decision*, *46*(2), 223–232. doi:10.1108/00251740810854131

OpenDemocracy. (2017). *Innovación abierta en el sector público*. Author.

Ortíz, J.C. (2016). Diseñando el cambio. La innovación social y sus retos. *Economía Creativa, 6*, 9-35.

Osterwalder, A., & Pigneur, Y. (2011). *Generación de modelos de negocio*. Editorial Deusto.

Papanek, V. (1985). *Design for the real world* (2nd ed.). Thames and Hudson.

Pardo, C., & Alfonso, W. (2018). Por qué los negocios fracasan en Colombia? (U. d. Colciencias, Ed.). Academic Press.

Parenti, M., Ushchev, P., & Thisse, J.-F. (2017). Toward a theory of monopolistic competition. *Journal of Economic Theory*, *167*, 86–115. doi:10.1016/j.jet.2016.10.005

Pavón Vieyra, M. A. (2017). *Administración de la moda MX: básicos para la gestión de pequeñas empresas de nueva creación*. NEILSA.

Pavón, L. (2010). *Financiamiento a las microempresas y las pymes en México (2000-2009)*. Cepal.

Pereira, F. (2007). *La evolución del espíritu empresarial como campo del conocimiento. Hacia una visión sistémica y humanista. Cuadernos de Administración*. Universidad Javeriana.

Pirson, M. (2015). *Social Entrepreneurship and all that Funk, Research Paper Series*. Fordham University Schools of Business Research; Humanistic Management Network.

Portales, L., & Pérez, O. (2016). Emprendimiento y Empresa Social como estrategia de desarrollo local. *Institut de Socio-Économie des Entreprises et des Organisations*, *144*, 45–56.

Posner, H. (2016). *Marketing de moda*. Gustavo Gili.

Poundstone, W. (1992). Prisoner's Dilemma. Academic Press.

Pudukudy, M., Yaakob, Z., Mohammad, M., Narayanan, B., & Sopian, K. (2014). Renewable hydrogen economy in Asia - Opportunities and challenges: An overview. *Renewable & Sustainable Energy Reviews*, *30*, 743–757. doi:10.1016/j.rser.2013.11.015

PwC. (2018). *Report Millennials vs. Generation Z.* Available online: https://www.pwc.com/it/it/press-room/assets/docs/cs_pwc_food.pdf

Quinn, R., & Rohrbaugh, J. (1983). A spatial model of effectiveness criteria: Towards a competing values approach to organizational analysis. *Management Science*, *29*(3), 363–377. doi:10.1287/mnsc.29.3.363

Rabellotti, R. (1997). *External Economies and Cooperation in Industrial Districts: a Comparison of Italy and Mexico*. Macmillan. doi:10.1007/978-1-349-25794-2

Ramírez, A. (2011). *Gobierno abierto y modernización de la gestión pública: tendencias actuales y el inevitable camino que viene*. Instituto Universitario de Investigación Ortega y Gasset.

Ramírez-Salazar, M. P. (2015). *Modelo de innovación abierta colaborativa para la banca de fomento: Caso Bancoldex* (PhD Thesis). Universidad Nebrija.

Rifkin, J. (2010). *La economía del hidrógeno*. Academic Press.

Roberts, P. (2004). The End of Oil: On the Edge of a Perilous New World. *Journal of Ecological Anthropology*, *9*. doi:10.5038/2162-4593.9.1.8

Robertson, H. (2018). *No Sign of Landing: Airbus, Boeing, the WTO, and the Expanding Large Civil Aircraft Battle* (SSRN Scholarly Paper ID 3114942). Social Science Research Network. https://papers.ssrn.com/abstract=3114942

Roberts, R., & Woods, C. (2005). Changing the world on a shoestring: The concept of social entrepreneurship. *University of Auckland Business Review*, *7*(1), 45–51.

Rodríguez Moreno, D. C. (2016). Emprendimiento sostenible, significado y dimensiones. *Katharsis*, (21), 449. doi:10.25057/25005731.775

Rosener, J. B. (2011). Ways women lead. In *Leadership, Gender, and Organization* (pp. 19–29). Springer. doi:10.1007/978-90-481-9014-0_3

Ruíz, C., Patiño, O., & Echeverry, P. (2018). *Emprendimiento social en comunidades indígenas*. Ponencia.

Rumelt, R. (2011). *Good Strategy, Bad Strategy: The Difference and Why it Matters*. Profile Books.

Saiz-Álvarez, J. M. (Ed.). (2019). Handbook of Research on Digital Marketing Innovations in Social Entrepreneurship and Solidarity Economics. Hershey, PA: Information Science Reference (IGI Global). doi:10.4018/978-1-5225-8939-6

Saiz-Álvarez, J. M., & Coduras, A. (2020). Aspects of Work-life Balance of Women in Entrepreneurship. In M. T. Lepeley, K. Kuschel, E. Eijdenberg, & N. Pouw (Eds.), *Exploring Wellbeing of Women in Entrepreneurship. A Global Perspective* (pp. 123–142). Routledge.

Salop, S. C. (1979). Monopolistic Competition with Outside Goods. *The Bell Journal of Economics*, *10*(1), 141–156. JSTOR. doi:10.2307/3003323

Sanabria A., S. E., Pedraza, P. A., & Hurtado A., E. (2014). El emprendimiento como fuente de desarrollo y fortalecimiento de las capacidades endógenas para el aprovechamiento de las energías renovables. *Revista EAN*, (77), 152. doi:10.21158/01208160.n77.2014.821

Sanabria, N. (2012). *Perdurabilidad empresarial. Anotaciones teóricas*. Universidad Autónoma del Caribe.

Sánchez, P. (2014). *Mercado de suelo informal y políticas públicas de habitat urbano en la ciudad de Guayaquil*. Quito: Flacso.

Sánchez, R. (2018). *Panorama laboral en Colombia: situación reciente y desafíos*. UN Periódico, Bogota, Colombia.

Sanders, E., & Stappers, P. (2008). Co-creation and the new landscapes of design. *CoDesign*, *4*(1), 5–18. doi:10.1080/15710880701875068

Santos, F. J., Barroso, M. d l O., & Guzmán, C. (2013). *La economía global y los emprendimientos sociales*. Academic Press.

Say, J. B. (1821). *Tratado de Economía Política o Exposición sencilla del modo con que se forman, se distribuyen y se consumen las riquezas*. Academic Press.

Schumpeter, J. (1939). *Ciclos económicos. Análisis teórico, histórico y estadístico del proceso capitalista*. Prensas Universitarias de Zaragoza.

Schumpeter, J. A. (1934). *The theory of economic development: An inquiry into profits, capital, credit, interest, and the business cycle*. Harvard University Press.

Scipioni, A., Manzardo, A., & Ren, J. (2017). Hydrogen Economy: Supply Chain, Life Cycle Analysis and Energy Transition for Sustainability. *The American Historical Review, 40*. doi:10.1086/ahr/40.1.128

Seco, C. (2018). *Aging and Entrepreneurship: Firm Creation and Performance among Older Individuals*. Universidade de Lisboa.

Sedeke, K., & Arora, P. (2013). Top ranking fashion blogs and their role in the current fashion industry. *First Monday, 18*(8). doi:10.5210/fm.v18i8.4314

Seeger, J. A. (1984). Reversing the Images of BCG's Growth/Share Matrix. *Strategic Management Journal*, *5*(1), 93–97. doi:10.1002mj.4250050107

Shamsuzzoha, A., Kankaanpaa, T., Carneiro, L. M., Almeida, R., Chiodi, A., & Fornasiero, R. (2013). Dynamic and collaborative business networks in the fashion industry. *International Journal of Computer Integrated Manufacturing*, *26*(1-2), 125–139. doi:10.1080/0951192X.2012.681916

Shane, S., & Venkataraman, S. (2000). Note As the Promise of Entrepreneurship. *Academy of Management Review*, *25*(1), 217–226. doi:10.2307/259271

Shirvanimoghaddam, K., Motamed, B., Ramakrishna, S., & Naebe, M. (2020). Death by waste: Fashion and textile circular economy case. *The Science of the Total Environment*, *718*, 137317. doi:10.1016/j.scitotenv.2020.137317 PMID:32088483

Siegel, P. H., Naser-Tavakolian, M., & O'Shaughnessy, J. J. (2008). *Factors Influencing Auditor Switching in the European Union* (SSRN Scholarly Paper ID 1612540). Social Science Research Network. https://papers.ssrn.com/abstract=1612540

Silva, S. C., Duarte, P., & Sundetova, A. (2020). Multichannel versus omnichannel: A price-segmented comparison from the fashion industry. *International Journal of Retail & Distribution Management*, *48*(4), 417–430. doi:10.1108/IJRDM-07-2019-0232

Simón Moya, V., Sastre Sánchez, O., & Revuelto Taboada, L. (2015). El emprendedor social: Análisis de la alerta social. *Suma de Negocios*, *6*(14), 155–165. doi:10.1016/j.sumneg.2015.07.001

Solano, J. (2004). Hacia una economía basada en el hidrógeno. *Anales de La Universidad Metropolitana*, *4*(1), 165–180.

Song, J. S., & Zipkin, P. H. (1996). Inventory control with information about supply conditions. *Management Science*, *42*(10), 1409–1419. doi:10.1287/mnsc.42.10.1409

Sperling, D., & Cannon, J. (2004a). Hydrogen Hope or Hype? In The Hydrogen Economy Transition (Vol. 17, pp. 235–239). doi:10.1016/B978-012656881-3/50017-4

Sperling, D., & Cannon, J. (2004b). *The Hydrogen Energy Transition. Moving toward the post-petroleum age in transportation. Growth*. Lakeland.

Staffell, I., Scamman, D., Velazquez Abad, A., Balcombe, P., Dodds, P. E., Ekins, P., Shah, N., & Ward, K. R. (2019). The role of hydrogen and fuel cells in the global energy system. *Energy & Environmental Science*, *12*(2), 463–491. doi:10.1039/C8EE01157E

Steele, V., & Major, J. S. (2019). *Fashion industry*. Retrieved from https://www.britannica.com/art/fashion-industry

Stringer, T., Mortimer, G., & Payne, A. R. (2020). Do ethical concerns and personal values influence the purchase intention of fast-fashion clothing? *Journal of Fashion Marketing and Management*, *24*(1), 99–120. doi:10.1108/JFMM-01-2019-0011

Surie, G. (2017). Creating the innovation ecosystem for renewable energy via social entrepreneurship: Insights from India. *Technological Forecasting and Social Change*, *121*, 184–195. doi:10.1016/j.techfore.2017.03.006

Tao, F., Fan, T., Lai, K. K., & Li, L. (2017). Impact of RFID technology on inventory control policy. *The Journal of the Operational Research Society*, *68*(2), 207–220. doi:10.105741274-016-0030-5

Tapscott, D. (1998). *Growing up digital: The rise of the Net generation*. McGraw-Hill.

Távara, L. (2017). Director Social Hogar de Cristo. In Informalidad Urbana: Comprendiendo el Problema de la Tenencia de la Tierra en Promesa de Dios, Monte Sinai, Guayaquil. Tesis de Grado. Universidad Católica del Ecuador.

Tavizón, A., & Cortes, K. (2016). *Vinculación estratégica en las organizaciones*. Pearson.

Tayal, S., Singh, S. R., & Sharma, R. (2016). An integrated production inventory model for perishable products with trade credit period and investment in preservation technology. *International Journal of Mathematics in Operational Research*, *8*(2), 137–163. doi:10.1504/IJMOR.2016.074852

Thackara, J. (2013). *Diseñando para un mundo complejo. Acciones para lograr la sustentabilidad*. Designio.

Thompson, E. (2014). *The Wedding Dress: The 50 Designs that Changed the Course of Bridal Fashion*. Prestel.

Thornquist, C. (2014). Basic research in art: Foundational problems in fashion design explored through the art itself. *Fashion Practice*, *6*(1), 37–57. doi:10.2752/175693814X13916967094795

Tromp, N., & Hekkert, P. (2016). Assessing methods for effect-driven design: Evaluation of a social design method. *Design Studies*, *43*, 24–47. doi:10.1016/j.destud.2015.12.002

Trujillo Blanco, W. G., Hernández, J. J. R., Hernández, A. M. L., Falco, E. R., Naite, O. F. A., Porro, E. M., & Valdivieso Romero, J. F. (2014). Adaptación del cuestionario SF-36 para medir calidad de vida relacionada con la salud en trabajadores cubanos. *Revista Cubana de Salud y Trabajo*, *15*(1), 62–70.

Trujillo Dávila, M. A., & Guzmán Vásquez, A. (2008). Intraemprendimiento: una revisión al constructo teórico, sus implicaciones y agenda de investigación futura. *Cuad. Adm. Bogotá (Colombia)*, *21*(2135), 37–63.

Tu, M. (2018). *An exploratory study of internet of things (IoT) adoption intention in logistics and supply chain management*. Retrieved from https://nls.ldls.org.uk/welcome.html?ark:/81055/vdc_100057944694.0x00002c

Turker, D., & Altuntas, C. (2014). Sustainable supply chain management in the fast fashion industry: An analysis of corporate reports. *European Management Journal*, *32*(5), 837–849. doi:10.1016/j.emj.2014.02.001

Ünay, F. G., & Zehir, C. (2012). Innovation intelligence and entrepreneurship in the fashion industry. *Procedia: Social and Behavioral Sciences*, *41*, 315–321. doi:10.1016/j.sbspro.2012.04.036

UN-Cepal. (2004). *Pequeñas y medianas empresas y eficiencia colectiva: estudios de caso en América Latina*. Mexico: Siglo veintiuno editores.

UNESCO. (2004). Las tecnologías de la información y la comunicación en la formación docente. Guía de Planificación. Organización de las Naciones Unidas para la Educación, la Ciencia y la Cultura. UNESCO.

United Nations Department of Public Information & Center for Indigenous People's Autonomy and Development (CADPI). (2010). *State of the world's indigenous people*. Author.

United States Fashion Industry Association. (2019). *About the fashion industry*. Retrieved from https://www.usfashionindustry.com/about/about-the-fashion-industry

Valenciano, J., & Urube, J. (2017). *Experiencias de Emprendimiento Social en Iberoamérica*. Editorial Universidad de Almería.

Valero, J. A. (2010). El Espejismo De Una Energía Social: La Economía Del Hidrógeno. *Revista Internacional de Sociologia*, *68*(2), 429–452. doi:10.3989/ris.2008.08.13

Vallejo Peña, A. (2017). *La Generación Y ante el desafío de su incersión laboral: Realidades frente a estereotipos*. Arbor.

Van der Laan, E., & Salomon, M. (1997). Production planning and inventory control with remanufacturing and disposal. *European Journal of Operational Research*, *102*(2), 264–278. doi:10.1016/S0377-2217(97)00108-2

Vangundy, A. (2007). *Getting to Innovation: How Asking the Right Questions Generates Great Ideas Your Company Needs*. Amacom.

Varela, R. (1998). El espiritu empresarial y la generación de empleos. *Univalle - ICESI*, 8.

Varela, R., Moreno, J., & Bedoya, M. (2014). *Colombian Entrepreneurial Dynamics*. Global Entrepreneurship Monitor.

Vásquez, C. O. (2002). La idónea implementación estratégica es condición necesaria para aspirar al éxito de la empresa. *Estudios Gerenciales, 18*(85), 41–66.

Velásquez, L. J., & Armas, M. (2015). Requerimientos estadísticos para la determinación de criterios e indicadores de desarrollo sostenible del Municipio Autónomo Caroní. *Universidad, Ciencia y Tecnología, 19*(75), 82–97.

Verne, J. (1874). La Isla Misteriosa. *Historia, 4*(1935), 1–27.

Vía Plural. (2011). *Desplazamiento forzado comunidad Wounaan-Nonam en Bogotá*. https://es.scribd.com/document/54865446/Desplazamiento-Forzado-ComunidadWounaan-Nonam-en-Bogota

Vorobiyenko, P., Tikhonov, V., & Taher, A. (2015). The LTE technology perspectives in multimedia applications. *Цифрові Технології, 17*, 7–14.

Walsh, P. R. (2012). Innovation Nirvana or Innovation Wasteland? Identifying commercialization strategies for small and medium renewable energy enterprises. *Technovation, 32*(1), 32–42. doi:10.1016/j.technovation.2011.09.002

Want, R. (2006). An introduction to RFID technology. *IEEE Pervasive Computing, 5*(1), 25–33. doi:10.1109/MPRV.2006.2

Weber, J., Willenborg, M., & Zhang, J. (2008). Does Auditor Reputation Matter? The Case of KPMG Germany and ComROAD AG. *Journal of Accounting Research, 46*(4), 941–972. doi:10.1111/j.1475-679X.2008.00298.x

Wen, X., Choi, T., & Chung, S. (2019). Fashion retail supply chain management: A review of operational models. *International Journal of Production Economics, 207*(C), 34–55. doi:10.1016/j.ijpe.2018.10.012

White, P. (2014). An assessment of the Competition Commission report and subsequent outcomes. *Research in Transportation Economics, 48*, 277–285. doi:10.1016/j.retrec.2014.09.053

Whittle, A., Carter, C., & Mueller, F. (2014). 'Above the fray': Interests, discourse and legitimacy in the audit field. *Critical Perspectives on Accounting, 25*(8), 783–802. doi:10.1016/j.cpa.2013.09.001

World Bank. (2015). *Indigenous people's policy brief. Still among the poorest of the poor.* Author.

WRAP. (2018). *Sustainable Clothing Action Plan 2020 Commitment: progress against footprint reduction targets 2012–2017*. WRAP.

Wren-Lewis, S. (2018, January 20). *What Carillion's collapse tells us about public sector outsourcing*. British Politics and Policy at LSE. https://blogs.lse.ac.uk/politicsandpolicy

Yang, S., Song, Y., & Tong, S. (2017). Sustainable Retailing in the Fashion Industry: A Systematic Literature Review. *Sustainability*, *9*(7), 1266. doi:10.3390u9071266

Zahra, S., Rawhouser, H., Bhawe, N., Neubaum, D., & Hayton, J. (2008). Globalization of Social Entrepreneurship opportunities. *Strategic Entrepreneurship Journal*, *2*(2), 117–131. doi:10.1002ej.43

Zapata Guerrero, E. (2004). Las Pymes y su problemática empresarial. Analisis de Casos. *Revista EAN*, *52*, 119–135.

Zarta Ávila, P. (2018). La sustentabilidad o sostenibilidad: un concepto poderoso para la humanidad. *Tabula Rasa*, (28), 409–423. doi:10.25058/20112742.n28.18

Zhou, S., Song, B., & Gavirneni, S. (2020). Bundling Decisions in a Two-Product Duopoly—Lead or Follow? *European Journal of Operational Research*, *284*(3), 980–989. Advance online publication. doi:10.1016/j.ejor.2020.01.030

Zhu, L., Zhang, L., & Zhao, J. (2019). The study on China civil aviation manufacturing industry's development Strategy facing international industrial transfer. *2019 3rd International Seminar on Education, Management and Social Sciences (ISEMSS 2019)*. 10.2991/isemss-19.2019.2

About the Contributors

Jorge Gamez-Gutierrez is an Economist and PhD specialized in entrepreneurship and family businesses. Author of books and articles, consultant and researcher of Uniagustiniana Bogota (Colombia), Uniminuto Bogotá (Colombia) and Universidad de la Costa (Colombia).

Jose Manuel Saiz-Alvarez, Ph.D. in Economics & Business Administration, Autonomous University of Madrid (Spain). Ph.D. in Sociology, Pontifical University of Salamanca (Spain). He has also studied at the Royal Complutense College at Harvard, University of South Florida, University Lumière-Lyon II (France), and Tallinn University (Estonia). He was Academic Director for Business Administration Doctoral Studies, Nebrija University (Spain). He was Visiting Professor at TEC de Monterrey (Mexico), EAN University (Colombia), and he is now Visiting Professor at the Catholic University of Santiago de Guayaquil (Ecuador), Autonomous University of Manizales (Colombia), and CEIEF-University of Santiago de Chile. Honorary Professor, Autonomous University of Madrid (Spain). President of FIEC Institute. Member of the Latin-American Family Business Net. Co-founder of the International Center of Research on Solidarity Economy. Certificate of Recognition, Capitol House of Representatives of Puerto Rico. Diploma of Honor, Valahia University of Targoviste (Romania). Member of the Scientific Research Council, Kielce University (Poland). Member of the Editorial Board and referee of numerous national and international journals. Who's Who in the World, from the 2011 Edition. He has given more than one hundred lectures in Europe and America, and is author of more than a two hundred publications in his specialty. To date he has supervised 75 doctoral theses from students from Argentina, Chile, Colombia, Ecuador, Guatemala, Italy, Mexico, Paraguay, Spain, USA, and Venezuela.

* * *

María Teresa Alcívar Avilés, Ph.D. in Business Sciences from Nebrija University, Spain. She is the director of the M.Sc. in Finance and Business Economics, Catholic University of Guayaquil, Ecuador. Specialized in International Commerce, she was a president and founder of ASOFLEX (Association of Producers and Exporters of Tropical Flowers) and COPEI (Ecuadorian Organization of Exports and Investment). Also, she has worked for the Chilean/Ecuadorian Chamber of Commerce and has been awarded the Top-ten Women Economists in the Region of Guayas, Ecuador.

Daniela Bellon Monsalve, Industrial Engineer, master's in Advanced Energy Systems, and doctoral student in Energy and Materials Sciences. Professor and researcher at the University of Santander (UDES), Bucaramanga, Colombia.

Robinson Ernesto Calvo is a Mathematician and a specialist in Applied Statistics. Professor and researcher at ECCI University of Bogota, Colombia.

Kiara Carranza Gudiel is an international student from Peru. She is soon to graduate with a B.S in Global Business at Kean/Wenzhou-Kean University.

Sara Esperanza Castañeda Valenzuela is a Business Administrator, Market Management Specialist, and Master in Business Administration, leading issues of management, planning, quality, projects, and customer service for over 16 years, contributing to organizational optimization in important companies in different economic sectors. She has a strong knowledge and skills in Strategic Management, Quality Audit and Implementation and Certification of Quality Systems, Leadership of the Customer Service Area, and Project Management. She has an outstanding trajectory on internal and external audit processes and leadership of audit teams.

Uriel Hitamar Castillo-Nazareno has a Ph.D. in Business Sciences from Nebrija University, Spain, with post-graduate studies in Argentina, Israel, and Spain. He has been a Provost at Universidad Técnica 'Luis Vargas Torres' de Esmeraldas, Ecuador, and has worked for the Ecuadorian government as a counselor for SENPLADES (National Planning and Development System for Ecuador). He teaches at the Catholic University of Santiago de Guayaquil, Ecuador, and he is an evaluator of the Higher Education in Ecuador.

Paula Echeverry Pérez, MSc in Strategic Design. Researcher and, designer of services and experiences that are centered on the human being. His background is in the field of social innovation, working mainly with rural communities.

Jossie Esteban Garzón Baquero, Business Administrator, Specialist in Pedagogy and University Teaching, and master's in Educational Sciences. Professor and researcher at the University of Santander (UDES), Bucaramanga, Colombia.

Gustavo Adolfo Gil Angel, Director of the Areandina Psychology Program in Bogotá from 2018, he is a graduate of the Catholic University of Colombia, has a Master's in Administration from the University of La Salle, and is an expert in the management of Higher Education Institutions. His expertise in the education sector began with his participation in governmental socio-educational projects in the city of Bogotá. Being a professor in different private universities, he has directed some research chairs for undergraduate students from various areas of knowledge. As in-charge of academic-administrative processes, he has designed and implemented educational quality management systems under local and international standards.

Miguel Angel Gil Robles is a Research Professor at Tecnologico de Monterrey, Guadalajara campus, where he teaches Accounting and Finance. He holds a B.A. in Accounting and Finance and an M.A. in Finance, both from Tecnologico de Monterrey, and a Ph.D. in Accounting and Finance from the University of Manchester, U.K. His research interests focus on Management Accounting, Organizational Learning in Accounting and Accounting, and Management in High-tech Industries.

Rob Kim Marjerison is Asst Professor of Global Business at Wenzhou-Kean University in Wenzhou, China. His previous affiliations include teaching internationally at Universities in Bhutan, Mexico, India and Korea. Dr. Marjerison has a PhD in International Business from the International School of Management in Paris France, a Master of Science in Information Systems from Louisiana State University, and a Masters in Public Administration from California State University. His research interests include Sino-US Trade, Sustainable Economic Development, Organizational and New Venture Assessment and Social Entrepreneurship.

Jessica Silvana Matute-Petroche is an Administration Engineer and MBA at the University of Guayaquil, Ecuador. Ph.D. candidate at the Catholic University of Argentina. Research professor and the Director of Treasury, Catholic University of Guayaquil, Ecuador.

Raul F. Montalvo Corzo is the Director of EGADE Business School in Guadalajara. His fields include Applied Microeconomics, Global Management, Industrial Organization, Marketing (Applied and Theory), Game Theory, Econometrics, and Business Analytics. Also, he has worked as a business consultant and has taught at different campuses of Tecnologico de Monterrey throughout Mexico, and as a visiting professor in countries such as Colombia, Ecuador, Peru, Panama, France, Japan, England, and the United States.

Omar Alonso Patiño Castro, Business Administrator, Doctor in Business Sciences and Master in Organization Management. He has been Dean, Program Director, Research Group Director and Department Director at EAN University, with experience in the services and financial sector. Research mainly in finances informality, microcredit, and entrepreneurship.

Md. Jahid Rahman has earned a PhD in Accountancy from the City University of Hong Kong, an MBA in Business Management from Ritsumeikan Asia Pacific University, Japan, an MBA from the University of Dhaka, Bangladesh and is a Certified Public Accountant (CPA, Australia). Presently an Asst Professor at the College of Business and Public Management at Wenzhou-Kean University, China, his previous teaching affiliation includes the City University of Hong Kong.

María del Pilar Ramírez Salazar, Ph.D. in Management, EAN University (Colombia) Ph.D. in Entrepreneurial Sciences, Nebrija University (Spain), and M.Sc. in Business Management, Quebec University (Canada). She is a RISE model consultant, as an innovation, and a sustainability path for organizations to show managers better ways to lead their organizations. She is a researcher from the G3Pymes Research Group, EAN University (Colombia). Professor in entrepreneurship, management and innovation topics, and expert on online teaching. She is a leader of the EAN-BIZLAB, a program aimed at developing intrapreneurship challenges, such as Collaborative Open Innovation in organizations.

Catalina Lucía Ruiz Arias, Master of Science in Strategic Product Design from Delft University of Technology (Netherlands), a Specialist in Design and Product Management for Export, and an Industrial Designer. She has obtained her business experience in product design, development, and consultancy at national and international companies from various sectors (including companies located in Brazil and the Netherlands). Ms. Ruiz has also worked as a professor at multiple universities in the country. At present, she works for Universidad EAN as an Associate Professor and as Director at the Institute for Sustainable Entrepreneurship, where she leads projects associated with consulting and training on innovation and design thinking for entrepreneurs, business people, and the government.

Carlos Salcedo-Perez, Business administrator. Master in Economic Development. PhD in Managerial Science. Professor at Universidad EAN since March 2005.

Jairo Alberto Vasquez Bernal is a full-time professor at Uniagustiana, Colombia, where he teaches and researches about Management and Business Development, Innovation, and Entrepreneurship. He holds an M.Sc. in Marketing, Universidad de Viña del Mar, Chile, and a B.A. in Advertising and Marketing at Corporación Universitaria de Colombia.

Yuxi Zhao is a Lecturer of Economics at Wenzhou-Kean University. She received her PhD from the Ohio State University. Her research interests include entrepreneurship, sustainability, commercialization of natural resources, and connecting landscape pixels with the market to create new ventures.

Index

X

Y

Z

www.ingramcontent.com/pod-product-compliance
Lightning Source LLC
LaVergne TN
LVHW081326300926
849161LV00008B/1888